Managing international risk

Managing international risk

Essays commissioned in
honor of the centenary of the
Wharton School, University of
Pennsylvania

Edited by RICHARD J. HERRING
The Wharton School, University of Pennsylvania

CAMBRIDGE UNIVERSITY PRESS
Cambridge
London   New York   New Rochelle
Melbourne   Sydney

Published by the Press Syndicate of the University of Cambridge
The Pitt Building, Trumpington Street, Cambridge CB2 1RP
32 East 57th Street, New York, NY 10022, USA
296 Beaconsfield Parade, Middle Park, Melbourne 3206, Australia

First published 1983

Printed in the United States of America

Library of Congress Cataloging in Publication Data
Main entry under title:
Managing international risk.
Based on essays and perspectives presented at a
conference entitled "Managing international risk," held
in Philadelphia, Oct. 26–27, 1981, sponsored jointly by
the Global Interdependence Center, the Group of Thirty,
and the Wharton School, University of Pennsylvania.
Includes bibliographical references.
Contents: Introduction and overview / Richard J.
Herring – Managing risks to the international
economic system / Richard N. Cooper – Perspective:
political threats to the international economic system /
Robert O. Keohane – [etc.]
1. International business enterprises – Finance –
Congresses. 2. International finance – Congresses.
3. Risk management – Congresses. I. Herring, Richard.
II. Global Interdependence Center. III. Group of
Thirty. IV. Wharton School.
HG4027.5.M36 1983 658.1′5 82–19930
ISBN 0 521 25078 1

Contents

v

List of contributors

RICHARD N. COOPER is Maurits C. Boas Professor of International Economics at Harvard University. Previously he was Frank Altschul Professor of International Economics and Provost at Yale University. He has served as Under Secretary for Economic Affairs, U.S. Department of State, and has been a consultant to several U.S. government and international agencies.

RIMMER de VRIES is Senior Vice-President of Morgan Guaranty Trust Company. He is in charge of the bank's international economics department, which has responsibility for analyzing economies other than the United States', especially in connection with the bank's foreign lending, examining developments affecting the balance-of-payments position of the United States, and publication of *World Financial Markets.* Mr. de Vries has served as a foreign research economist with the Federal Reserve Bank of New York.

JOHN DUNN is a Reader in Politics at Cambridge University. He has served as a visiting professor at the University of Bombay, the University of British Columbia, and the University of Ghana. He has written extensively on political theory and modern revolution.

JONATHAN EATON is Associate Professor of Economics at Yale University. He was a visitor at the Graduate Institute of International Economic Studies in Stockholm and a visiting fellow at the Australian National University. He has written widely on the impact of uncertainty on international trade and financial flows.

MARK GERSOVITZ is Research Economist and Public Affairs Analyst at the Woodrow Wilson School at Princeton University. His main area of interest is economic development. He has written on land reform, urban unemployment, inflation in LDCs, and international aspects of development including trade, investment, default, and expropriation.

RICHARD J. HERRING is Associate Professor of Finance at the Wharton School, University of Pennsylvania. He has been an International

Affairs Fellow at the Council on Foreign Relations, an IBM Postdoctoral Fellow, and a consultant to several firms and government agencies. He has written on interest rate determination, capital flows, and public policy toward international banking.

HELEN HUGHES is Director of the Economic Analysis and Projections Department at the World Bank. She has served as a Senior Fellow at the Australian National University and has taught and conducted research at the universities of New South Wales and Queensland. She has been a consultant to the Australian government and to Australian mining and manufacturing firms. Dr. Hughes has written widely on economic development.

ROBERT O. KEOHANE is Professor of Politics at Brandeis University. Previously he was Chairman of the Political Science Department at Stanford University, where he established and chaired the program in international relations. He was editor of *International Organization* and has served on the board of editors of *World Politics*. He has written widely on the interface between international politics and international economics.

PAUL KLEINDORFER is Professor and Chairman of Decision Sciences at the Wharton School, University of Pennsylvania, where he also holds a secondary appointment in the Department of Economics. His current research is concerned with incentives and regulations, with special emphasis on the relationship between decision processes and policy.

HOWARD KUNREUTHER is Professor of Decision Sciences at the Wharton School, University of Pennsylvania. He is presently directing the activities of the risk analysis group at the International Institute of Applied Systems Analysis (IIASA). He is particularly interested in the decision processes of individuals and groups with respect to low-probability events and the relative performance of the private market and social programs for protecting and insuring against such events.

TOMMASO PADOA-SCHIOPPA is Director-General for Economic and Financial Affairs at the Commission of the European Communities, Brussels. He is a member of the board of directors of the European Investment Bank and a member of the Group of Thirty. He has served as economic adviser to the Italian Ministry for the

Treasury and as head of the Banca d'Italia's money market department and economist in the bank's research department.

JOHN T. REID is Vice-President of Planning and Projects at Pfizer International. He received his Ph.D. in agricultural economics from Oxford University. Dr. Reid has extensive international experience in corporate planning.

MARTIN SHUBIK is Seymour H. Knox Professor of Mathematical Institutional Economics at Yale University. He has served as Director of the Cowles Foundation for Research in Economics at Yale and as a visiting professor at the University of Melbourne, the Institute for Advanced Studies in Vienna, and at the University of Chile. An expert in game theory, he has acted as a consultant to the U.S. government and many foundations.

JAMES R. STREET is Vice-President of Chemical Products at Shell Chemical Company. Mr. Street has served in many capacities at Shell, including Director of Exploratory Science, Director of Corporate R & D Engineering, Manager of Lubricants Business Center – Oil Products, General Manager of Products Economics, and Vice-President of Corporate Planning. He received his Ph.D. in chemical engineering from the University of Michigan.

RAYMOND VERNON is Clarence Dillon Professor of International Affairs at the Center for International Affairs at Harvard University and was previously Herbert F. Johnson Professor of International Business Management at the Harvard Business School. He has served in various capacities at the Department of State and as consultant to several U.S. government and international agencies. He is editor of the *American Journal of Public Policy and Management*.

JAMES M. WYBAR, CPCU, is Vice-President, Product and Market Development of the Harleysville Mutual Insurance Company and Vice-Chairman of its UK affiliate, Harleysville Insurance (UK) Ltd. He is past chairman and continues as a member of the board of the National Committee on Property Insurance and has been active in other industry affairs. His company responsibilities include the management of its reinsurance program, both ceded and assumed.

Acknowledgments

Earlier versions of these papers and perspectives were presented at a conference entitled "Managing International Risk" held in Philadephia on October 26 and 27, 1981. The conference was sponsored jointly by the Global Interdependence Center, the Group of Thirty, and the Wharton School, University of Pennsylvania. This joint venture arose from complementary interests and a coincidence of plans.

In forming the Wharton Center for International Management Studies during 1980, the Wharton School began by taking an inventory of international research in progress at the school. The survey disclosed that in almost every academic department researchers were attempting to deal with some aspects of international risk and uncertainty. But despite the common concern with international risk, there was regrettably little interchange or cross-fertilization among disciplines. The celebration of the centenary of the Wharton School presented an opportunity to remedy this deficiency by planning an international conference that would bring an interdisciplinary perspective to the problem of managing international risk. Meanwhile, in developing plans for their third international conference, the Global Interdependence Center and the Group of Thirty found that their constituents were also concerned with how to assess and manage international risk. In order to avoid duplication of effort and to take advantage of a wider range of resources, the leaders of the three organizations – Donald C. Carroll, Dean of the Wharton School; Frederick Heldring, President of the Global Interdependence Center; and Johannes Witteveen, Chairman of the Group of Thirty – decided to join forces in sponsoring the conference.

As editor, my greatest debt is to the authors, who managed to meet deadlines despite the pressure of busy schedules. I am also grateful for help from Jerry Wind, Karen Freedman, and Anne Hearn at the Wharton School, and from Reine Dempsey and Anne Grace and Brewster Grace at the Global Interdependence Center. JoLynn Horvath skillfully typed draft upon draft of material for the conference and this volume.

The Global Interdependence Center and the Wharton School

gratefully acknowledge financial assistance for this undertaking from BankAmerica Foundation, Delaware Steel Company, Inc., Exxon Education Foundation, First National Bank in St. Louis, Hunt Manufacturing Company, International Business Machines Corporation, INA Foundation, Pfizer, Inc., Rorer Group, Inc., SmithKline Corporation, and Xerox Corporation.

Introduction and overview

RICHARD J. HERRING

The importance of managing international risks has grown as the volume of international activity has increased. Over the past two decades, international transactions have expanded more rapidly than domestic transactions in almost every country. Profits, opportunities for growth, and, indeed, corporate survival have increasingly come to depend on how effectively managers cope with international uncertainties. Yet, relative to the earlier postwar period, the international environment seems to have become less predictable. Over the last decade, exchange rate volatility has increased as have divergences in national rates of growth and inflation. Moreover, economic, social, and political changes, such as the Iranian revolution and the manipulation of oil prices by the Organization of Petroleum Exporting Countries, have reshaped the international environment in dramatic and unexpected ways. The importance of managing international risks has grown even as our ability to anticipate such risks has seemed to diminish.

Inadequate information impedes the effectiveness of all decision makers, but because knowledge about foreign events is especially limited, costly, and uncertain, international managers are particularly hampered. Moreover, managers of international enterprises must cope not only with the hazards that jeopardize the success of ordinary domestic transactions but also with additional perils that do not affect purely domestic transactions. Three of the most important of these uniquely international risks are: (1) foreign exchange risk – the risk that an unanticipated change in the exchange rate will affect the profitability of a transaction or a stream of transactions; (2) country risk – the risk that a sovereign power will interfere with the repatriation of profits, interest payments, principal repayments, or the control of foreign assets; and (3) the risk of a breakdown in the rules and practices that govern international trade and investment flows. This book focuses on the latter two risks. The problem of managing foreign exchange risk is addressed in a companion volume.[1]

---

[1] See R. J. Herring, ed., *Managing Foreign Exchange Risk* (Cambridge: Cambridge University Press, 1983).

1

2   **Richard J. Herring**

This collection of essays is intended to contribute to an improved understanding of international risk and uncertainty by bringing together the reflections of academic experts from several different fields and the views of distinguished practitioners from multinational manufacturing firms, international financial institutions, and official international organizations. The academic contributors were asked to write broad, conceptual essays and the practitioners were invited to prepare perspectives that would expand and illuminate some aspect of the topic from the vantage point of their experience. Because of the primitive state of knowledge about international risk, we have chosen to present a variety of provocative ideas rather than attempt a more integrated, textbooklike treatment of the subject.

The diversity of viewpoints represented here will present something of a challenge to the reader because of unavoidable differences in style and usage among the contributors. Experts, whether in academia, corporations, government, or international organizations, inevitably develop jargon that is extremely efficient for communicating with the initiated, but a barrier to comprehension by nonspecialists. As editor, I have encouraged the authors to avoid jargon where possible and I have insisted that they define specialized terminology when it cannot be avoided, but I have not attempted to impose uniform usage. Rather, I have sought the more modest goal of ensuring that the meaning of each term is clear even if it differs a bit from author to author. In that spirit, I will begin by explaining the use of the term "risk" in the title.

Risk is the possibility of an outcome that is less favorable than the expected outcome. The concept is relevant only when an option must be implemented before its precise outcome can be known. In accordance with popular usage, it is used only with regard to events that may cause shortfalls or losses that are greater than anticipated.[2]

It could be argued that uncertainty is a more appropriate description of the subject of this book than risk. A venerable tradition in economics extending from J. M. Keynes and F. H. Knight draws a sharp distinction between risk and uncertainty, in which risk refers to the chance of the occurrence of some event determined by some objectively verifiable probability distribution, and uncertainty pertains to the chance occurrence of some event where the probability distribution is not known. To use Keynes's illustration, risk applies to

---

[2] This is in contrast to usage in the literature on finance in which risk is the dispersion of possible outcomes, both more and less favorable, around the expected outcome.

a game of roulette, whereas uncertainty applies to the prospect of a European war.[3] Although the phenomena investigated in this book are much more like the latter than the former, I have found it convenient to follow the more common usage in which risk is synonymous with uncertainty.

The logical possibilities for managing risk follow from the definition. Risk can be reduced to the extent that the possibility of an outcome less favorable than the expected outcome can be reduced, or the impact of an unfavorable outcome on decision makers can be mitigated by insurance, diversification, or government support. One approach to reducing risk is to improve decision makers' abilities to forecast the occurrence of the risky event. The contributors to this volume are not optimistic about prospects for substantially improving the prediction of international risks, although several suggestions are made with regard to improving the flow of information. Another approach is to improve the decision makers' control over the occurrence of the event, perhaps by restructuring their activities. For example, joint ventures or management contracts may be used to reduce the probability of expropriation by the host government. The purchase of insurance can mitigate risk by converting an uncertain loss into a known insurance premium. Diversification of exposure across a number of (not perfectly correlated) risks will lessen the decision makers' vulnerability to risks they cannot reduce or insure against. Government policies may attempt to reduce the burden of uncertainty on decision makers by providing subsidized insurance, by making assistance available after the realization of unfavorable outcomes, or by attempting to stabilize various prices and/or quantities. The authors examine these various measures for dealing with risk, as well as the factors that give rise to international risks.

The following is a selective summary, highlighting some of the issues raised by each of the contributors.

Richard Cooper begins with an essay that deals with large-scale nightmares that could face the international manager. He examines disturbances sufficiently large not only to lead to crises for firms and some governments, but also to threaten a rupture of the framework within which firms and nations undertake international transactions. Cooper argues that we are in a period of heightened uncertainty. Technological changes in transportation and communication have

3 John Maynard Keynes, *The Collected Writings of John Maynard Keynes, The General Theory and After*, Part 2: *Defense and Development*, vol. 14, ed. Donald Moggridge (Cambridge: Cambridge University Press, 1973), pp. 112–13.

created new opportunities, but have also intensified competition and uncertainty about the economic prospects of particular firms, regions, and countries. Decolonization and the thawing of the Cold War have opened new markets, but these events have also increased uncertainties about the rules that govern trade and financial relationships. Cooper assesses the threats to the international economic system that arise from this uncertainty.

Cooper identifies four kinds of disturbances that are most likely to jeopardize the stability of the international economic system: (1) balance-of-payments crises, (2) an international banking crisis, (3) an oil crisis, and (4) a trade war. With regard to each, he examines the mechanisms that have been developed to prevent or contain a crisis and the scope for improving existing arrangements. He emphasizes that the principal effort to deal with risk in the international economic system (as in his hang-gliding analogy) is to try to influence the probabilities of various outcomes.

Cooper believes that adequate arrangements are in place for dealing with all of these potential disturbances except, perhaps, an oil crisis. In his view, the most serious danger to the international economic system is not a major international disturbance, but rather a gradual unraveling of the fabric of international cooperation that has been painstakingly woven over the past thirty years. In industrialized countries, this danger arises from the attempts of governments to protect employment patterns and industrial structures against international competition and shifts in the structure of the world economy. Among developing countries, the danger arises from the possibility that the more successful newly industrialized developing countries will choose to take advantage of the opportunities offered by the international economic system without accepting the responsibilities for maintaining the system that are commensurate with their new status.

Robert Keohane provides a political perspective on Cooper's chapter, asserting that the greatest threat to the international economic system is not economic, but rather political–military in nature. He argues that the acceleration of the arms race jeopardizes the international economy because it aggravates the risk of nuclear war and because it undermines the leadership of the United States in the world economy. He is concerned that emphasis on defense expenditures in the United States will diminish the growth of productivity in high-technology, civilian industries and thereby increase the pressure for protectionist policies in the United States.

With regard to the prospect of an international banking crisis, Keohane is less sanguine than Cooper. He is particularly concerned about political pressures on leaders of many developing countries attributable to the large volume of external indebtedness. He questions whether authorities have the political resources to sustain the macroeconomic policies that will ensure an orderly flow of debt service payments, and he sketches a scenario in which developing countries would have strong incentives to repudiate their debts (a topic that Eaton and Gersovitz explore in greater detail in Chapter 2). He urges policy makers to recognize that the international banking system rests on a fragile foundation of confidence that, if fractured, would require prompt remedial action.

Keohane shares Cooper's concern about a gradual erosion of the international rules, conventions, and institutions that govern the international economic system. But he also sees a danger in the system's failing to adapt to the needs of developing countries, noting that political antagonisms between developed and developing countries can prevent efficient solutions to international economic problems.

In his perspective on Cooper's analysis, Tammaso Padoa-Schioppa argues that contemporary concern over international economic risk is due less to the condition of the world economy than to a sense that the ability of policy makers to affect the economy is diminishing and less certain. As a consequence, the threat of a disturbance is doubly alarming because there is uncertainty about the appropriate policy response and there is greater risk that a policy error may exacerbate the impact of the disturbance. Moreover, Padoa-Schioppa warns that the frustration over ineffective economic policies may also lead to pressures for more authoritarian policy measures and, consequently, to risks for liberal, democratic institutions.

Padoa-Schioppa evaluates a variety of reasons for the decline in the effectiveness of economic policy, such as anticipation of policy actions, the growth of underground economy, the diffusion of economic power beyond the Group of Ten, and the growing gap between the jurisdiction of governments and the decision-making domain of corporations. He emphasizes, however, that the underlying cause is a decline in the "exogeneity" of economic policy. He attributes this to a deterioration in the government's ability to influence the economy relative to that of other economic agents and to a weakening of the will of policy makers to pursue policies that are opposed by special interest groups.

Padoa-Schioppa favors policy coordination as a way of countering the decline of exogeneity, by expanding the policy domain of governments relative to the decision-making horizons of the private sector. But as an experienced international civil servant, he is conscious of the limitations of this remedy. He notes that the necessity of achieving unanimity among sovereign nations for each policy initiative severely circumscribes the scope for coordinated policy actions.

Chapters 2, 3, and 4 address different aspects of country risk. Although the term "country risk" applies to a broad range of actions taken by (or permitted by) the sovereign power that have unfavorable consequences for foreign investors, the authors usually focus on the extreme cases: the nationalization of direct investment without compensation (expropriation) and the disavowal of a debt (repudiation). In Chapter 2, Jonathan Eaton and Mark Gersovitz investigate economic determinants of country risk. Martin Shubik emphasizes political factors in Chapter 3, and John Dunn explores social and cultural dimensions of country risk in Chapter 4. These three essays on particular sources of country risk are followed by three perspectives that consider country risk from the respective vantage points of an official international organization, an international financial institution, and a multinational manufacturing corporation.

Jonathan Eaton and Mark Gersovitz develop a conceptual framework that identifies fundamental economic sources of country risk. The framework has novel implications for country risk analysis, as well as for appropriate policies to improve the allocation of capital to developing countries. The authors treat political and social factors as given in order to focus on country risks that arise from the host government's careful calculation of the costs and benefits of interfering with the contractual rights of the foreign investor.

Eaton and Gersovitz view the difficulty in enforcing contracts between foreign investors and host governments (or entities protected by host governments) as a crucial determinant of foreign investment decisions. Since investors understand that it may not be possible to compel compliance with the investment contract, prudent investors will invest only to the extent that they are convinced that it is in the government's interest to permit the contract to be fulfilled. Because investors will focus on the country's willingness to repay as well as its ability to repay, a country may be rationed in international capital markets. Since the costs and benefits of fulfilling the investment contract may vary with the particular characteristics of the investment, country risk is often project specific; nonetheless, Eaton and Gersovitz find it useful to distinguish between two broad categories of investment: direct investment (in which the foreign investor has control over production within the host country) and indirect or portfolio investment, which they exemplify as bank lending.

Bank lenders have fewer (but perhaps more powerful) options for defending themselves against repudiation by foreign borrowers than do direct investors. Bank lenders can influence the benefits of repudiation to a borrower only by limiting the amounts lent, but they can make repudiation costly to the borrower by making it difficult to borrow from foreign banks in the future and by denying the borrower access to the international payments system. These costs will vary depending on the country's prospects for growth and its economic structure. Eaton and Gersovitz identify four motives for borrowing that suggest empirical proxies for the costs of repudiating foreign loans. Countries may wish to maintain access to international capital markets in order to: (1) smooth consumption, (2) invest, (3) ease adjustment to balance-of-payments disturbances, and (4) provide liquidity for performing international transactions. Their analysis leads to some novel interpretations of traditional country risk indicators. For example, greater export instability may, other things equal, enhance a country's creditworthiness because it increases the prospective costs to such a country of losing access to foreign loans, thereby increasing the country's willingness to repay in order to protect that access. This is in sharp contrast to the usual interpretation of export instability as a factor increasing the riskiness of a loan by increasing the variability of the borrower's capacity to repay.

Eaton and Gersovitz argue that direct investors ordinarily have much greater scope for influencing the cost–benefit calculations of the host government with respect to a particular investment. Direct investors can pursue several different strategies for protecting their assets, all of which have in common the general objective of structuring the investment so that it is much less valuable to the host government if it is expropriated than if the foreign investor is permitted to maintain control. This may be accomplished by adopting a technology that cannot be efficiently used by alternative local managers, by retaining the ability to withdraw skilled labor in the event of expropriation, or by locating different aspects of the production process in different countries.

Country risk imposes costs on both foreign investors and on host countries. The defensive measures taken by foreign investors reduce the efficiency of investment or limit the volume of investment below the optimal level. The authors conclude that developing countries could grow more rapidly if country risk could be reduced. They recommend an improved flow of information to enable investors to assess country risk, a better-designed role for insurance against country risk, and, more controversially, tougher sanctions against countries that expropriate direct investments or repudiate foreign loans. Eaton and Gersovitz argue that tougher penalties on hostile actions taken against foreign investors could benefit both foreign investors and country borrowers. Raising the costs and hostile actions by borrowers will make investors less apprehensive that countries will view such actions as in their best interests and thereby increase the supply of external financing.

Martin Shubik defines political risk as the hazards faced by foreign institutions or individuals due to the unforeseen actions or influence of host country political powers. The actualization of political risk may be associated with changes in policies caused by elections, public pressure, coup d'etat, revolution, or civil war. Shubik emphasizes that the protective veneer of international law is very thin and that the consequences of failing to cope with political risk may be even graver than that of failing to cope with economic risk since personnel, as well as real and financial assets, may be at stake.

Shubik asserts that effective management of political risk begins with an assessment of the resources at risk and their sensitivity to changes in the political climate. As an illustration, he contrasts the exposure of an international bank to that of a nonfinancial corporation. The bank has relatively few employees or real assets exposed; at risk are mainly financial assets. The nonbank firm is likely to have much greater exposure in terms of personnel and real assets and, consequently, has a much more complicated risk management problem.

Shubik argues that the management of political risk must be strategic. A large foreign institution cannot realistically expect to maintain a low profile and thereby escape notice by the local authorities (or rivals of the local authorities). Rather, its options are to leave the country, or to accommodate, resist, or influence the political change. The corporation must not only attempt to predict changes in the political environment, but it must also influence the environment or its exposure to the environment. Thus, coherent risk assessment depends not only on estimates of probabilities and possibilities of various outcomes of the political process, but also on an evaluation of the importance of outcomes to the corporation. Shubik emphasizes this point by noting that some firms guessed correctly about Castro's rise to power in Cuba, but suffered losses nonetheless because they failed to comprehend the consequences of that event for their operations in Cuba.

Shubik advocates strategic planning in which the institution considers not only contingencies, but also how its own actions may influence those contingencies. Shubik assesses a wide variety of inputs into the strategic planning process. He considers qualitative approaches to political assessment and prediction such as the use of advisers, briefings, newsletters, situation reports, and grand tours by corporate decision makers. He also examines more quantitative approaches such as the formation of political indexes, Delphi techniques, scenarios, games, and simulation. He emphasizes the limitations of each approach, but concludes that each is worth considering since there is no evidence that one approach is clearly best. He recommends coordination and integration of both quantitative and qualitative approaches.

Shubik believes that the greatest scope for improving the management of political risk is less in the refinement of techniques of political risk assessment than in the integration of political assessment in the decision-making process. The managerial challenge is greater the more far flung the institution and the more volatile the environment because the techniques available for political risk assessment remain the same, but the difficulties of incorporating political risk assessments into operating decisions increase, as do the dangers of not dealing with political risk effectively.

John Dunn begins by distinguishing social and cultural risk from political risk. Political risk refers to hazards faced by foreign investors due to actions of the incumbent host government or any reasonably predictable, constitutional successor.[4] Social and cultural risk connotes hazards faced by foreign investors due to the beliefs, values, and attitudes of the host country population that have not yet found an effective voice in the political process. Imminent social and cultural risk is thus risk on the very point of becoming political risk. Revolution is the most striking manifestation of the realization of social and cultural risk.

It is extremely difficult to deal with social and cultural risk because it is a set of actual and potential responses for which no legitimate representation has been found. Moreover, even where such responses can be identified, the foreign investor may be severely restricted by the host government from contacts with rivals for power, particularly when such rivals are not represented in the political establishment. These difficulties notwithstanding, the assessment of social and cul-

---

[4] Note that Dunn's definition of political risk is narrower than Shubik's. Shubik implicitly treats revolution as an aspect of political risk, whereas Dunn regards it as the essence of social and cultural risk.

tural risk is of substantial importance. The long list of across-the-board expropriations of foreign investment by revolutionary governments in the twentieth century and the substantial payments made by many corporations to insure against the risk of ransom payments for their executives are tangible indications of the cost and importance of social and cultural risk.

Dunn has little sympathy for quantitative approaches to explaining political or social and cultural risk, although like Shubik he would seem to grant quantitative analysis the role of "sweetening the intuition" of experts. He argues that such risks cannot be quantified, but they can be understood.

Dunn begins by asking what in a society or culture facilitates foreign investment. He finds an answer in the writings of Adam Smith and David Hume on the conditions that enable capitalism to flourish. The requirements for a healthy climate for foreign investment are secure and predictable property rights and a government with the will and capacity to defend those rights. Dunn argues that what the classical economists failed to perceive, however, was the ideological fragility of such a system. Perceptions of distributive injustice may undercut its legitimacy. Nationalism, he argues, is to some extent a refusal to regard the property rights of foreigners as compatible with the requirements of distributive justice and consequently a refusal to recognize such rights at all.[5] He observes that most of the large-scale confiscations of foreign property in this century – Russia after 1917, Mexico in the late 1930s, Eastern Europe and China after 1945, Vietnam, Algeria, Cuba, Chile, and Angola – have occurred in the aftermath of an anticapitalist or anticolonialist revolution. Dunn concludes that social and cultural risk is highest in countries where repressive governments are perceived as protecting the property rights of foreigners rather than representing the interests of the indigenous population. This has the disconcerting implication for the foreign investor who must deal with the unpleasant irony that a host government that is too solicitous of the interests of foreign investors may place those interests in jeopardy.

To illustrate his analysis, Dunn presents a case study of the Iranian

[5] These are some of the important "other things" that Eaton and Gersovitz explicitly held equal in their analysis of optimizing behavior by the host country government. But the government that carefully weighs the economic costs and benefits of taking hostile actions against foreign investors a la Eaton and Gersovitz may well find itself in jeopardy in Dunn's world of social and cultural risk.

revolution, which is arguably the epitome of social and cultural risk for Americans. He emphasizes that the Shah's government was very weakly articulated with Iranian society, but strongly identified with U.S. interests.

Dunn's assessment of responses to social and cultural risk shows that there are no easy solutions. He notes that one tempting response is to "take the money and run" – to extract high profits over a very short period. But he warns that although such a strategy may serve the interests of an individual firm, it undercuts the longer-term interests of foreign investors as a group and may imperil liberal political traditions. Since the incidence of social and cultural risk cannot be predicted, the investor has strong incentives to pass on the risk to third parties through insurance or guarantees, or to diversify.

Dunn asserts that, collectively, foreign investors ultimately get the social and cultural risk they deserve, and thus the best protection against political risk is a careful assessment of the impact of their activities on the host country population. And since revolutionary governments generally do not make fine distinctions among foreigners, the foreign investor must also take into account what other foreigners are doing in the host country.

Helen Hughes takes issue with two of the presumptions that underlie most discussions of managing country risk. She questions whether lending to developing countries is unduly risky or even riskier than lending to industrial countries or domestic borrowers. In addition, she expresses skepticism over whether the extensive governmental measures taken since World War II to mitigate country risks have had a beneficial impact on the flow of capital to the developing countries.

Hughes observes that because of the perception that country risk would impede the flow of capital to developing countries a broad network of guarantees and insurance has been developed. Most industrial nations insure their residents for some direct investments and trade-related and other banking flows to developing countries. Official guarantees and insurance are buttressed by a network of private guarantees by parent corporations of transactions with their subsidiaries in developing countries. And governments of developing countries guarantee more than 75 percent of the public and private debt of developing countries to private foreign lenders.

As evidence that country risk is not a significant deterrent to foreign investors, Hughes reviews the sustained growth of commercial capital flows to developing countries since World War II. The composition of capital flows has shifted through time from official development assistance to nonconcessional official lending to direct investment to supplier's credits to bank loans to portfolio investment. Within the broad trend of increasing developing country access to private capital markets, there have been sharp shifts among forms of capital flows, often in response to shifts in relative costs. Hughes asserts that the fundamental reason for the steady growth in commercial capital flows has been profits; on average, investment in developing countries has been more profitable than investment in alternative domestic opportunities.

Hughes argues that the valid case for public insurance or guarantees against country risk rests on three propositions: (1) Enforcing contracts abroad is more difficult than within the domestic legal system; (2) political instability is inherent in the condition of underdevelopment; and (3) there is an ideological bias in favor of expropriation or repudiation in many developing countries. She asserts that the first proposition has no more special relevance to developing countries than to developed countries,[6] and that the second and third propositions are declining in importance as development proceeds and as more countries shift to market-oriented development strategies. She rejects several additional rationales for public insurance or guarantees, such as to compensate for poor information about risks in developing countries, to supplement foreign aid, or to subsidize exports.

Hughes urges that officials not overlook the useful role played by the private sector in allocating resources under uncertainty. If foreign investment is to be efficient, then the profits of foreign investors must depend on their judgments about the borrower's ability to manage resources efficiently and productively. Otherwise, if foreign investors are protected against the unprofitable consequences of their decisions, they may be less careful in their judgments. She argues that country risks are neither so much greater than nor different in kind from business risks in domestic transactions that they require special public intervention or subsidy.

Hughes concludes by agreeing with Cooper that developing country debt is not an important threat to the stability of the international financial system. She argues that, for the most part, developing countries, especially those that have borrowed most heavily, have managed their economies prudently. Moreover, she notes that the developing

---

6 Eaton and Gersovitz maintain that constitutional and institutional safeguards are sometimes (but not always) stronger in industrialized countries than in developing countries.

countries have an important stake in the survival of the international financial system; as a group, they hold assets in the system almost equal to their liabilities.

Rimmer de Vries observes that although country risks loom larger than at any time during the last two decades, bank managers are relatively unperturbed by them. Indeed, international lending has grown faster than bank capital and it has grown fastest to those countries that have already incurred the greatest indebtedness. Foreign exchange risk and interest rate risk are of much greater concern, perhaps because they have contributed much more to losses in the postwar era than country risk.

De Vries attributes this relaxed attitude toward country risks to a number of factors. First, most banks hold well-diversified portfolios of international loans. Even Brazil and Mexico, the heaviest borrowers among developing countries, each account for only about 10 percent of total international lending. (As de Vries notes later in his perspective, however, these loans comprise a much larger share of bank capital.) Second, the entrance of new banks, particularly Arab banks, in international loan syndications has spread country risks more widely. Third, the rate of growth of international lending is declining both in absolute terms and relative to the growth of exports in the borrowing country. Fourth, the International Monetary Fund has played a constructive role in helping countries devise adjustment policies and thereby strengthen confidence in the system. And most importantly, experience has shown that the international adjustment process works. Japan, Italy, and more recently, Brazil have demonstrated that countries with substantial current account deficits can reduce their imbalances, accelerate export growth, reduce oil consumption, and maintain economic growth. De Vries regards the experience with two major oil price increases as strong evidence that the market can work effectively in bringing about adjustment.

Despite these favorable factors, de Vries warns that bank managers should not underestimate country risks. He sees dangers to international lending from a number of sources. Although several countries have demonstrated that they can carry out effective balance-of-payments adjustments programs, many developing countries remain extremely vulnerable to disturbances in the world economy. Political instability in the Middle East could easily give rise to another sharp increase in oil prices (or a continuing drop in the inflation-adjusted price of oil could lead to a serious balance-of-payments problem for some oil-exporting countries). Sustained high interest rates could cause substantial difficulties for some of the heaviest borrowers in international markets, such as Mexico and Brazil.

De Vries argues that in country risk analysis, political or social and cultural factors are much more menacing than economic factors because the erosion of a country's creditworthiness due to economic factors tends to occur slowly whereas an unanticipated political change, such as in Poland, Iran, or Nicaragua, can affect a country's creditworthiness suddenly. This may reflect in part his judgment that banks can assess economic risks more effectively than political or social and cultural risks.

In reviewing recent experience with managing country risk, de Vries applauds the role of the International Monetary Fund in facilitating balance-of-payments adjustment, but he urges a greater role for the IMF in providing data and information necessary to assess country risks. He argues that improved data on government budgets, real exchange rates, real interest rates, and short-term debt would be especially useful.

John Reid evaluates the role of country risk analysis from the perspective of a manufacturing–marketing firm. He argues that predictions yielded by such analysis are seldom sufficiently precise or different from conventional wisdom to motivate action and that, in any event, after an investment has been made, there is little scope for defensive action.

Reid emphasizes that direct investors face quite different problems in risk management than do banks or portfolio investors. In general, direct investors have much less flexibility to adjust their asset exposure in response to changes in perceptions of country risk. Although investment decisions can be reversed and facilities can be abandoned, the costs of deviating from an investment plan are usually very high. Moreover, it is extremely difficult to enter, leave, and then reenter a foreign market, even if country risk assessments could yield reliable short-term information. Because start-up costs are large and investment projects tend to be irreversible and require large expenditures, direct investors must take a long view.

Reid characterizes the entry decision of a direct investor as a bargain between a corporation and the host government over access to the local market. Both parties to the bargain expect to profit from the investment. Reid stresses that country risk analysis is most useful before the bargain is made. Before direct investors have committed their resources, they have bargaining leverage – the threat of withholding their resources – and they may be able to obtain clarifications, guarantees, and concessions from the host government that will reduce their exposure to country risk, subject to the major uncertainty that the host government (or its successor, however determined) may alter the terms of the bargain after the investment has been made. But Reid argues that this uncertainty is different only in degree, not in kind, from risks investors customarily face in their home market. Unanticipated shifts in home government policies may have even greater impacts on corporate profits than shifts in the policies of foreign governments. Moreover, as recent events in France have made clear, the risk of expropriation is not limited to foreign investments in developing countries (although, presumably, compensation is more easily arranged when expropriation is by the home government).

Reid concludes that although direct investors have a variety of options for managing country risk before they enter a particular market, direct investors who have committed resources to a market must rely primarily on diversifying their investments across countries. Although diversification cannot prevent the realization of country risk, it can lessen the consequences for overall corporate activity.

Raymond Vernon focuses on organizational and institutional approaches to reducing country risk. He emphasizes that direct investment is a way of internalizing within the firm what would otherwise be international market transactions. He notes the irony that the decision to establish a foreign subsidiary (which is implicitly a decision to expose the firm to country risk) is often part of a strategy to reduce the firm's exposure to some other risk. The extensive work of Vernon and others has shown that direct investors are predominantly from industries with relatively small numbers of firms in which each firm can affect prices and each is vulnerable to actions taken by its competitors.

In industries that exploit and process oil and minerals, direct investment is often a way of achieving vertical integration – integrating all stages of the production process within the firm from exploration for and acquisition of raw materials to delivery to the consumer – in order to neutralize similar preemptive measures by a competitor that could otherwise jeopardize the firm's position in the industry. In industries that develop and apply advanced technologies or that market differentiated consumer products, the establishment of foreign subsidiaries is often a way of surmounting trade barriers that the host country has erected (or threatened to erect) while avoiding risks that might result from a sale of the technology or trademark to a host country firm. Such risks include disclosure of valuable information to third parties, competition with the firm in other markets, or erosion of the firm's reputation through failure of the foreign firm to maintain quality. Vernon also notes that some direct investment may be aptly characterized as follow-the-leader behavior: If a firm follows other firms in the industry into foreign markets it will not be put at a competitive disadvantage (although if the leader makes an error the industry may do badly relative to other industries). Thus the establishment of a foreign subsidiary is often a way of managing competitive risks that confront the firm, but it is a strategy that leaves the firm with a new problem of managing country risk.

Vernon surveys the various defensive measures that firms have taken as protection against country risk. Although joint ventures are often imposed on the firm by the host country government either implicitly or explicitly, they are sometimes chosen as a device for minimizing country risk. He identifies three kinds of joint ventures. The first is a consortium of foreign investors from several countries joining together to form a subsidiary in the host country. This approach may reduce country risk by blurring the identity of the home country of the subsidiary and may deter unfavorable actions by the host government by implicitly jeopardizing the host government's relations with several other governments instead of one. (But this is obviously not appealing to a firm with a differentiated product or a unique technological advantage.) The second is a joint venture with a local entrepreneur who may be able to give the firm better information about country risk or who may reduce the subsidiary's vulnerability to country risk by enhancing its image as a local firm. The third is a joint venture with a state-owned enterprise, which at least on the surface would seem to offer ideal protection against unfavorable actions by the host country government. Vernon, however, is very skeptical that any of these types of joint ventures provide effective protection against country risks or that the protection provided is worth the loss of flexibility and control over the activities of the foreign subsidiary.

Another approach to dealing with country risk may be viewed as an attempt to gain some of the advantages of direct investment without the vulnerability that results from owning assets in foreign countries. One such tactic is the long-term management contract. Vernon is in accord with Shubik that control over assets does not necessarily require ownership of assets. The present value of the flow of prospective fees from management contracts may be as attractive as the flow of prospective profits from a subsidiary, yet less vulnerable to country risk. Similarly, long-term supply contracts may be a less vulnerable substitute for direct investment. And long-term licensing agreements may be drawn up to provide adequate protection against disclosure to third parties, competition in third markets, and erosion of quality. But Vernon warns that such arrangements should be regarded as statements of intent rather than firm contracts. The difficulties in enforcing international contracts are so great that evasion of contractual obligations is easily accomplished whenever their fulfillment becomes burdensome.

Finally, Vernon examines a more tenuous approach to protecting against country risk – bribery. He notes that bribery may poison the climate for all direct investment in a country, but that differences in customs and traditions create difficulties in interpretation. Many measures firms take that are applauded by some observers as evidence of the firm's responsiveness to local sensibilities, such as offering blocks of stock to influential local figures at less than market value and appointing local government officials to lucrative directorships, may be viewed less charitably by others as bribes.

Vernon concludes that different institutional and organizational arrangements offer the firm a choice among different combinations of risks, but that no arrangements eliminate risk. The firm's problem is thus selecting the combination of risks with which it feels most comfortable.

James Street illustrates many of Vernon's points from his experience in a raw materials industry – oil – and a high-technology industry – agricultural chemicals. He emphasizes that foreign investment and the consequent exposure to country risk are essential for the survival of firms in these industries. Without foreign investment, the firm risks loss of access to raw materials, loss of access to opportunities for growth in booming foreign markets, and loss of position in the home market relative to foreign producers or home country producers who have invested abroad.

Street notes that focusing exports on the foreign market in order to obtain a significant market share is often a useful preparation for the establishment of a joint venture. His firm's experience indicates that developing a joint venture with the local government can take considerable time. Street reports that negotiations for his firm's establishment of a joint venture with Saudi Arabia to build a petrochemical complex took six years.

Chapter 6 addresses the problem of insuring against country risks. In their analysis, Howard Kunreuther and Paul Kleindorfer emphasize the decision processes through which investors and insurers deal with risk. They examine the way in which decision makers gather and assimilate data and identify and structure the alternatives before evaluating the alternatives to arrive at a final choice. They argue that in order to deal with the paucity of reliable information and the complexity of causal relationships that are often not clearly understood, decision makers will rely on simplified rules rather than attempt to specify all alternative outcomes and their consequences for the decision at hand. Such rules economize on scarce information and executive time, but they may also lead to biases in decision making. Kunreuther and Kleindorfer argue that these biases are especially important in decisions involving country risk because the information base is sparse and causal relationships are particularly obscure.

In the absence of appropriate information, the formulation of probabilities for various outcomes may be heavily influenced by recent experience. The term "availability bias" refers to the tendency of decision makers to assess the probability of some future event by the ease with which they can remember similar past events. Events that are vivid, concrete, and therefore easily recalled may be given much greater weight than less dramatic occurrences. For example, greater importance may be attached to insurrections, student strikes, or coups d'etat than to a humdrum shift in regulations and administrative decisions that may have much greater significance for the profitability of investments. In much the same way that motorists tend to drive much more cautiously than usual just after having witnessed an accident, corporate decision makers may be much less willing to undertake an investment in country A just after they have suffered an expropriation of their investment in country Z. Low-probability events that have devastating outcomes may be overestimated if a similar event has occurred recently, or they may be underestimated if, as will usually be the case for low-probability events, recent experience has been favorable.

In order to reduce the range of options that need to be considered, decision makers often employ threshold criteria. For example, if the probability of some event is sufficiently small, it will be treated as if it were zero and disregarded in further deliberations. Or projects with a probability of loss greater than some rate will be rejected summarily. A consequence of this technique is that little or no attention is paid to the way in which risks associated with different investments may interact, and inadequate diversification of country risks may result.

The reluctance to take responsibility for decisions that may result in loss leads to a tendency to avoid new markets or activities and to share the responsibility for risky decisions as widely as possible. This may result in a preference for investments in countries where the corporation has had previous experience, to the detriment of diversification considerations.

The authors illustrate their analysis with reference to an actual international investment decision that was selected to emphasize the universal nature of the problem of managing country risk. The usual presumption in country risk analysis is that an investor based in a developed nation is contemplating an investment in a developing nation; but the authors examine a decision in which a corporation based in a developing country – Pertamina in Indonesia – is considering an investment that is dependent on conditions in a developed country – the United States. Not only does the example illuminate their analysis, but it also demonstrates that country risk is not confined to developing countries.

Kunreuther and Kleindorfer argue that both investment decisions made by corporations and insurance decisions made by insurance companies may be subject to biases. But, insurance companies may be subject to two additional risks: adverse selection and moral hazard. These risks are inherent in all insurance contracts, but they may be more difficult to control in the case of country risk insurance.

Adverse selection may occur in a situation where investors know more about the risk characteristics of the project for which they are seeking insurance than the insurers. If the insurers cannot discriminate adequately among projects in terms of their probability of loss, they may find that they have inadvertently insured the highest risks because, given the premium per dollar of coverage set by the insurers, investors will determine whether to buy insurance by comparing their estimate of the probability of loss with the insurance premium. If the investors' estimate of the probability of loss is higher than the premium per dollar of coverage, they will buy insurance; if their estimate is lower, they will probably not buy insurance. Since, by assumption, investors know more about the risk characteristics of their project than the insurers, the insurers will find that they have collected less in premiums than they must pay out in claims. Kunreuther and Kleindorfer think that this risk is an especially serious obstacle to the provision of country risk insurance.

Moral hazard results from the fact that insurers have only a very limited ability to monitor and influence the behavior of investors after a project has been insured. Since the insurance contract permits investors to transfer risk to the insurers, investors may be less prudent in avoiding hazards than if they were to bear the full consequences of an unfavorable outcome. If insurers have not anticipated such behavior in setting the premium, losses will result. Kunreuther and Klein-dorfer observe that because of the difficulties in monitoring international activities, the problem of guarding against moral hazard in country risk insurance is at least as great as that encountered in providing traditional kinds of insurance.

Kunreuther and Kleindorfer argue in favor of two public policy measures to increase the availability of country risk insurance. First, they favor a pooling of information between private insurers and the government to facilitate a more accurate assessment of country risk and to reduce barriers to entry of smaller firms that face large information costs on entering the country risk insurance market. Second, they endorse the development of a government reinsurance program that would enable smaller insurance companies to take a more active role in the provision of country risk insurance by allowing them to reduce their exposure through the reinsurance market to amounts commensurate with their capacity to bear risk.

James Wybar takes issue with Kunreuther and Kleindorfer's assumption that insurance premiums should be based on firm statistical evidence. Mortality tables, he argues, are the exception rather than the rule. Wybar stresses that actuarial practice is an art as much as a science. He contends that providing insurance against country risks is very much like providing insurance against natural catastrophes. The fact that estimates of the incidence of the hazard are somewhat subjective has not been a substantial obstacle to the provision of insurance against such hazards and should not obstruct the provision of country risk insurance.

The basic difficulty in dealing with low-probability events that cause heavy losses is that it is impossible to predict their incidence over short intervals. It is only by aggregating large numbers of exposures over long periods of time that general risk characteristics can be assessed. In this sense, country risks are more insurable the larger the number of different exposures that are insured.

Neither does Wybar regard the risk of adverse selection or moral hazard as especially important deterrents to the provision of country risk insurance. He thinks that insurers have adequate information to guard against adverse selection and that coinsurance, which requires the insured to bear a portion of all losses realized, is effective protection against moral hazard. As long as the share of the loss borne by the insured is greater than the cost of managing risk exposure prudently, the insured will have a sufficient incentive to behave in the insurers' best interests.

Wybar identifies the main obstacle to greater participation by smaller insurance companies in underwriting country risks as information costs and inadequate reinsurance arrangements for spreading large country risks across many insurers. He thinks that both obstacles can be readily overcome so long as risk-adjusted rates of return for underwriting country risk insurance are attractive relative to those obtainable for insuring against other risks. He is not enthusiastic about Kunreuther and Kleindorfer's suggestions for government involvement in country risk insurance. He argues instead for a revision of tax laws to facilitate accumulation of large reserves over long periods of time against those risks, such as country risks, that have a low probability of high loss.

Although it would be gratifying to conclude this highly synoptic introduction with a statement of the optimal way to manage international risks, it is apparent that there are no definitive answers. Nor, in view of the pervasive and irreducible uncertainty that surrounds the future, are there likely to be. Even though it is sometimes possible to influence the likelihood of prospective events – several such strategies are suggested by the contributors – there are few situations of any real importance in which future developments can be fully controlled. Consequently, insurance and diversification strategies are always likely to play a useful role in dealing with international risks. In addition, uncertainty can be reduced to some extent through a better understanding of the forces that give rise to international disturbances and country risks. It is hoped that these essays and perspectives will contribute to that end.

CHAPTER 1

Managing risks to the international economic system

RICHARD N. COOPER

Introduction: clarifying terms

We live in a period of high uncertainty, some would say exceptional uncertainty. John Kenneth Galbraith has called it the "Age of Uncertainty." The purpose of this chapter is to assess the risks, or one might better say, the threats, to the international economic system that arise from this uncertainty, and the suitability of present institutional arrangements to deal with those risks.

By "risk" I mean the possibility of an unforeseen development that influences our welfare. Risk as used here bears little relationship to the risk involved in games of chance, where the outcome is uncertain before the dice are rolled, but the nature of the outcomes is understood and their relative likelihood, or probability, is known. One might say there is statistical certainty in games of chance. In sharp contrast, the principal effort to deal with risk in social systems, as with hang gliding, is to try to influence the probabilities.

If the development is foreseen, it can be allowed for and is not a risk. For the most part, we will be dealing with unforeseen adverse developments. Favorable developments are generally of less concern, although in some cases, if they are mishandled, they may influence the future adversely, as when a firm finds itself with demand for its products that it cannot satisfy and thereby loses customers, or a country discovers oil, which creates public expectations it cannot satisfy.

A period of change almost always creates uncertainty, for the field of possible outcomes is wider than during a period of relative stability. The current international economy is in a period of rapid change. Some of those changes are driven by technology, such as improvements in transportation and communication, that integrate the world market and thereby reduce the natural protection of regional or national markets. Greater integration occurs partly by simply removing barriers of ignorance so that the "foreignness" is going out of foreign trade and investment. These developments create new opportunities for business firms, but they also stiffen the competitive environment in which firms must operate. Governments too are affected, for the globalization of markets undermines some of their traditional modes of intervention into economic activity; but it also creates new opportunities to exploit the mobility of business firms.[1]

Rapid change has also emanated from the political arena, mainly from decolonization and its continuing aftermath, during which the political framework in which economic transactions take place is in a constant state of flux. Breaking political ties with former colonial powers removed an element of stability and relative certainty, but it also reduced the privileged position of the colonial power, thus creating new opportunities (with their attendant uncertainties) for outsiders.

During the past decade, developing countries have not merely altered the basis for doing business at home; they have also become important actors on the world scene, partly as rapidly growing exporters of manufactured goods (Korea, Brazil, etc.), and partly as political actors calling for fundamental changes in the international economic system, thus creating uncertainties about the durability of the existing "rules of the game."

Finally, the thawing of the Cold War and the emergence of détente removed a comprehensible (if not always sensible) framework for East–West relations. Again, new opportunities for trade have been created, but they remain uncertain because of continuing ambivalence on the part of American officials and the American public toward trade with Communist countries. A decline in temperature again, especially after the Soviet Union's invasion of Afghanistan and the imposition of martial law in Poland, introduces new uncertainty for Western economies arising from the possibility of politically induced reductions in East–West trade. But, in fact, trade between Western and Eastern Europe (including the Soviet Union), although important to individual firms, has never reached such a scale that even major reductions would pose a serious threat to Western economies or to the economic system as a whole.

It will prove useful to distinguish among different degrees of adverse development, ranging from a *disturbance,* which is an unfortunate event but one we can take in stride; to a *crisis,* which is a disturbance that threatens more serious consequences and the possibility of a *breakdown,* or *collapse,* which causes us to change, in some fundamental way, how we do things; to a *catastrophe,* which is a breakdown from

---

[1] This theme is developed at greater length in R. N. Cooper (1974).

which recovery is difficult, prolonged, and very painful, if indeed the process can be spoken of as "recovery" at all.

Other chapters in this book will be concerned with the risks that particular firms or, possibly, nations confront; this chapter will deal with the international economic system as a whole, by which I mean the framework in which firms and nations undertake international transactions. The framework comprises the formal rules, the informal conventions, and the accepted practices that govern international economic transactions, along with the institutional arrangements for policing the rules, resolving disputes, and changing the rules in the face of altered circumstances.

Obviously, some participants in the international economic system can be in crisis or even experience a breakdown (as when a firm declares bankruptcy) while leaving other participants, and the system as a whole, free of crisis and far from collapse. Indeed, the system can be said to be resilient precisely to the extent that it is able to absorb disturbances and even crises and breakdowns among its participants without generating a systemwide crisis, much less a breakdown. A system is supportive to the extent that it assists its participants in avoiding a disturbance from becoming a crisis, or a crisis from leading to a breakdown for the participants.

The time dimension must also be mentioned. A series of crises may seem to have been absorbed satisfactorily, yet leads over time to important changes, none of them dramatic but nonetheless cumulatively substantial. Do we call this a breakdown of the old system if the cumulative changes are sufficiently large? In historical perspective, the answer will almost surely be yes. But contemporary participants may have no sense of such a breakdown, only adaptation to altered circumstances and/or new information. Thus, both crisis and collapse have a time dimension; to warrant the label, events must occur rapidly. But how rapid is rapid will itself vary with the time perspective of the observer.

This chapter, then, will be concerned with disturbances that are sufficiently large and concentrated in time that they lead to crises for firms and perhaps governments of such a magnitude that they threaten to cause a breakdown of the international economic system or some substantial part of it. We must then ask the following questions: (1) What types of disturbances are most likely to do this? (2) What mechanisms do we have in place to prevent a crisis for the system? (3) What mechanisms do we have in place to mitigate the effects of a crisis and prevent a breakdown? (4) What improvements are possible to prevent systemwide crises and to mitigate the effects of those that occur? Implicit in these questions is the judgment that breakdowns are undesirable and should be avoided. Some breakdowns, however, will be welcome to some observers, and they may even be preferable (if the damage is limited) to continuation of a crisis-prone regime. The shift to flexible exchange rates following the partial breakdown of the Bretton Woods system in the early 1970s, for instance, may fall into this category.

The Great Depression: a catastrophe

The Great Depression offers examples of complete breakdowns in several parts of the economic system, and a brief examination of those aspects also provides background for the institutional innovations arising from the Great Depression that still form the core of the existing international economic system.

The basic causes of the depression are still a source of controversy and dispute.[2] For our purposes, it involved three separate but mutually reinforcing kinds of crisis: a tariff war, a banking crisis, and a balance-of-payments crisis. They all contributed to, but were also aggravated by, the sharp decline in industrial production and prices, which in turn were worsened by restrictive fiscal policies and efforts to deflate in the mistaken notion that if only factor costs, especially wages, could be reduced enough, national economies would right themselves.

Consider first the tariff war. Tariffs had already been raised after World War I to protect industries that had expanded during the war and now experienced new postwar competition. After 1925, world agricultural prices began to slump under pressure of large supplies, farm income dropped, and pleas for support of agricultural prices spread. Herbert Hoover campaigned in 1928 on a platform that promised tariff protection to American farmers, and Congress started hearings in January 1929 on a terms of reference that was not confined to agriculture. The Hawley-Smoot Tariff Act wound its way through Congress, passing the House in May 1929, to the growing anxiety and formal protest of foreign governments. In June 1930 (against the advice of 1,028 petitioning American economists), President Hoover signed into law the highest tariff in American history. Other countries – Spain, Canada, Italy, Cuba, Mexico, France, Aus-

---

[2] See, e.g., Peter Temin, *Did Monetary Forces Cause the Great Depression?* Temin's answer to his title's question is unambiguously negative, but he leaves the depression basically unexplained.

tralia, and New Zealand – retaliated with higher tariffs on American (and other) goods within a few months. Others followed later. Switzerland even promoted a boycott of American goods (Kindleberger 1973, p. 132).

Under the combined onslaught of falling real income, falling prices, and higher tariffs, international trade fell by two-thirds between 1929 and early 1933. Tariffs no doubt were the least important of the three causes, but they made a contribution to the decline and, more important, they both reflected and reinforced inward-looking national perspectives that made difficult international cooperation of any kind in mitigating the forces that were pushing the world into ever deeper depression. Kindleberger attributes the breakdown to a lack of world leadership; Britain (which supported a tariff freeze and maintained its economy open until 1932) was unable to provide it and the United States was unwilling to.

A second crisis was in banking. Also under the pressure of declining agricultural prices and incomes, a number of small American banks failed in 1929 and 1930 in the rural areas of the country. More serious was the failure of the Bank of the United States in December 1930. It had fifty-seven branches in New York and a capital of $25 million, so its failure was a major event. This failure was due to fraudulent and illegal activities by its owner, Bernard Marcus, who was subsequently sentenced to jail; it cannot be attributed directly to the depression. But it surely lessened public confidence in banks.[3]

Two French banks failed at about the same time, one also involving fraud and the complicity of several French officials (Kindleberger 1973, p. 146). But the major banking crisis came the following spring. Foreign lenders began to withdraw their funds from German banks, which had borrowed heavily abroad at short term, after the German election of September 1930 in which both the Communists and the Nazis greatly increased their representation in the German parliament, the Reichstag. This weakened the German banks. A second wave of withdrawals started in May 1931, both slightly before and

---

[3] Curiously, in their massive *Monetary History of the United States* (1964, pp. 309–11), Milton Friedman and Anna Schwartz argue that the Bank of the United States was fundamentally sound, despite the fact that it was insolvent, and fail to mention that its top officers were convicted of illegal activities, although it was a cause célèbre at the time – perhaps because such malfeasance did not fit into their thesis that all the major mistakes were made by government, and especially by the Federal Reserve Board.

massively after the announcement of the collapse of Austria's largest private bank, the Kreditanstalt. This bank had made some bad acquisitions in the preceding two years, and its weak financial position gradually came to light. The wave of distrust spread to banks in Hungary, Czechoslovakia, and Rumania, parts of the former Austro-Hungarian Empire, as well as to Poland and Germany, as though American lenders lumped all of these countries together, unaware of their separate identities. In June 1931, a German firm, Nordwolle, which had speculated unsuccessfully on a rise in the price of wool, went into bankruptcy. In July, the great extent of its losses, and the exposure of its creditors, especially the large Danatbank, became known; the withdrawals accelerated. Banks had to be closed temporarily, emergency loans raised, and support extended, but the damage to confidence in banks had been done, and the continued withdrawal of foreign deposits and loans led to a balance-of-payments crisis.

The major countries in this period adhered to the gold standard, which meant that gold provided the legal backing for the issue of currency and that each central bank would pay out gold on demand at a fixed price in exchange for its currency. The practice had become widespread during the 1920s for some central banks to hold as reserves the currencies of other countries, most notably sterling, on the understanding that those currencies could readily be converted into gold. Hence the regime has been called the gold exchange standard. France chafed under this arrangement (which had been advocated to conserve monetary gold), and after the French franc was stabilized in 1926 (at an undervalued rate), France began to convert some of its holdings of sterling into gold on a more or less regular basis. These conversions accelerated in the second half of 1928, and in 1929 the extent of U.S. lending abroad slackened to the point that the United States, too, began to pull in gold from the rest of the world. Between early 1929 and the summer of 1931, France and the United States together acquired $1.7 billion in gold, about 10 percent of world gold reserves. This occurred when London was still the acknowledged financial capital of the world and the Bank of England the principal regulator. Britain burdened itself with an overvalued currency when it returned to the gold standard at prewar parity in 1925, and Germany was burdened with reparations payments as stipulated in the Dawes Plan of 1924. Both countries borrowed abroad to cover their payments, and both were financially vulnerable to the withdrawal of foreign funds that came in 1931.

Hoover proposed a moratorium on all payments of reparations and intergovernmental war loans, but it was too late. Funds streamed out of Germany until a standstill on the withdrawal of all foreign funds was agreed to in July. The pressure then shifted to London, where the Reports of the Macmillan Committee and the May Committee had just been released, respectively indicating the extent of Britain's foreign liabilities and the extent of the upcoming budget deficit, along with sharp disagreement among its members on how to reduce it, but urging new loans from abroad. Two emergency loans were raised from France and the United States, but they were not enough to stem the wave of distrust and pessimism among both private holders of sterling and among the smaller central banks. Following erroneous press reports of a mutiny in the Royal Navy, withdrawals accelerated, and Britain went off the gold standard on September 21, 1931 (Kindleberger 1973, pp. 158–60). Two dozen countries followed and the international monetary system, as it had been known until then, collapsed. The United States held onto gold until 1933, France and the continental "gold bloc" until 1936. Germany declined to allow the mark to depreciate with sterling, as some recommended, out of continuing fear of inflation engendered by the hyperinflation of 1923. Instead, it introduced controls over international payments, a practice that was to be emulated widely during the subsequent three decades, continuing in some countries even today.

Once countries left gold, the possibility arose for exchange rate manipulation, active or passive. Under financial pressure, sterling depreciated by one-third by December, far more than was necessary to correct Britain's trading imbalance, and the drop stimulated Britain's sluggish economy. Japan, too, enjoyed the stimulus of an undervalued currency, and in 1933 the United States abandoned gold with the deliberate aim of "raising prices" within the United States. The dollar was repegged to gold at thirty-five dollars an ounce the following year, resulting in an undervaluation of the dollar relative to continental European currencies.

International cooperation was not wholly lacking during this turbulent period; it was merely hopelessly inadequate. Few national governments had the courage or the domestic political support for international cooperation that seemed to involve any sacrifice. Hoover did, it is true, successfully propose a moratorium on intergovernmental debts, but it came only in July 1931, and even then France had to be threatened with isolation before it agreed to go along. A series of special loans was arranged, usually with the Bank of England in the lead, to help countries in distress – Austria, Germany, then Britain itself. Central banks were the principal parties, and when the question of a massive new loan for Germany was raised in the summer of 1931, Hoover declined on the grounds that the U.S. budget deficit was already too large. France on several occasions stipulated political conditions on new loans, especially in an attempt to head off economic cooperation between Germany and Austria.

Once banks were seen to be in serious trouble, the distrust spread to other, unrelated banks, and withdrawals, both domestic and foreign, occurred apace. Finally, the decline of commodity prices and export earnings, plus the related drying up of the international bond market, led a number of primary producing countries to default on international bonds they had issued during the more buoyant 1920s (although other countries went through extraordinary deflation at home in order to continue payments on their bonds).[4]

Rebuilding the international economic system

The experience of the Great Depression governed the institutional arrangements that were established during and immediately after World War II and that in crucial respects prevail at the present time. Much, of course, was done in domestic legislation. The Glass-Steagall Act, the Banking Act, the Securities and Exchange Act, and the creation of the Federal Deposit Insurance Corporation were all designed to strengthen the U.S. financial system to prevent a repetition of stock market excesses and the rash of U.S. bank failures that had taken place during 1928–33. The Agricultural Adjustment Act aimed to prevent a collapse of farm prices and incomes. Above all, the Full Employment Act of 1946, and its counterparts in other countries, committed governments to act as the balance wheel of national economies, to prevent the kind of deflation of prices and incomes, the loss of production, and the rise in unemployment that had taken place during the depression.

On the international front, the main institutional arrangements are set out in the Bretton Woods Agreements and in the General Agreement on Tariffs and Trade. These agreements establish both general norms of international behavior, enjoining cooperation and a concern for the system as a whole, and particular rules designed to avoid what was thought to have been the worst behavior of the depression. They also established institutions to perform a facilitating role and to police the new norms and rules.

Briefly, the Bretton Woods Agreements required that each country

---

[4] For a brief discussion of the experience with defaults, see R. N. Cooper and E. M. Truman (1971); also Carlos F. Diaz-Alejandro (in press); and Jeffrey Sachs (in press).

establish a "par value" for its currency, which it would alter only to correct a fundamental disequilibrium in its international payments, and then only on notification and with approval of other countries. These provisions were designed to prevent the evil of competitive depreciation of currencies. Moreover, each country was to make its currency freely available both to residents and to nonresidents for payments for goods and services, a reaction to the exchange controls of the 1930s (but note the significant omission of a requirement for currency convertibility for capital movements). Each country was also obliged to convert its currency on demand from other *monetary* authorities (but not the public) into gold or some currency itself convertible into gold. Finally, two new institutions were to be established. The International Monetary Fund (IMF) would police the rules and would lend to countries at medium term in order to tide them over temporary balance-of-payments difficulties, thus providing a source of balance-of-payments support that was absent in the 1930s.

In addition, the International Bank for Reconstruction and Development (now known as the World Bank) was created to provide long-term loans to countries, to be raised in private capital markets. It did so by providing guarantees to the buyers of World Bank bonds backed by all the members of the World Bank. This arrangement permitted the resumption of long-term international lending.

With respect to trade, the General Agreement on Tariffs and Trade (GATT) established the principle of nondiscrimination in international trade, aimed to avoid bilateral trade agreements of the type set up by Germany and other countries during the 1930s. It prohibited quantitative restrictions on international trade (except for balance-of-payments reasons, with the approval of the IMF) and subsidies to exports. It involved a commitment to reduce tariffs over time through a process of multilateral negotiation, and a commitment not to raise tariffs previously in place. Finally, it established procedures for resolving disputes between contracting parties and for controlled retaliation in the event that disputes could not be resolved satisfactorily. The last feature was a novel one, designed to limit sharply any "trade wars" that might develop and to keep them on their own track, so they would not sour other cooperative relations among countries.

These various agreements made allowance for exceptions, and they have been administered flexibly over time – some observers would say too flexibly in the case of the GATT (see Curzon and Price 1979). But they nonetheless established a framework of norms that, along with the domestic legislation already mentioned, laid the basis for a remarkable world economic prosperity over a quarter of a century, probably the most prosperous period of that length the world has ever experienced.

The "breakdown" of the Bretton Woods system

The threats to the present international economic system are similar in kind to those that contributed to its breakdown in the 1930s: banking crises, balance-of-payments crises, and trade wars. In addition, because we have experienced a taste of it, we can now contemplate an oil crisis. We will return to these possible sources of disturbance in a contemporary setting. But first it will be useful to digress briefly on the alleged breakdown of the Bretton Woods system that occurred in the early 1970s.

The breakdown arose, like the collapse of the gold exchange standard forty years earlier, from a balance-of-payments crisis in the world's leading economy and financial center, now the United States. For a variety of reasons that need not concern us here, the U.S. dollar had become overvalued by the early 1970s. The U.S. payments position deteriorated both on current and on long-term capital account (especially direct investment), and when the protection provided by high interest rates in 1969 melted during the recession of 1970 and the recovery of 1971, capital began to flow out of the United States on a massive scale. Alarmed by the inflow of dollars (which, under the rules of the Bretton Woods regime, they were obliged to purchase at the going exchange rate), many central banks began to convert their dollar acquisitions into gold on a considerable scale. U.S. gold reserves were inadequate to cover the large outstanding dollar liabilities, a point that had been obvious for some time, and in August 1971, the United States ceased to convert dollars into gold for foreign monetary authorities. It also imposed a 10 percent surcharge on all dutiable imports in order to improve the competitive position of American firms, at least in the home market.

In December the surcharge was removed following a negotiated depreciation of the dollar and appreciation of other leading currencies amounting to a net (weighted) depreciation of the dollar by about 7 percent, an amount American officials considered inadequate. The par value system was salvaged, but with the important difference that the United States did not undertake to convert dollars into gold. When in early 1973 a large outflow of dollars resumed, other countries thus faced a choice of accumulating dollars without limit or allowing their currencies to "float" against the dollar. In March they chose the latter course, and the world entered an era of floating exchange rates, at least among the major currencies.[5] This system was formally sanctified in 1978.

It is an error to believe, however, that this development represented the demise of the Bretton Woods system. Rather, it represented the loss, and some would say a welcome loss, of one feature of the Bretton Woods system, namely the commitment to fixed exchange rates. The other features of the Bretton Woods system – the convertibility of one currency into another and the role of the IMF as a guiding hand and a lender to countries in difficulty – continued, in addition to the IMF's newly acquired role as an issuer of Special Drawing Rights, a new form of international reserves.

Although pressures on the dollar precipitated the move away from fixed exchange rates, tensions in the old system had been evident for some time – around sterling in the mid-1960s and around the German mark in 1969. These tensions were relieved with revaluations of those currencies (downward in the case of sterling, upward in the case of the mark), but only after much turbulence in foreign exchange and financial markets and after much disturbance to monetary policy.

Indeed, the fixed exchange rate feature of the Bretton Woods system contained a fatal flaw: National autonomy in monetary policy, fixed exchange rates, and free movement of capital are incompatible. One of the three had to give way. The Bretton Woods system did not require the freedom of capital movements, but as a practical matter it was impossible to separate capital from current transactions, and in any case several countries, including the United States, were committed to a high degree of freedom of capital movements. This remained true in spite of the restraint that the United States imposed on outward movement of some forms of capital after 1963. Nations were not yet ready to give up their autonomy in monetary policy, in effect, a return to the domestic version of the "gold standard" without the actual use of gold. That left the fixed exchange rates to give way, and they did.[6]

The collapse of the system of fixed exchange rates was long foreseen by a number of specialists in international finance – and urged

5 For an illuminating history of this breakdown, see Robert Solomon (1977, ch. 9–11).
6 Given this flaw, the interesting question is not why the Bretton Woods system broke down, but why it took so long to break down. One possible explanation, based on the fact that it took nearly fifteen years to implement the Bretton Woods system fully, is given in Cooper (1968, ch. 2, and pp. 234–42).

by some of them – but it nonetheless came as a surprise and a shock to the much wider public, and to this day is still usually considered a "breakdown," with its unfavorable connotations, rather than an improvement in the international economic system that, to be sure, was brought about in a disorderly fashion under the pressure of events.

Current threats to the international economic system

Let us return to the 1980s. Four possible sources of crisis are frequently mentioned, and we will take up in turn the nature of each threat and the institutional arrangements in place to prevent or contain it. These four are foreign exchange crisis, banking crisis, oil crisis, and trade wars.[7] As will become clear in the course of the following discussion, I believe that these possible threats are real, but that governments are well aware of them and, with the possible exception of a major oil crisis, they are manageable. The most serious threat to the existing system does not come from an international crisis at all – although there will certainly be crises from time to time – but from a gradual, piecemeal erosion of the international rules and conventions under the pressure of various national economic crises, such that after a period of, say, a decade the fabric of international transactions and international economic cooperation that has been successfully built up over the past thirty years may have disintegrated. But let us first turn to the possible sources of crisis.

Foreign exchange crisis

A foreign exchange crisis arises when there is a rush, for whatever reason, from one currency to another or, when the option is available, from a currency into monetary gold at a central bank. Foreign exchange crises brought down the gold standard in 1931 and part of the Bretton Woods system in 1971. These days, a foreign exchange crisis could be precipitated by an attempt by any large holder of liquid funds to convert them into some other currency, such as Iran threatened to do with its dollar holdings in November 1979. Or it could be precipitated by market perception that monetary policy in one country is way out of line with that in other major countries. Whatever the

---

[7] I leave to one side a major real war as a source of crisis. Full discussion of that remote possibility and its economic consequences would take this chapter on a quite different course.

reason, once the movement starts it is subject to bandwagon effects, that is, foreign exchange dealers initially buy or sell in sympathy with the initial impetus, rather than counter to it.[8]

Then what happens? We will leave for later discussion the possibility that some banks might run into difficulty because of large-scale conversions from one currency to another. With floating exchange rates among major currencies, large-scale conversions will lead to a depreciation of the currency being sold initially (it is, of course, also purchased – the rate moves enough to induce a purchase). Psychological bandwagon effects for or against a currency may lead to a sharp movement in its exchange rate. But sooner or later buyers will appear for a depreciating currency (and sellers for an appreciating one). The exchange rate will move until they do. Flexible exchange rates thus provide a safety valve – not always a comfortable one – in balance-of-payments crises; a country cannot be "driven off gold" now as in 1931 or 1971. The dilemmas for policy are more subtle, involving management of the domestic economy (a depreciating currency aggravates inflation) and export competitiveness (which is reduced by a currency that appreciates more rapidly than differential inflation rates would require). Countries with rapidly appreciating currencies will find imports more competitive and exports less competitive, and their governments may be called upon to protect imports, even though import restrictions would perversely accelerate the appreciation of the currency and worsen the position of exports. Countries with depreciating currencies will be tempted to restrict outflows of capital (as Germany did informally in 1980–1) or to tighten monetary conditions (as the United States did in October 1978).

Central banks can brake the movement in exchange rates, and sometimes even reverse it, by intervening directly in exchange markets. They act as counterspeculators. For an appreciating currency, there is no limit to the possible intervention, since the central bank is selling its own currency of issue; but large sales entail expansionist monetary policy that cannot always be easily or fully offset by open-market sales of securities.

For a depreciating currency the extent of intervention is limited by the country's foreign exchange reserves and its capacity to borrow abroad, including credit lines with other central banks. The major

---

[8] See the comment by Dennis Weatherstone, an important participant in the foreign exchange market, on John Rutledge, "An Economist's View of the Foreign Exchange Market," in J. S. Dreye et al. (1978).

central banks now have extensive access to funds. Once again, exchange market intervention influences monetary conditions, in this instance in a contractionary direction.

Some countries still peg their currencies to the dollar or to a weighted average of other currencies. A number of European currencies are confined within a series of bilateral exchange rate limits by the European Monetary System. In these cases a country can, of course, be forced off its previous rate by sufficiently large movements of funds across the foreign exchange market. But that is not likely to represent a threat to the monetary system as a whole, however traumatic it may be for the particular country. We have now had many cases of exchange rate adjustment. The International Monetary Fund often oversees, and indeed recommends, such a change and accompanies it by a loan to help the postdevaluation adjustment. Recently the IMF has greatly augmented the amount of funds it will make available during these stabilization programs, and it has also adapted the conditions it lays down for a loan to fit the diverse circumstances that may lead a country into balance-of-payments difficulty.

One inhibition to currency devaluation these days may be the large amount of external indebtedness denominated in foreign currency. Currency devaluation increases the local-currency cost of servicing these debts, and unless that possibility has been allowed for (e.g., through reserve funds), a nongovernmental debtor may be forced into bankruptcy. The problem of external indebtedness will be discussed further in the next section.

To sum up, flexible exchange rates provide a considerable shock absorber for the international economy. Balance-of-payments crises are not likely to threaten the system as a whole, except insofar as they give rise to banking crises or lead to trade restrictions.

Banking crisis

A bank insolvency can ricochet through the banking community, leaving a field of illiquidity and even further insolvency. This is because of the great extent to which interbank transactions dominate bank lending, especially international banking. The so-called Eurocurrency market had grown to an astounding $1.4 trillion by the end of 1981, of which over $1 trillion was in interbank deposits. Thus, if one bank becomes insolvent, it freezes and perhaps reduces the assets of other banks. Moreover, the insolvency can influence other banks by reducing confidence in them, and thus lead depositors to withdraw their funds.

The precipitating events may be a withdrawal of funds by a major depositor, default by a major debtor, or losses in operations of the bank by its management's bad judgment, bad luck, or malfeasance.

Despite the attention it has received in recent years in connection with the massing of large surplus funds by oil-exporting countries, a major withdrawal of funds is not likely to cause a banking crisis these days. If we are dealing with a single currency, any withdrawal of funds must be redeposited, directly or indirectly, elsewhere in the banking system. Unlike in the 1930s, withdrawals cannot take place in gold, and large depositors are unlikely to withdraw banknotes. So banking funds will be moved about, but not reduced except through contractive central bank action. A run by small depositors into bank-notes is, of course, conceivable, but in the United States this is inhibited by deposit insurance, an institutional bulwark that many other countries have not yet adopted.

Large withdrawals do, of course, create a problem for the particular bank that is subject to the withdrawals, but so long as it is perceived to be sound, it can borrow funds in the interbank market to cover the withdrawals to the extent that it cannot liquidate some of its assets. Thus, large-scale withdrawals become a serious problem only if the bank is in trouble for other reasons and has effectively lost access to the interbank market. Even then it will generally have access to the discount window of its central bank. Understandings on this point with respect to foreign banking will be taken up later in this section.

More serious is default by a major debtor. During the past decade, and especially since the oil price increases of 1974, there has been an enormous increase in international debt. Although the increase has been virtually universal, the increase to developing countries (other than members of OPEC) has been the source of the most articulated concern. Official institutions have greatly increased their lending, but bank lending has increased even more, by a factor of 6 between 1973 and 1981 (see Table 1.1). The largest single debtor countries were Brazil and Mexico, whose external debts were huge, both absolutely and relative to the capital of some lending banks. These figures are somewhat misleading, since a consequential amount of bank lending involves guarantees by third parties (68 percent of loans to non–OPEC developing countries in 1981), typically governments of the major exporting countries, and this is even more true of non–U.S. bank loans than of U.S. bank loans. Still, there is no question that banks these days are highly leveraged. The ratio of equity capital to total assets of the nine U.S. banks most heavily engaged in interna-

Table 1.1. *Long-term external debt, 1973–81 (in $ billion)*

	1973	1981
East European countries (bank claims only)	9.0	55.1[b]
OPEC members (bank claims only)	3.0	59.8[b]
Non–OPEC developing countries	96.8	436.9
Official creditors	48.3	175.6
Private creditors	48.5	261.4
financial institutions	34.6	223.6
Oil-exporters	15.6	90.6
Others	81.2	346.3
Debt service payments	15.3	92.3
Ratio of debt service to exports[a] (percent)	14.0	21.0

[a] Exports of goods and services.   [b] 1979.

Source: From IMF (1982, Tables 30, 33); and IMF (1980, Tables 2, 3).

tional business was only around 4 percent.[9] Lending to all non–OPEC developing countries by these nine U.S. banks amounted to 204 percent of their capital by the end of 1980, up from 156 percent in 1977. Moreover, there were eighty instances in which loans by U.S. banks to a single developing country exceeded 30 percent of its capital (up from thirty-six instances in mid-1979) (see Wallich 1981).

Given the magnitude of external debt, and the varied economic and political disturbances to which countries around the world are subject, default is a major source of concern. At the end of 1980, a total of twenty-six countries, mostly African and Central American, had payments in arrears amounting in total to over $6 billion, the equivalent of 42 percent of the 1980 export earnings of the countries involved. This represented an increase in arrears from just under $1 billion in 1975, involving thirteen countries (see IMF 1981, p. 22).

In one respect the situation today is intrinsically more precarious than it was in the 1930s, when most lending to developing countries was in the form of bonds, most of which were held by households and institutions other than banks. Under those circumstances, a domino effect through the banking system was less likely. Defaults to bond holders could be taken more or less in stride (Sachs, in press). Even banks can absorb defaults, if they are sound and well diversified. But the possibility of multiple defaults and the resulting interruption of

[9] This compares with equity–asset ratios for U.S. banks of around 13 percent in 1929.

the continuing flow of funds through international markets lead banks and debtors alike to go to considerable length to avoid formal defaults. The practice of rescheduling debts that are in threat of imminent default has developed precisely to avoid the possible consequences of default, both for creditors and for debtors. Under these arrangements, a debtor country for which default threatens asks for a meeting of major creditor nations (known as the "Paris Club"), usually under the chairmanship of the French Ministry of Finance. The debts in question are official and officially guaranteed claims with maturity over one year, including official export credits or guarantees. An assessment of the economic prospects of the debtor is made, and the creditors agree to reschedule the principal payments of the outstanding debt due in the coming year, often with a grace period of several years during which no payment of principal is required. An agreement with the IMF on a stabilization program has been required as a condition for rescheduling (except in the recent case of Poland, which is not a member of the IMF). Moreover, the debtor undertakes to reschedule its debts to private creditors, mainly banks, on terms no more favorable to the creditors than was the case for the official debts. Thus a framework is established for working out a rescheduling with the leading bank creditors.

This system, which falls short of the "standstills" that were introduced in several instances in the 1930s (because interest and some nonrescheduled principal continue to be paid), has the advantage of avoiding formal default, keeping the debtor country formally creditworthy and maintaining the loans on the balance sheets of the lending banks at full value. The possibility of insolvency is thus avoided, albeit at the expense of increased maturities on the loans and reduced liquidity for the lending banks.

Over thirty debt reschedulings have taken place during the past decade, involving amounts in excess of $1 billion for Turkey (1978 and again in 1980), Zaire (1979), and Poland (1981), as well as Indonesia in 1970 (see Table 1.2).

The banks are rather well diversified in their international lending, with their loans spread among developed countries, Eastern European countries, oil-exporting developing countries, and oil-importing developing countries. They have tended to avoid lending to the poorest countries, leaving them to official institutions such as the World Bank. Default thus would become a major problem only if several substantial ones occurred at the same time, due most likely to a common cause such as another large increase in oil prices or a major world recession, or both.

Table 1.2. *Multilateral debt reschedulings, 1972–81*

Year	Number of debtor countries	Total amount rescheduled ($ million)
1972	5	650
1973	2	290
1974	4	1,594
1975	2	397
1976	2	330
1977	2	200
1978	2	1,780
1979	4	2,750
1980	3	3,036
1981	8	4,116

Note: Data refer to official and officially guaranteed debt.

Withdrawals of deposits or default by a major borrower can become a serious problem if a particular bank is already in trouble for other reasons, such as having incurred large losses on foreign exchange dealings or on real estate loans. In that case the bank in question may not have access to adequate liquidity through the interbank market. It may even become insolvent in the traditional way, through bad commercial loans or operating losses. Two examples of bank failures, Bankhaus I.D. Herstatt and the Franklin National Bank, did greatly disturb the international banking system during 1974, a year of rapid change in banking because of the fourfold increase in oil prices and the consequent OPEC surpluses and general economic uncertainty.

Herstatt had suffered large losses on foreign exchange transactions, which it had concealed through false bookkeeping. When this was discovered the German banking authorities declared Herstatt bankrupt in June 1974. It was a medium-sized bank, with $800 million in assets, but it had $200 million in outstanding spot foreign exchange contracts. The difficulty arose because the bank was closed immediately after the close of business, European time, after it had been credited for its purchases, but several hours before the close of business, New York time, before it had been debited. Thus, numerous banks found themselves without expected receipts on a spot transaction, and as a consequence the foreign exchange market virtually came to a halt for several days. It was resumed (on a scale reportedly only about one-third of what it had been) through the expedient by the New York Clearing House of allowing payments to be recalled up to a day after they had been made. Moreover, smaller and less well-known banks had great difficulty dealing both in foreign exchange and in the Eurocurrency market for some time thereafter and had to pay a premium on transactions when they were readmitted to the markets.

The Franklin National Bank had also lost substantial sums in its foreign exchange dealing and had attempted to conceal the loss through manipulation of its books. Rumors about the difficulties of Franklin had been circulating for some months after December 1973, but the difficulties did not become public until May 1974, whereupon there was a rapid withdrawal of funds, both domestic and foreign, from Franklin and its London and Nassau branches. The scale of Franklin (the ninety-fourth largest American bank, with assets totaling $4.8 billion), and in particular its foreign exchange commitments of $2 billion, caused concern in the Federal Reserve about the impact of a precipitous collapse by Franklin on the international financial system. To avoid this, the Federal Reserve lent to Franklin through its discount window on an unprecedented scale ($1.8 billion by the time Franklin actually closed its doors). The loan was also unprecedented in its duration and in its availability to cover deposit withdrawals from Franklin's foreign branches as well as from the home office. Finally, once it became impossible for Franklin to carry out foreign exchange transactions, the Federal Reserve purchased and sold foreign exchange on its behalf, and in the end took over Franklin's remaining foreign exchange book of some $800 million for settlement, subject to indemnification for losses or nonperformance by the other parties.[10] Without this assistance from the Federal Reserve, the ramifications of Franklin's failure would no doubt have been very wide indeed.

Both Herstatt and Franklin operated within their home jurisdictions, although foreign exchange transactions played a crucial role in the demise of each and Franklin was heavily in debt in the Eurocurrency market as well. Both thus had important connections beyond national boundaries. But what about the possible failure of banks operating outside their home jurisdiction? How would the difficulties of, say, an Italian bank operating in London in U.S. dollars have been handled?

The possible problems created by the growth of international banking were brought home to central bankers during the banking crises

---

[10] For an excellent and detailed account of the collapse of Franklin National, how it got into its difficulties, and the interagency and international cooperation that was involved in isolating and resolving the problems, see Joan Edelman Spero (1980).

of 1974, but they were unable in several meetings at the Bank for International Settlements to resolve their differences fully. They issued a communiqué after their September 1974 meeting saying that "they recognized that it would not be practical to lay down in advance detailed rules and procedures for the provision of temporary liquidity. But they were satisfied that means are available for that purpose and will be used if and when necessary" (Spero 1980, p. 155). This vague statement was not entirely comforting to the banking community and others concerned with the stability of international banking. As host to the largest international banking center, the Bank of England attempted a more precise definition of responsibilities, one that would limit its own exposure. It stated that branch banks were clearly the responsibility of their parents and, through their parents, of the regulatory authorities of the home country of the parents, which the Federal Reserve implicitly acknowledged in its handling of the Franklin case. It went on to suggest that in the case of subsidiaries and consortium banks the parent–owners had a moral responsibility for their support, defined as "responsibility to support those investments beyond the narrow limits laid down by laws of limited liability and, above all, as responsibility to protect depositors with those banks" (Bank of England 1975, pp. 188–94). The Bank of England sent letters to owners of consortium banks and parents of subsidiaries operating in London, asking them to accept such moral responsibility, and they did so.

It is unclear whether the central banks in the home countries take a similar view of their responsibility. In summarizing the extensive cooperation that has developed among national bank supervisors, also arising out of the banking crises of 1974, and in particular the division of responsibility between home and host countries (home countries are to worry about the solvency of their banks on a worldwide consolidated basis, host countries are to worry about the liquidity of the banks operating under their jurisdiction), Peter Cooke has stated that the agreed division of responsibility "is not, and was never intended to be, an agreement about responsibilities for the provision of lender of last resort facilities to the international banking system, and there should not necessarily be considered to be any automatic link between acceptance of responsibility for ongoing supervision and the assumption of a lender of last resort role" (Bank of England 1981, p. 240).

Thus, despite the important strides that have been made in international cooperation, most notably in data collection and consolidation and in exchange of information among bank supervisory authorities, important ambiguities remain. These are perhaps necessarily present because of the potential inability of any central bank to be a lender of last resort in a currency other than its own and also because of an understandable reluctance by the Federal Reserve (and other central banks whose currencies are used internationally) to take on that responsibility for banks around the world that fall wholly outside of its regulatory reach and involve no American ownership.

Despite the remaining ambiguities, the fabric of cooperation among central banks and their sense of common purpose in preventing a collapse of international banking are both sufficiently strong that the banking crises that will surely arise from time to time are not likely to lead to a collapse of international banking. Given the extensive swap network between the Federal Reserve and other central banks – now amounting to over $30 billion – as well as the unlimited short-term credit that is afforded between central banks that are members of the European Monetary System, even the lender of last resort function in another currency can be carried quite far.

An oil crisis

Modern economies are extremely dependent on petroleum, and by 1977, 53 percent of the petroleum for the non-Communist world originated in the Persian Gulf plus Libya and Algeria. A cutoff of all or even a substantial fraction of this oil would have devastating effects on the economies and even the political systems of the Western world. Even the fear of a cutoff, or a price increase based on those fears, is a major disturbance to Western economies.[11]

An oil crisis is no longer hypothetical. The world experienced two during the 1970s. The first was in 1974 when, following a brief embargo by the Arab oil producers of the United States and the Netherlands for their support of Israel in connection with the Yom Kippur War, the Organization of Petroleum Exporting Countries, led by Iran (which had not participated in the embargo), raised the posted price of Persian Gulf crude oil by a factor of four. The second was in 1979, when the revolution in Iran deposed the Shah and led to a reduction in Iranian production by about two million barrels a day – although the immediate reduction was considerably larger – and a worldwide scramble for oil.

It is worth recalling that the world has been subjected to four other

[11] A good review of the possibilities can be found in David Deese and Joseph Nye (1981).

interruptions of oil from the Middle East, although none of them caused the widespread damage of the 1974 and 1979 price increases. Iran nationalized its oil production in 1951, whereupon Iranian oil was boycotted by Western firms for nearly three years. The Suez Canal, through which most Persian Gulf oil was transported to Europe, was closed in 1956–7 and again in 1967 (for eight years). And Iraq invaded Iran in September 1980, with the result that Iraqi and Iranian oil exports together declined for a time by about 3.5 million barrels a day. Although these interruptions, particularly the one in 1956, created some turbulence, they did not create the devastation of the 1974 and 1979 disturbances. In each case, new or excess productive capacity was brought into production. Moreover, in 1967, Europe was already reducing its dependence on the Suez Canal, with large tankers going around the Cape of Good Hope, and in 1980, there were exceptionally large stocks (built up in panic buying during 1979) combined with a downturn in demand for oil brought about by the 1979 price increases and the attendant economic recession.

Because of the importance of oil, major increases in oil prices greatly complicate the management of modern economies. An immediate effect is to raise the general price indexes, such as the consumer price index. That in turn may stimulate demands for higher wages and for higher prices of items not directly related to oil. At the same time, higher oil prices involve a tremendous transfer of wealth from oil-importing to oil-exporting countries – over $90 billion a year in 1974 and about twice that in 1980. This transfer reduces the real standard of living in oil-importing countries (which wage earners and others may fruitlessly attempt to recover through higher wages and prices) and creates large imbalances in international payments until the oil-exporting countries are able to adapt their expenditures to their new levels of income, a process that may take several years. Moreover, until this adjustment takes place, the world is likely to experience contractionary tendencies, since oil consumers (because of the inelasticity of their demand for oil) will reduce their purchases of other goods and services faster than the oil producers will increase their demand. Thus, the economic decisionmakers in industrial countries are faced with a sharp dilemma. To maintain demand and avoid an unnecessary rise in unemployment, they should for a time pursue an expansionist economy policy. To do so, however, will provide an environment in which heightened wage demands are more likely to be satisfied, thus converting the oil price increase into a wage–price spiral. The extent of this latter danger, of course, depends on the state of the economy at the time of the oil price disturbance and on the extent to which wage settlements are responsive to slack in the labor market.

Future disturbances in the oil sector cannot be ruled out; on the contrary, they are likely to occur, although it is difficult to predict just how they will occur (as late as mid-1978 few were predicting a revolution in Iran). No preparation can be fully adequate to deal with a stoppage once it occurs, but without any preparation an oil stoppage would threaten the smooth functioning of modern economies and even the basic political institutions in many countries. The loss of real income and the secondary impact on economies would provide fertile ground for radical political movements offering panaceas and making scapegoats of established political figures for the inflation and unemployment. The rise of Hitler through democratic processes in depression-ridden Germany comes to mind. Or there may be military coups as parliamentary governments demonstrate their inability to cope with the economic distress, as in Turkey in 1980.

Most governments are aware of these dangers, but it remains sadly the case that national policies and international cooperation are not fully adequate to deal with the risks. The failure to act arises from the high costs of the various possible courses of action to reduce dependence on Middle East oil, from the distributional consequences of some of those actions, and from sharp disagreements over which actions would be most efficacious. One school of thought, dominant in Germany and, since January 1981, in the U.S. government, holds that allowing the market free rein offers the best approach to allocating scarce resources, even in an emergency. (Despite its philosophy, the German government has prepared for emergency allocation, should the need arise. The U.S. government has not been so wise.) There are, however, several factors that market participants will not take into account without some kind of government interference. Market participants will of course take actions to prevent damage to their own direct interests from any likely interruption. But they will not, in their individual decisions regarding consumption of oil or its substitutes, allow for the dangers to our institutional structures arising from excessive dependence on imports from an unstable part of the world. Neither will they allow for the undesirable macroeconomic effects of excessive dependence on imported oil. Finally, market participants do not allow for the collective impact that they can have on the price of oil (their monopsony power, taken together). It is the role of government to look after these external effects, particularly those (such as macroeconomics and national security, broadly defined) that fall directly under their charge.

The United States in 1980 (a year of recession) accounted for 37 percent of non-Communist world oil consumption and about 20 percent of world oil imports. Thus, active U.S. participation is necessary in any scheme to reduce the Western world's dependence on Middle East oil, but moderate action by the United States alone would not be sufficient. To deal with the possible risks adequately, some kind of collective action is necessary. The objectives of such action should be threefold: (1) to avoid disturbances to the oil market insofar as that is possible; (2) to reduce dependence on potentially uncertain sources of oil, so as to reduce the impact of a disturbance in the oil market; and (3) to take emergency measures in the event of an oil crisis to mitigate both its immediate impact and its longer range impact through the racheting up of prices.

The first of these objectives is the task of general foreign policy. We have learned in recent years that some disturbances are beyond the control or even influence of Western governments, and in any case, foreign policy has its own conflicts and dilemmas such that it cannot typically be directed at a single, exclusive objective, however important that may be. But avoiding turbulence in world oil markets should be a major objective of U.S. (and European) foreign policy in the 1980s.

The second and third objectives have become sources of lively discussion and action in the International Energy Agency, a Paris-based, twenty-nation organization of industrial countries created in the wake of the 1974 energy crisis, as well as within the European Economic Community and at the seven-nation economic summit meetings in 1979 and 1980. With respect to the second objective, the IEA established medium-range (1985 and 1990) collective objectives for oil imports, along with a reporting and monitoring framework for national actions designed to achieve these collective objectives. It established year-by-year national "yardsticks" in order to measure national performance against the collective objectives. The heart of this program is, of course, the national actions taken to reduce dependence on imported oil, but the IEA mechanism provided an international framework for assessing the adequacy of those national actions and for encouraging all IEA member countries to take actions. This avoids the tendency of small countries to adopt the "free rider" position of allowing the larger countries to take the difficult actions alone and solve the problem for all.

This medium-range program now seems to be in abeyance, since the U.S. government under President Reagan has taken a negative view of medium-range targets for oil consumption and of national actions to reduce oil consumption, other than simply allowing the price to rise or fall with conditions of supply and demand. If other governments adopt a similar position, we leave ourselves open to the same risks of large disturbance that have already been experienced, unless one takes the view (which was also taken by some observers after the 1974 price increase) that at *today's* oil prices, conservation and switching to substitutes are sufficiently attractive that an adequate reduction in import dependence will take place even in the absence of additional actions.

The third objective, coping during an oil interruption, has been addressed by the IEA in two ways. First, it has established minimum oil inventory targets for all member countries – ninety days of imports – so that there will be some cushion against an interruption in supply.

Second, the IEA has established an emergency sharing scheme to be brought into play for a shortfall in supply that exceeds 7 percent of IEA consumption. Under this scheme, each member country would undertake to reduce home consumption by the amount of the shortfall; this would be accompanied by a prorated sharing of the available oil among all participating countries, if possible on a voluntary basis (through the leading oil firms), if necessary on a mandatory basis. This emergency sharing scheme is designed not only to assure the availability of oil to friendly nations, but also to offer them enough security that they will not engage in a competitive scramble for limited oil supplies in a fashion that sharply drives up not only the spot market price of oil but also the posted OPEC (term contract) prices, as happened in 1979.

The emergency sharing scheme was not invoked in 1979 because the global shortfall did not in fact reach 7 percent, since other oil producers, notably Saudi Arabia, increased their production to make up for the loss of Iranian production. But the uncertainties generated by the loss of Iranian production (combined with the low level of stocks, which had been depleted during the "oil glut" of 1978) induced firms and countries to build stocks during a period of prospective shortage. The heightened demand for stocks in turn bid up prices on the thin spot market for crude oil, which in turn induced the members of OPEC to raise their posted prices several times during the course of the year.

The U.S. government remains formally committed to the IEA sharing scheme, but with great ambivalence because of its working assumption that the market can allocate scarce resources in a superior way even during an emergency. Apart from its professed willingness to draw down the Strategic Petroleum Reserve in an emergency short-fall, therefore, it leaves the international system exposed to the considerable risks in the oil domain that have already materialized twice in the past decade.[12]

The assumption sometimes made that a major disturbance in the Persian Gulf would be so threatening to the Western world as to call for military action overlooks the nature of the problem. Military force is necessary in sufficient strength to deter the Soviet Union from engaging in military action or even plausible (and perhaps implicit) military threats to the area. And an effective U.S. military presence in the area might well deter takeovers by radical political minorities. But a military presence cannot ensure the continued functioning of the oil facilities, wherein Western interest lies. Military preparedness is therefore not a substitute for energy preparedness.

Trade wars

Countries are tempted to protect their economies from import competition for a variety of reasons: to encourage "infant industries" with the prospect of development, to improve their international payments position, to protect employment in particular sectors that are experiencing import competition, to grant favors to particular firms or individuals who have supported the government in power, to retaliate against similar actions by trading partners, and so on. Some of these reasons are relatively unchanging over time. But calls for import protection are likely to be more strident and more favorably received − or more difficult to resist politically − during times when economic growth is sluggish, unemployment is high, and international payments are in deficit. Unhappily, these are the consequences, as we have just seen, of an oil crisis. Thus, the prospect of trade wars is enhanced by an oil crisis. But they could also arise simply from the efforts of countries to maintain tight monetary and fiscal policies in order to combat inflation.

Fortunately, there are several countervailing tendencies. First, governments are much better apprised these days of the strong positive links between trade and economic growth that have benefited the world economy during the past three decades. They are also aware that because major actions to restrict imports are likely to be emulated elsewhere, exports would suffer. This factor is reinforced by the pres-

---

[12] For an official statement reflecting a desire for exclusive reliance on market prices, see Department of Energy (1981).

ence of flexible exchange rates, whereby import restrictions would lead to a currency appreciation and thus would discourage exports. (Erratic movements in exchange rates that affect a country's competitiveness adversely have however led to some pleas for protection against seemingly arbitrary movements of currency value.) And governments are aware that import protection both in reality and in perception is not consistent with fighting inflation. Finally, since the 1940s we have had institutional mechanisms – mainly the GATT, but the IMF and the Organization for Economic Cooperation and Development (OECD) have also played important roles – which serve as forums for reminding governments of the consequences of protectionist actions, for strengthening their collective resolve not to engage in them, for settling trade disputes that arise, and finally, for maintaining some momentum toward continuing trade liberalization, even in difficult times.

On the whole, governments have behaved well during the extreme provocations of the two oil crises and the economic recessions they aggravated. The industrialized countries, through the OECD, pledged in June 1974 not to introduce trade-restricting measures to help them out of their current difficulties, recognizing that a round of such restrictions would in fact hurt rather than help. This pledge was repeated annually (and broadened and made permanent in 1980). The by now annual economic summit meetings among the seven heads of government of the leading industrial democracies have also recognized the importance of avoiding restrictions. And the Multilateral Trade Negotiations, launched in 1973, were successfully completed during 1979. They also extended the trade rules into some new areas (such as government procurement), clarified and tightened them in some old areas (such as the role of subsidies in industry and their impact on trade), and introduced new dispute settlement mechanisms associated with the seven codes that were negotiated as part of the MTN.

Given this recent experience, the prospect of an open trade war does not seem great. Rather, the risk is that there will be creeping protectionism, a gradual erosion of the relatively liberal trading environment that has been established since World War II. This erosion could take place through government takeovers of commercial enterprise and subsequent manipulation of their purchases and sales abroad, which would lead to different results from those achieved under a private, competitive regime; through "voluntary" restraint agreements under which a successful exporting country restrains its exports under the threat of more onerous restrictions imposed by importing countries; and through the misuse for restricting imports of the growing number of health, safety, and environmental regulations that national governments may quite legitimately impose on both imported and domestically produced goods.[13]

Gradual erosion of the system of cooperation

On the whole the institutional bulwarks are reasonably strong against breakdowns arising from crises in the four areas that have been discussed: balance-of-payments difficulties, banking difficulties, oil, and trade – with the possible exception of oil, where cooperation in the process of development now seems to have been set aside. But the bulwarks are less strong against a gradual erosion of the international economic system. From the perspective of, say, the year 2020, observers may look back on the 1970s and 1980s as a period of major transformation of the international economic system, and they may well speak of a "breakdown" of the post–World War II system of international economic cooperation.

But those of us who are living through it may not recognize any such breakdown. Crises, yes, because people are always impressed with their own difficult moments and tend to underrate the difficulties of past periods provided they turned out reasonably well. But not breakdowns. For those who live through this period, it will appear as an evolution of the international economic system, sometimes in an orderly way and sometimes as ad hoc responses to urgent and pressing developments.

The most important question will be the nature of the response to an oil disruption, already discussed briefly. Whether, and if so when, and if so how large, an oil disruption will be a major source of uncertainty through the 1980s and perhaps beyond. For many, an equally large source of uncertainty will be how governments of consuming nations respond to an oil disruption – by economic contraction, by introducing price and allocation controls – and even whether they will survive such a disruption politically.

A second major source of uncertainty will be the changing role of developing countries. Despite all the rhetoric that suggests they are being victimized by the industrialized nations, some of them have done extraordinarily well; others have been positioning themselves to

[13] For a discussion of some of these developments, see Curzon and Price (1979). For a brief description of the results of the MTN and their bearing on these developments, see Thomas R. Graham (1979, pp. 49–63).

grow faster through changes in their own economic policies and can be expected to do well during the 1980s, barring major disruptions to the world economy. Still others, in contrast, continue to blame the international economic system and the industrialized nations for their economic backwardness.

There is bound to be much economic transformation during the next decade whatever happens, and as noted at the outset, change creates uncertainty. How will developing countries actually develop? As they develop, will they see it in their interest to integrate more fully into the existing and evolving international economic system, or will they call for radical changes in it? Or will they simply take advantage of the opportunities it permits without actually supporting it by taking on its obligations, and thereby induce an erosion in the system as it becomes more difficult for developed nations to ignore deviations from its rules?[14]

How the industrialized countries will respond is another source of uncertainty, both with respect to maintaining open markets for the products of developing countries and with respect to admitting them into the circle of decision making on changes in the international rules as the developing countries are able and willing to take on the obligations of full membership.

The large and growing disparity of circumstances and views among developing countries is a further source of uncertainty. They have learned the advantages of bloc voting in the international political arena, and the Group of Seventy-seven, as it is called, has shown remarkable cohesiveness. But will the "moderates" or the "radicals" come to dominate the G-77? Or will it be a standoff, resulting in an incompatible and contradictory mixture of proposals for moderate and radical change, combined with indecisiveness that leads to immobilism by the international community? And how much difference will that actually make? The international economy has its own dy-

---

[14] A similar problem in principle, but on a much smaller scale, arises from the gradual integration of Communist countries into the international economic system. Trade and capital movements between market and nonmarket economies have grown sharply in the past decade. One after another has applied for membership in the GATT and the IMF, with Rumania entering the IMF in 1972, China in 1980, and Poland and Hungary probably in 1982. These developments, assuming they are not reversed, pose problems of adaptation for the guardian institutions, but they will not be insurmountable, nor will they alter radically the operation of those institutions.

namics of change, clearly influenced but not fully determined by the actions of national governments, and certainly not fully determined by international agreements or their absence. The evolution of the international monetary system took quite a different course in the mid-1970s, for instance, from the direction in which the Committee of Twenty, set up to reform the system, was pointing. On the other hand, continuing international disagreements over the nature of a seabed regime – disagreements between those countries in the G-77 who want maximum governmental involvement in management and even mining of the seabed, and those, mainly developed countries, who want maximum reliance on private enterprise – have almost certainly postponed by five or more years the inauguration of manganese module mining from the deep seabed. Moreover, radical rhetoric concerning "national sovereignty over natural resources," even when not embodied in damaging fashion in international agreements, fosters a climate of uncertainty about the security of investment in mineral industries in developing countries by helping to legitimate the future abrogation of contracts that seem (after successful development of a mine or well) to be inconsistent with one or another interpretation of this imprecise phrase.

Finally, continuing and sharp disagreements among developing countries may influence future decisions of OPEC, particularly insofar as some of the moderate members of OPEC feel politically insecure and must from time to time balance their generally moderate stance with more aggressive actions.

It is the function of diplomacy to manage these sometimes imponderable processes as skillfully as possible, trying to secure a moderate, evolutionary course that is more conducive to economic prosperity. But whether diplomacy will succeed is itself uncertain.

References

Bank of England. "Developments in Co-operation Among Banking Supervisory Authorities." *Quarterly Bulletin,* June 1981, pp. 238–44.
"The Supervision of the U.K. Banking System." *Quarterly Bulletin,* June 1975, pp. 188–94.
Cooper, Richard N. *The Economics of Interdependence.* New York: McGraw-Hill, 1968.
Economic Mobility and National Economic Policy. Stockholm: Almqvist and Wiksell, 1974.
Cooper, Richard N., and E. M. Truman. "International Capital Markets as a Source of Funds for Developing Countries." *Weltwirtschaftliches Archiv,* 1971, vol. 106, no. 2, pp. 153–83.
Curzon, Gerard, and Victoria Curzon Price. "The Undermining of the World Trade Order." *Ordo,* 1979, vol. 30, pp. 383–407.

Deese, David, and Joseph Nye (eds.). *Energy and Security*. Cambridge, Mass.: Ballinger, 1981.

Department of Energy. "Domestic and International Energy Preparedness." July 1981 (processed).

Diaz-Alejandro, Carlos F. "Stories of the 1930s for the 1980s," in P. Aspe, R. Dornbusch, and M. Obstfeld (eds.), *Financial Policies and the World Capital Market: The Problem of Latin American Countries*. Chicago: University of Chicago Press, in press.

Dreye, J. S. *Exchange Rate Flexibility*. Washington, D.C.: American Enterprise Institute, 1978.

Friedman, Milton, and Anna Schwartz. *Monetary History of the United States*. Princeton, N.J.: Princeton University Press, 1964.

Graham, Thomas R. "Revolution in Trade Politics." *Foreign Policy*, Fall 1979, no. 36, pp. 49–63.

IMF. *International Capital Markets*. Occasional Paper No. 1, September 1980. Washington, D.C.

Annual Report on Exchange Arrangements and Exchange Restrictions 1981, Washington, D.C.

World Economic Outlook, April 1982, Washington, D.C.

Kindleberger, Charles P. *The World in Depression, 1929–1939*. Berkeley: University of California Press, 1973.

Sachs, Jeffrey. "LDC Debt in the 1980s: Risk and Reforms," in P. Wachtel (ed.), *Crisis in the Economic and Financial Structure*. Lexington, Mass.: Lexington Books, in press.

Solomon, Robert. *The International Monetary System 1945–1976: An Insider's View*. New York: Harper & Row, 1977.

Spero, Joan Edelman. *The Failure of the Franklin National Bank*. New York: Columbia University Press, 1980.

Temin, Peter. *Did Monetary Forces Cause the Great Depression?* New York: Norton, 1976.

Wallich, Henry C. "LDC – To Worry or not to Worry." Mimeographed. Remarks to the Bankers' Association for Foreign Trade, Boca Raton, Fla., June 2, 1981.

Perspective: Political threats to the international economic system

ROBERT O. KEOHANE

These remarks constitute a "perspective" and are not meant as a critique of Professor Richard Cooper's chapter. My perspective is that of the student of international politics, the true "dismal science," since the repeal of the Iron Law of Wages and the development of new technologies of destruction and oppression that strengthen the hands of repressive governments – and terrorists – around the world.

This may be a dismal way to begin my commentary. But putting matters this way suggests an initial perspective on Professor Cooper's chapter. The risks with which Professor Cooper is concerned all have their origins in actions that would directly affect economic transactions of specific types – foreign exchange dealings, debt repayments, and trade in manufactured goods and in oil. Political-military risks, most notably, the risk of nuclear war and of a continually accelerating arms race, are not considered. Yet in the past, the world economy has been disrupted by war as well as depression, as the experience of World War I suggests. And in the present state of Soviet–American relations, the risks of nuclear war and of an escalating arms race should not be underestimated. The chief military advisor to the National Security Council declared in October 1981 that the Soviet Union had achieved military superiority, was "on the move," and was "going to strike" (*New York Times,* Oct. 21, 1981). Earlier that same month, the president of the United States suggested that a tactical nuclear war was possible in Europe without, perhaps, leading to a nuclear exchange between the superpowers. And the current American arms buildup has, as its rationale, the need for "superiority" and a "war-fighting capacity." I need hardly point out that the consequences of nuclear war for the world economy would be devastating, although the notion of a "world economy" after a nuclear war might itself be absurd. We cannot address issues of risks in the world economy effectively without at least remembering this greatest of all risks to world order – the broad topic of this book – and to our very survival.

Even if we avoid this cataclysm, we should consider the implications of an accelerated arms race for risks of a breakdown in the world economic order. One aspect of this is the stimulus that an arms race between the Soviet Union and the United States may give to other arms races, in particular, the quest for nuclear weapons by countries such as Libya, Iraq, and Pakistan. The risks to world order of a world in which many countries have nuclear weapons will be appallingly high. Nevertheless, it is very difficult to halt the spread of nuclear weapons, and our current administration has greatly reduced the priority given, in U.S. policy, to this objective.

The accelerated arms race also threatens the international economic order indirectly by its effects in the United States economy. If the United States diverts much of its capital and technological competence into new armaments, while Japan and Germany refrain from making comparable efforts, we are likely to find ourselves at a greater competitive disadvantage in technologies that have principally civilian uses, including much of the semiconductor and computer industry. If the American industrial structure declines, and our exports suffer, the United States will be less and less able to exercise leadership among the industrialized market-economy countries. We will be tempted once again to seek shortcuts – "quick fixes" to our problems that only make them worse in the long run and antagonize our allies in the process. Increased protectionism would become a real possibility. So would an increase in public hostility toward our allies as they grew richer and more dexterous, while we "protected" them with armaments of questionable value to ourselves as well as to them.

On balance, I think that these political–military risks to world order, and to the international economic system, are at least as serious as the political–economic risks that Professor Cooper discusses. This is not a criticism – nothing is worse than the commentator who demands that the author have written on a different subject – but it does provide a "perspective."

Let me now turn to the discussion itself. I agree with Professor Cooper that foreign exchange crises do not pose major threats to the international economic system. In the short run to middle run, at least, protectionism also does not seem likely to provide a source of major disruption, although, as I have noted, if the United States should fall behind quickly, even in high-technology civilian industries, protectionist pressures might grow. This leaves problems of banking crises, in particular, international debt, and oil. I wish to comment briefly on both. In conclusion, I will briefly consider Professor Cooper's concern with long-term erosion of international rules and conventions.

With respect to international debt, Professor Cooper says that the situation is "intrinsically more precarious" than it was in the 1930s, since banks hold the bulk of the debts of less-developed countries and the magnitudes involved are huge. As he points out, "default would become a major problem only if several substantial ones occurred at the same time." He then concludes that the system seems quite strong, but the grounds for this conclusion are not clear to me. The evidence presented suggests that the volume of debt is huge and still growing. Morgan Guaranty Trust Co. reports that, "Since 1973, the total external debt of the twelve major non-oil LDCs has nearly quadrupled and in relative terms has risen from 19% to 25% of the group's aggregate GDP" (*World Financial Markets* 1981, p. 11). Sixty percent of this debt carries floating interest rates, so that interest costs alone will be equivalent, in 1981, to $26 billion for these countries – about 17 percent of exports. At the same time, recession and sluggish growth in the industrialized countries will limit export growth, although the exports of these developing countries have been very strong despite the sluggish industrialized economies (19 percent export growth in 1981, 9.9 percent in real terms).

I do not want to debate the *economic* capabilities of major LDC borrowers eventually to repay their debts, certainly not with Richard

Cooper! Adjustment efforts by many of these countries have been impressive. But as *World Financial Markets* puts it, "a major uncertainty is whether the authorities in some of these countries will be able politically to sustain policies which depress the rate of per capita income growth" (1981, p. 10). When we focus on their political decisions, one approach is to examine situations country by country, as analysts of "political risk" purport to do. But insofar as idiosyncratic features of particular countries may account for occasional defaults, the problem is unlikely to be critical for the international economy as a whole. As Professor Cooper points out, the banking system could withstand a few isolated defaults, especially if they were temporary; indeed, as he says, the negotiating arrangements for avoiding defaults in these circumstances are quite well developed.

The political questions are more pressing at the level of *aggregate* flows. As long as the flows of funds to finance LDC deficits continue to increase, debtors have strong incentives to repay their old debts, or at most to refinance. The flows of incoming funds exceed those of outgoing funds needed to service debts. Under these conditions, rescheduling efforts such as those of the "Paris Club" are likely to work.

But it is important to consider how the incentives would change if the incoming flows of funds dried up, as flows from the United States to Germany did at the beginning of the depression (Kindleberger 1974). At this point, debtors would no longer have the incentive to repay old debts so that they could borrow more anew. Incentives might shift toward default, even if that involved serious economic and political costs. If interest costs came to exceed net new borrowing, there would be a great temptation, if not for governments, then for opposition groups, to denounce the "international bankers" as greedy exploiters, and to default, or demand default, on outstanding debts.

Default would not be a *necessary* outcome even at this point. Optimists believe that there are multiple incentives not to default: To keep open the option of access to capital markets even if, in the foreseeable future, outflows will exceed inflows, or to maintain export markets that might also be threatened by default. My point is simply that repayment should not be taken for granted. In the past, lenders have become hostages to debtors, as the experience of France and Russia before 1914 illustrates (Feis 1931). This could happen again.

I suggest also that the international situation bears some resemblance to a "chain letter" or a "pyramiding" scheme. Such a system has peculiar equilibrium properties. Within a certain range, with new funds flowing in, and expectations of repayment widely held, the system is stable, and mechanisms exist to smooth out the disturbances that do exist. But once critical features of the system, which sustain it, change sufficiently — as new funds cease to be lent and creditors begin to worry about whether the loans will be repaid — a cycle of instability and default could set in. At some point, prompt action by industrialized country central banks and governments, preferably with some systematic advanced planning, would be needed to stop the panic. It is to be hoped that if that point comes, governments will not be so blinded by antiregulatory ideology that they are unable or unwilling to act effectively.[1]

With respect to the question of oil, I agree entirely with Professor Cooper's conclusion that collective action is necessary. The process of international consultation and policy coordination in the International Energy Agency is important to the world economy and to the United States — much more important than is usually recognized in this country. This does not mean that the IEA can "solve the problem." But leaving it to the market alone is *certainly* inadequate. During 1979, a maximum 4 percent shortfall in world oil supplies led to more than a doubling of prices in the course of a year. Speculation and stockbuilding *aggravated* the problem: Companies drew down their stocks in 1978, when oil was selling at around fourteen dollars per barrel, and built them up in 1979, at costs of twenty-five dollars or more per barrel. Fortunately, the Reagan administration has recognized the inadequacy of leaving matters entirely to the market by accelerating measures to fill the strategic petroleum reserve. This is a wise policy and reduces the risk of international disorder. It is to be hoped that the U.S. government will recognize the importance also of keeping informal consultative and negotiating arrangements in place at the IEA. These arrangements reduce risk by improving the information that governments and companies have about the world oil market and each others' intentions; they helped to avoid panic in the wake of the outbreak of the Iran–Iraq War in September 1980, and they may be useful again. International cooperation is so hard to achieve, and institutions to facilitate it take so long to develop, that it would be foolish to discard the mechanisms for policy coordination that have been built up over the last eight years in Paris. The real significance of international organizations such as the IEA does not lie in their formal powers, which are virtually nonexistent, but rather

---

[1] Since these words were written, in October 1981, actions have been taken, by international financial organizations and the United States Federal Reserve Board, to prevent panic as a result of Mexico's economic difficulties and to avert a Mexican default.

in the communications channels they provide for sharing information and therefore reducing uncertainty and risk in world politics.

Finally, let me take up the contention that a gradual erosion of international rules and conventions may be a greater threat to the system, in the long term, than crises of one sort or another. I also believe that the liberal world economic system is more likely to end with a whimper than with a bang. Yet the policies that determine the direction of the system, and that constrain the choices of its members, are principally those of industrialized countries, although as Professor Cooper emphasizes, a fair amount may depend on the attitudes taken by newly industrialized members of the club. Perhaps it is useful to reemphasize, however, that it has often been the developed, advanced countries who have broken the old rules and imposed new ones in their place. When developing countries have become *too* successful, as in textiles, quotas have been enacted, implemented, and progressively tightened. One may go a step farther and say that it is the responsibility of the industrialized countries to improve the current international economic system as it affects the developing countries, and not merely to take it as given. Development has often meant increasing internal inequalities in developing countries, and has frequently been accompanied by bureaucratic authoritarian political rule, rarely by liberal democracy. An international economic system that allows certain countries to industrialize but that creates pressures for doing so under authoritarian regimes that rigorously control labor is not entirely benign. We should look not only at the adjustment policies of developing countries, but also at the requirements for adjustment that constraints from the international political economy impose.

For many people in poor countries, the current system does not provide the goods essential to a healthy and productive life. For them, the relevant risk may seem to be not that the current system will break down, but that it will continue.

Thus, in broadest terms, I find myself in agreement with Professor Cooper: International cooperation among the industrialized countries is necessary for world order, in energy and other commodities and in manufactured goods trade and financial affairs. Specifically, however, I believe that the political dynamics of decisions to repay, or not to repay, international debts require more attention, and that thinking about them should make us more worried about the possibility, although not necessarily the likelihood, of widespread default. But in a broader framework, we should also be concerned about two other problems that the existing international economic order does not effectively address: the dangers of accelerating arms races and nuclear war, which could destroy in minutes everything we are considering here, and the dangers of failure to change the present system in ways that would improve the conditions of life of poor people around the world.

References

Kindleberger, Charles. *The World in Depression, 1929–1939.* Berkeley: University of California Press, 1974.

Feis, Herbert. *Europe: The World's Banker.* 1931. Reprint. New Haven, Conn.: Yale University Press, 1974.

World Financial Markets, May 1981, p. 11.

Perspective: The crisis of exogeneity, or our reduced ability to deal with risk

TOMMASO PADOA-SCHIOPPA

Introduction

In Chapter 1, Richard Cooper has given us a masterly description of the possible sources of crisis at the beginning of the 1980s. In all the areas he covered (foreign exchange crises, banking crises, trade wars, and oil crises) the source of the risk did not lie in nature but, at least in part, in voluntary human actions. I could not avoid comparing this description with some of his previous work (e.g., *The Economics of Interdependence*, 1968) where the problem was basically identified as a game against nature. In that framework, the conscious actors were national governments of industrialized countries who addressed their set of policy instruments to the attainment of economic targets. Other operators were not assumed to react significantly to the actions of governments. Rather, their behavior was, in the aggregate, analogous to that of impersonal, natural forces. Of course, the growing interdependence of Western industrialized economies was creating cross-dependencies between each nation's pursuit of legitimate objectives and a solution had to be found to this problem. The basic framework, however, was still one in which people, through their democratically elected governments, tried to manipulate impersonal forces to increase their welfare. In our day, instead, the game looks much more like one of humans against other humans, with every player reacting to the actions of all other players.

I think you would agree with me that this change of emphasis does not reflect some whim of Richard Cooper's, but rather a real change that has occurred in our economies. It is precisely on this change that I wish to concentrate my attention, as I am convinced that to the old problem of how to best use a given set of instruments, we now have to add the new problem of understanding why those instruments seem to have lost part of their effectiveness.

Consequently, risk is not just an unexpected event to which we have to adapt our response, manipulating the tools of economic policy. It is also a state of uncertainty as to the possibility and effect of our own manipulation. In both respects risk is higher now, as Cooper has pointed out, than it has been for many years after World War II. And the two types of risk are multiplicative rather than additive: An external shock is made more threatening if we are uncertain as to the response we can give it. In turn, precisely because of poor control over our economic policy machinery, we might provoke damage to the economic system over and above the effects of external shocks.

Why are we so dissatisfied with our economic performance?

As economists we are exposed to an ever-increasing number of learned articles that use data relating to a few years of economic history of a particular country to proclaim as proven, or refuted, fundamental economic hypotheses. As officials and citizens, we are exposed, through newspapers, to even shorter perspectives. The predominant message in both cases is "the poor state of our economies," which confirms how much economics deserves the name of "the dismal science," which it was given from its very beginnings. However, if we look at things from a broader historical perspective, the situation does not seem so unequivocally bad.

First of all, the amount of goods and services with which the economies are capable of providing us is higher than in any previous period of human history.

If goods and services can be disputed as indicators of welfare, health and education cannot: Life expectancy at birth in industrial countries is now seventy-four years compared with sixty-seven in 1950. The literacy rate is now 99 percent and was 95 percent in 1950 (World Bank 1981).

Finally, even if we take a more stringent performance criterion and look at rates of growth instead of income levels the situation does not seem bad.

Figures collected by the Italian economist Giorgio Fua (1976) suggest that the average per capita growth rate of a selected group of seven industrial countries (Italy, France, Germany, Japan, the United Kingdom, the United States, and Sweden) from the beginning of their industrial revolutions (mid-eighteenth century for the United Kingdom and various dates in the nineteenth for the others) up to 1913, has been between 1.1 percent (United Kingdom) and 3.1 percent (Sweden). In the following quarter of a century (1913–38) the figures range from a minimum of 0.5 percent (Germany) to a maximum of 2.9 percent (Japan). The 1938–70 period shows a minimum growth rate of 1.8 percent (United Kingdom) and a maximum of 4.3 percent (Japan); the overall country average in these thirty-odd years is less than 3 percent. If we consider that in the 1970s the per capita growth rate of all industrial countries was around 2.5 percent per annum, we can conclude that our recent economic performance is not significantly lower than in the period of fastest growth in the whole of the industrial era.

For the future, Lawrence Klein in his 1980 Nobel lecture forecast that the flow of goods and services in thirteen major Organization for Economic Cooperation and Development (OECD) countries in 1990 will be about one-third higher than in 1981, which means that the average growth rate in the decade will be equal to 3.2 percent. A slightly lower rate of growth (always per capita) is given by the World Bank in its 1981 *World Development Report*. Again these figures compare well with our historical performance.

Thus, it is only when looking at the "golden" and limited period of the 1960s (industrial countries grew at a 4.1 percent average annual rate in that decade) that the perspective for the 1980s and the experience of the 1970s may appear dismal. And the question is, then, why we take that exceptional decade as a standard, rather than the longer perspective I have just illustrated.

In my view we do so because the experience of the 1960s persuaded many that our societies could add to their collection of technological trophies the capacity to substantially improve, through policy, the performance of the economy. That bold conviction is now put in doubt not only by the slowdown in growth, but even more by the marked, almost universal, worsening of the performance in the two areas, inflation and unemployment, that have been highly "policy intensive" since even before the beginning of the industrial era.

Figures are eloquent. In the seven largest OECD countries inflation fluctuated in the 2–6 percent range until 1973, whereas unemployment was around 3 percent. From 1974 to 1981, inflation has fluctuated around a 10 percent trend but unemployment has shifted up to a plateau of about 6–7 percent. Again, Klein, our guide to the 1980s, does not forecast any marked improvement.

Surely our developed welfare systems have made unemployment much less costly in social terms than it used to be before World War II, but 25 million unemployed in the OECD area (OECD 1981) is nevertheless a dramatic social problem. As regards inflation, economists are not very clear about its welfare cost over and above its negative effect on output, but I certainly agree that persistent two-digit inflation indicates a failure of economic policy.

The crucial question, therefore, is what happened to economic policy. If we were to consider the experience of the 1960s merely an historical accident, then the wise attitude would be to accept the end of that fortunate period. If, however, we were to conclude that in the 1960s our positive experience was due to our improved economic policy, then we would have to find out why we no longer seem to be capable of the same achievements.

For these reasons, an analysis of the poor state of the art of *economic policy* is perhaps a more urgent task than an analysis of the poor state of the *economy*. And because in a democracy unfavorable events are more easily accepted when they can be attributed to external factors than when they are due to our own reduced ability to govern, there is the danger of looking for "authoritarian" measures that promise to recover lost efficiency. The risk of "policy failures" is thus both economic and political.

The crisis of economic policy

We were taught at university that, given an economic model, there are certain variables, called "instrumental variables," which are exogenous to the model itself and which may be manipulated to obtain the desired values for the target variables. Modern Western societies have developed a complex machinery to perform this regulatory function for the macrosystem. On one end we find popular will, as expressed in free elections, which ultimately dictates the instructions for steering the economy. At the opposite end we find "policy makers," holding the steering wheel to transform the general mandate given to them into day-to-day actions. It is also their duty to organize, interpret, and clarify the economic developments and the economic options among which the strategic choices have to be made. Unfortunately, and increasingly often, the knobs of the choice variables are stuck and refuse to move into the desired position; or they move according to desiderata but give results, in terms of endogenous variables, far removed from the ones desired; or, still, they seem to be moving on their own, completely outside the driver's will.

We have a variety of examples of these "policy failures," that is, circumstances in which the model that for years described economic policy satisfactorily has apparently ceased to function. One common element of these examples is the freedom private operators have acquired to avoid undesired policies. The result is the substantial reduction of the effectiveness of such policy measures.

A first and perhaps the clearest evidence in this direction is the growth of xenomarkets, that is, financial markets basically free from control or regulation. Domestic financial markets have grown in the United States and Germany at around 10 percent per annum between 1973 and 1980. International markets have grown, in the same period, by about 20 percent per annum. These markets are evidence of a massive avoidance of monetary and financial policies by operators who have preferred the unregulated, international habitat to the controlled, domestic one. The establishment of International Banking Facilities in New York is the latest important development in this direction and, in a sense, the seal of official approval of the phenomenon.

Domestically, an important area of avoidance of policies is the informal economy. A survey of the growing though still imprecise evidence has been recently carried out in the EC Commission (Smith 1981). Estimates of the "underground" economy in the United States range from 3 percent of GDP, as measured revising national accounts, to 27 percent, as measured using monetary statistics. For European countries, the estimates range from 2 percent of GDP in the United Kingdom, to 35 percent of the labor force in Italy. Even if not conclusive, these figures are sufficiently large and, what is more important, rising, giving some plausibility to E. Feige's suggestion that the most serious productivity slowdown that has occurred in our economies is in the statistical offices that leave larger and larger portions of economic activity unrecorded (Feige 1980). Also in this case we have had a massive avoidance of economic policies: Workers and employers have decided to participate in a black market just to avoid the effects of the action of the authorities.

Another source of policy failure is a concentration of economic power inside the economy so great that policy makers are decisively conditioned in their action. In a sense, the cost of stabilization policy is raised to such a level that the government gives up. Decades ago, the foremost examples of this phenomenon were provided by concentration of capital. Today, in many countries labor is often the conditioning variable.

Thus, money creation, instead of driving, is driven by wage negotiations. More generally, the monetary area is one in which policy failures have been very visible. The changes that intervened at the beginning of the 1970s were supposed to provide an additional "choice variable," the exchange rate, to pursue macroeconomic goals, and it was widely expected that it would be easier to manage the economy through the monetary levers. Now, after ten years, there are reasons to fear that we have lost rather than gained monetary control. Not only is the "real" effect of a given maneuver of monetary variables much more uncertain, but the assumed power of central banks to control nominal variables also often seems to be put into question.

Richard Cooper himself pointed out, in *The Economics of Interdependence* (1968), another example represented by the imbalance that has grown between the *decision-making domain* of a business enterprise and the *jurisdiction* of governments. He defined the former as "the geographical area over which its activities range. Obviously the domain of a firm will vary according to activity, and it is useful to distinguish a firm's domain with respect to: (a) sales; (b) sources of capital; (c) sources of management personnel; and (d) location of production facilities." He defined further: "A jurisdiction is the geographical area over which a given governmental unit governs or could govern in the various dimensions of economic policy" (pp. 91–2), and he noted that the former had grown relative to the latter. Since 1968 the internationalization of business has continued, although only very timid steps forward have been made in the enlargement of jurisdictions. The imbalance has thus increased.

The appearance of new actors on the international scene, such as oil-producing countries or newly industrialized ones, is of course another important aspect. Since Cooper discussed this topic extensively, I will not elaborate.

Finally, a particular way to evade policies is to anticipate them. Fully discounted policies become ineffective. The wider and more rapid disclosure of statistical evidence, the greater transparency of the analytical framework supporting decisions, and the establishment of a language common to policy and market operators have made it possible to anticipate policy actions to an extent that would have been inconceivable a generation ago.

If all these phenomena are undoubtedly causes (and sometimes effects) of policy failures, one should in no way infer that they are running *against* the general interest. Xenomarkets, the black economy, multinational corporations, trade unions, OPEC, and so on, all perform useful functions. Indeed, they contribute to satisfy needs that are of great concern to the authorities themselves, needs such as providing financial intermediation at the world level, assuring a degree of wage flexibility sufficient to reduce unemployment somewhat, and achieving a more efficient international division of labor. But if it is true that these phenomena are useful, it is no less true that they escape economic policies as they are organized today. In a sense, they run *ahead* of the present institutional setting of policies.

How has it become increasingly possible to evade policies? How can it happen that the textbook model more and more often fails to work?

Of the many answers that can be suggested to this question, I want to stress one that, for lack of a better expression, I would call a "crisis of exogeneity," to stress the fact that all the policy failures of which I have given examples have in common a weakening or disappearance of that very special link between exogenous and endogenous variables of the model on which the very essence of economic policy rests. To be sure, there is nothing in the formal presentation of our models that identifies for us the essence of that crucial economic operator we call government. We have, of course, symbols: T, for taxation; G, for government expenditure; M, for the quantity of money. And we assume, somewhere in the background, that these symbols are moved by the government, an economic agent for which we do not specify the systematic behavioral relationship. But what is "government"?

Exclusivity and *purpose* are two crucial features of the action of government in the field of economic policy. I use the term "exclusivity" to indicate the variety of factors that includes size, lack of substitutes, and monopoly. I use the word "purpose" to indicate that the action of government has objectives that are different in nature from those pursued by economic agents inside the economy. Now, I think, one can visualize the crisis of exogeneity as a decline or weakening of these two peculiar elements.

Exclusivity has been gradually eroded. The government used to have superior information, but it has now largely lost this advantage. It used to be bigger and stronger than individual economic agents; it is now often smaller than the markets on which the corporations that are supposed to be influenced by its decisions operate. It used to "surprise" economic agents by action often secret, unpredictable, per-

haps capricious; it is now more and more rational, more easily understood, and predictable. It used to produce goods and services that had
no substitutes in the economy and that were, so to speak, complementary in production and consumption by the private sector. Now, although the government has extended its intervention, at least in some
countries, to the production of goods and services that are in no way
of a public nature, we see true public goods, such as security, justice,
mail delivery, and medium of exchange to be produced inside the
economy, providing firms and households with substitutes for what
used to be a monopoly production by the public sector. True, this
vision may be influenced by the experience of countries in which a
special ingenuity has traditionally been developed in crossing the
border between public and private in either direction. But what I am
referring to is a general phenomenon, of which we have visible and
very important traces in all our countries.

Now it is clear that if the government offers goods and services that
are also offered, sometimes at better conditions, by other agents in the
economy, it has lost the main lever by which it could drive the economy to its policy goal.

If exclusivity has to do with instruments, purpose has to do with
objectives. Government is there to address itself to the pursuit of
objectives of a different nature from those that individual agents
inside the economy set themselves. Individual agents are not supposed, indeed they are not asked, to seek price stability, or full employment, or fast growth, or balance-of-payments equilibrium. The
economy would not work properly if those were their objectives.
Those are objectives for the system, not for individuals. When the
price index swells, private operators are expected to want more money to finance an increased volume of nominal transactions. It is up to
the government to reduce the volume, or the rate of growth, of money in order to stop the inflationary process. Similarly, if the wage rate
is too high to make it profitable for the private sector to employ the
whole labor force, firms are not supposed to suddenly become charity
institutions and offer unprofitable jobs with the result of going into
the red and eventually into bankruptcy. It is the government that
should, by various actions ranging from improvement of the functioning of the labor market to the stimulation of private investment,
re-create conditions in which it again becomes profitable for firms to
hire workers. Without a clear distinction in the very nature of the
respective purposes of the economic behavior of government and of
private agents, who act on the *same* markets, policy is not possible.

I am inclined to think that the purpose of government action in economic policy has undergone an evolution that is even more subtle and, in a sense, insidious for the functioning of policies, than the evolution we have seen in the feature of exclusivity. This evolution has to do with the functioning of our democratic system.

Democratic governments are elected. Today they are almost continuously campaigning to defend their position in the media, in polls, in by-elections, and so on. Economic and monetary matters have become, for many reasons, matters in which a very large part of the strength and popularity of governments is at stake. In these conditions, the exogeneity of economic policy becomes a slippery concept. When there is a sharp distinction between the "authority" of the public operator and the will of "the people," there is no doubt about the exogeneity of the purpose, although we have the strongest doubts about the desirability and the efficiency of an authoritarian basis for public intervention in the economy. However, in a democratic system the will of the public authorities is ultimately the will of the people. If this is so, is there not a contradiction between democracy and economic policy, a contradiction that becomes more and more visible as gaps in information, attention, control, and knowledge are closed? If the government wants exactly what its constituency wants, it would make the same choice as we would between unemployment and inflation, between guns and butter, between greater social security and increased equilibrium in the budget. How can its purpose then maintain the degree of peculiarity necessary for effective government action?

The answer rests on three different but interrelated arguments.

The first is quite technical and has to do with public goods. Even the staunchest supporters of private enterprise will admit, if one really forces them, that it is more efficient to have public armies than private ones, a public judiciary than a private one, and so on. The real argument starts when the area of public goods has to be defined. Some will give a very restrictive definition, others a wider one, and there is really no a priori way to settle the issue; a case-by-case empirical examination is the only way to deal with it.

The second argument is that the process by which "popular will" is expressed is by no means perfect, even, or maybe especially, in our "electronic" democracies. Policy makers, that is, public administrators, are not, and should not be, robots simply performing the tasks that a somewhat mythical democratic power dictates. They are necessary filters between the constituency and the economy and must filter both ways. On the one hand, they have to interpret and understand the message contained in the general choices made by the electorate and transform it into concrete, often highly technical policy actions. On the other hand, they must interpret and clarify the message the economy itself is sending, to make it understandable to the electorate. They have to make it clear, for instance, that if certain objectives are to be pursued certain instruments will have to be used and that there is no democratic sovereign power that can reconcile conflicting objectives. In short, they have an educational duty.

The third argument is that, in practice, it is often very difficult to separate the genuine general public will from that of pressure groups, given the natural tendencies these have to present their interests as general ones.

However, even if in principle there are both scope and need in a democratic system for some margin of autonomy by public authorities, our societies still have developed in a way that tends to reduce this independence and make the public intervention in the economy dependent on some very arguable expressions of general will.

In the field of money we often say (and I strongly share this view) that a certain degree of independence of the central bank is necessary to make the pursuit of monetary stability institutionally possible. Independence means independence from the government. Some think that is independence from demagoguery, from constituencies of governments, and fear that if the printing press were directly in the hands of such constituencies, too much money would be printed. But what does that mean, if not that monetary stability is too important a principle to be left exposed to the pressures of sectoral interests and to the short-term meanderings of public opinion? In our days, this independence has been eroded in many ways. The Federal Reserve may increasingly have the impression of being the prisoner of "Fed watchers," of being increasingly dependent on a system of conventional signals that may have little relationship with the hard facts of economic behavior but that still conditions its choices in a decisive way. They are still called "watchers" but they could soon be called "drivers." A degree of separation, of independence, of educational relationship is necessary between monetary authorities and the public if monetary policy is to perform its function. One could characterize this delicate balance by saying that money is exogenous, but central bank governors are not. If central bank governors had to fight for their position every Friday when the money supply figures are published, money too would become endogenous and monetary policy would disappear.

Answers to the "exogeneity crisis"

Various answers have been proposed, and tried, to deal with the exogeneity crisis. Some are activist in nature, and others are more passive. None of them, I think, provides the decisive answer to the problem.

In the activist domain responses have been sought in the two directions of policy coordination and direct controls.

Policy coordination can be seen as an attempt to regain exclusivity by reassembling the pieces of policy power scattered in many different hands throughout the economy. I have recalled the phenomenon of fragmentation of the monopolistic power that governments used to have. It is quite natural to try a reconstitution of the "monopolistic" position through what we could call, furthering the analogy, a "cartel." To expand the domain of policy in line with the enlarged decision-making domain of private operators, authorities in charge of only segments of each market now coordinate their interventions.

Compared with the past, the institutional embodiments of international coordination, such as the IMF, General Agreement on Tariffs and Trade (GATT), OECD, EC, and similar organizations have grown in importance and relevance. Some of the visions of their founding fathers have vanished but, in terms of hard facts, it is fair to say that there is, by and large, more genuine coordination now than in the 1950s. However, even so, a very partial answer to the exogeneity crisis was provided by improved coordination.

What is interesting in this respect is that coordination is not only the most common answer at the international level, but it has also increasingly been used *inside* countries to cope with the difficulties of managing the economy.

In many countries public authorities have proved unable, or unwilling, to impose the desired economic policy and have looked for various forms of voluntary incomes policies, social contracts, and so on to achieve noninflationary and investment-fostering wage-profits-prices configurations. Price controls of the voluntary kind are just another example in this direction.

A general assessment of these experiences is hard to give. It seems that they have some effectiveness in situations where the competing claims on national product are not too inconsistent. In certain countries flexible forms of income–price policies seem to have made a long-term contribution to favorable economic developments. However, when the task was more challenging these instruments proved to be simply ineffective.

Coordination among sovereign powers (whether inside one country, or at the international level) has inherent limitations that prevent it from being an adequate answer to the crisis of exogeneity. One could say that the main problem is precisely the one confronting participants in a cartel: Although everybody gains from cooperation, anyone can gain even more by cheating, but generalized cheating would destroy the agreement and its benefits. In other words, if the essence of policy is the provision of public goods that transcend individual cost–benefit analysis, then the method of seeking unanimous consensus anew for each policy decision is as inefficient and doomed to failure as would be a political system without laws or constitution, that is, without an agreed and generally nonrenegotiable set of rules that organizes the process of collective decisions. In short, coordination may well restore exclusivity, but it seldom generates purpose. Purpose needs to be embodied in institutions.

The other activist answer to the exogeneity crisis has been *direct controls* or, more generally, an escalation of authoritarian public interventions in the economy. This has taken the form of more frequent controls, more severe sanctions for transgressors, and an increasing number of variables subject to control. One can say that, when it becomes incapable of conducting policies in the physiological way described by the relationship between exogenous and target variables, the government bypasses this relationship and uses its general (noneconomic) power to directly impose (by decree) the desired value of the target variable. Price and wage controls, credit ceilings, and foreign exchange controls are examples of this type of response.

As with coordination, with direct controls one should avoid being dogmatic and condemning them in all circumstances, regardless of the available alternatives. I am not sure that such measures produce only negative results and that their dismantling will always be immediately beneficial. Cutting the throat of a patient is not generally regarded as a wise medical practice, but tracheotomy is sometimes necessary to save a life.

However, although recognizing their marginal merits and occasional inevitability, it must be firmly said that direct controls, a latent sign of economic weakness on the side of governments, are both an inadequate answer to the crisis of exogeneity and a disruptive factor of the desirable order of economic and political relationships.

The essence of direct controls is the recourse to force, an "instrument" of which the government has the ultimate monopoly, to compensate for the lack or insufficiency of normal instruments of economic policy. The police replace the trading desk. But in doing so the government crosses the line that must separate managing the economy from other public functions and their corresponding instruments. In this intrusion I see a danger potentially as serious as, say, a contamination between the executive and the judiciary power.

Besides being inappropriate, direct controls are in the end ineffective. Although they apparently strengthen the grasp of governmental over final economic variables, they further entrench the very same phenomena that originally caused the inability of the government to manage the economy by normal procedures. More financial intermediation goes through xenocurrency markets as credit controls are applied. More production and distribution go into the black market as wages and prices are frozen. Statistics become less and less reliable as they are transformed from sources of information into instruments of control. And so on. From an economic point of view one could say that direct controls replace exclusivity with purpose, but by doing so they set the process of economic policy into a gear that imposes further substitutions of the same kind, with the final result of aggravating the crisis of exogeneity.

The most pervasive and fashionable answer to the exogeneity crisis today, however, is in the passive domain and takes the form of a regained strength of laissez-faire.

According to the supporters of the new laissez-faire the right answer to the economic policy crisis is a downgrading of the objectives that were nonsensically high anyway. In their view, any tampering by the public authorities with the market mechanism (except for some well-defined cases such as defense or justice) is either ineffective or harmful, and therefore a reduction in their "tampering ability" (what I called, more respectfully, a crisis in exogeneity) is either immaterial or even welcome.

It is now clear to both supporters and opponents of public intervention in the economy, and I limit myself to economic considerations, that its utility depends on an assessment of the efficiency of the public sector relative to that of the private sector. And this general argument is presented today in terms that can be usefully split into two main components: the rationality, or information, issue and the flexibility issue. Let us examine them in turn.

Supporters of the futility, and potential danger, of public intervention have always been aware that their case rested on the assumption that public operators had no informational advantage over private ones. For instance, Friedman founded his case on the historically accidental ignorance of the economic model. "So I am led to suggest as a rule the simple rule of a steady rate of growth in the stock of money . . . while this is by no means necessarily an ideal gadget, it seems, in looking at the record, that it would work pretty well . . . I think we do not really know enough under present circumstances to do much better – and this has nothing to do with the particular people who are in control. I do not believe anybody here, including myself knows enough to do any better" (1960, p. 209).

Rational expectations theories, instead, underline an economic mechanism that rules out the possibility of any informational advantage public operators may have: Maximizing private operators will outguess any systematic behavior of the public authorities and pre-empt it. The futility of macroeconomic stabilization policy is no historical accident but rather a result of the maximizing behavior of economic agents and, as such, a permanent feature.

Friedman's argument is turned upside down: It is not the ignorance of the public sector but the wisdom of the private one that makes active stabilization policies undesirable. The practical result, however, is not reversed, but rather is reinforced.

The "flexibility" issue can be developed along similar lines. Opponents of public intervention maintain that there exists an "optimal" degree of flexibility and that private operators are perfectly capable of producing this optimal amount. According to this analysis, for instance, the duration of wage contracts will be no historical or institutional accident, but rather the outcome of an optimization process. In theory it could not be excluded that the optimal duration of a wage contract is five minutes and that recontracting should go on twelve times per hour.

In my view there is a basic contradiction in the argument of the extreme supporters of the laissez-faire idea. In fact, many of them also maintain that institutions are "endogenous" to the economic system and they are what they should be, given the economic opportunities and tastes. In a sense institutions, which of course should include public ones, are optimal. However, if this were strictly the case, there would be no need for anyone to wave the laissez-faire flag: If the "nontampering" option were "optimal," then public authorities would spontaneously not tamper and the issue would not even be raised.

The actual situation is slightly different from this. The Thatcher experiment in the United Kingdom and the Reagan one in the United

States suggest that the most forceful political will has to be applied to put in practice the laissez-faire recipe, or even to marginally reduce the amount of public intervention in the economy.

Of course, one could maintain that only "private" institutions are endogenous and optimal whereas public ones are not necessarily so. However, to reach the conclusion that public intervention is *always* inopportune we should implicitly pass a very negative judgment on our political systems. We should in fact, conclude that our democratic process systematically produces nonsatisfactory outcomes. In purely economic terms this could perhaps be a legitimate position: But who could accept it as the basis of a personal political philosophy?

Conclusion

This chapter began with the consideration that, from a historical perspective, our economic performance is not that worrying. It then put forward the suggestion that our preoccupation does not really depend on the actual state of our economies but rather on the ominous feeling of having lost control of economic developments. Several cases of policy failures have been illustrated and summarized in a concept of "exogeneity crisis." Finally, some reasons were given for doubting the adequacy of the answers tried so far to the crisis of economic policy.

The optimistic note of the beginning has thus been dissipated and reasons have been supplied for us to be more preoccupied than when we began.

The excuse could be that my assignment was to point out rather than to solve problems. But the true reason is that I do not see a ready-made solution for the problems and difficulties our policies face. And since we all have a tendency to forget the problems for which we have no solution, I think it is necessary to pay attention to the risks that may follow from such a disregard or from excessive reliance on inadequate, though popular solutions.

First of all we have to be aware of the danger in acritically transferring the gospel of "new laissez-faire" to the international sphere, forgetting that such a sphere is already, almost by definition, one in which policies and policy institutions are lacking. This lack is even more acute now that some of the few governmental instruments that had worked for decades, such as the gold standard or the Bretton Woods system, have been dismantled. An attempt to restore these instruments as they were would be impractical. But there is an even greater and more insidious lack of realism in believing that no act of international government is necessary to help organize extremely complex monetary, financial, and trade relationships among 130 countries in the world.

On the other hand, for reasons I have tried to explain, one should not be unduly optimistic about what can be achieved through policy coordination. It is our daily task to help get the best out of this rather weak instrument of policy, and all possible efforts should continue to be made in this direction. But those who are engaged in it are also well placed to see the limits of the exercise.

Finally, direct controls are not available at the international level. We may be satisfied with that, because misuses of intrinsically inappropriate instruments are thus impossible. But we also have to be aware that this may entail a greater use of direct controls domestically, and particularly a use of domestic direct controls for objectives related to the external sector of the economy. The various forms of creeping protectionism that we see proliferating are an example.

If awareness of dangers is the first condition for safety, then some of these remarks may not be totally unconstructive for those who are involved in managing international risks.

References

Cooper, R. N. *The Economics of Interdependence.* New York: McGraw-Hill, 1968.

Feige, E. L. "A New Perspective on Macroeconomic Phenomena." Mimeographed. August 1980.

Friedman, Milton. *A Program for Monetary Stability.* New York: Fordham University Press, 1960.

Fua, Giorgio. *Occupazione e-capacità produttive: La realtà italiana.* Bologna: Universale Paperbacks, 1976.

OECD. *Economic Outlook.* July 1981.

Smith, A. "A Review of the Informal Economy in the EC." EP no. 3, July 1981.

World Bank. *World Development Report, 1981.*

CHAPTER 2

Country risk: economic aspects

JONATHAN EATON AND MARK GERSOVITZ

Introduction

From a U.S. or West European perspective investment in the Second and Third Worlds looks very much riskier than investment at home. Recent events in Poland and Mexico, among other places, seem to provide dramatic confirmation that this perception is well founded. There is a lot to worry about: The increased internationalization of investment in the last decade has enormously raised the exposure of investors to risks associated with events in many different countries.

As a consequence of this situation, institutional investors and public organizations concerned with international investment are devoting substantial resources to analyzing the risks of investment abroad. There have been significant improvements in the collection and dissemination of data on foreign investment. Some investors have developed statistical models that attempt to evaluate the safety of loans to particular countries.

We believe, however, that this activity is unfortunately taking place without an adequately articulated conceptual framework that identifies the fundamental sources of country risk. This analysis is unlikely to be very robust if it is not based on appropriate theoretical notions. Without a good specification of what motivates borrowers and lenders it is difficult to identify which data are important for analyzing country risk. In addition, there is no reason to believe that apparent regularities derived from past data using econometric models will continue in the future unless these models are specified using an appropriate theory.

To make these points more concrete, consider the conceptual underpinnings of the debt–service ratio, a widely used indicator of the safety of loans to LDCs. Other things equal it seems reasonable that a country has more to gain from default if the ratio of its debt service to its exports is high. Yet countries with the highest ratios may instead be the best risks. A high ratio may merely reflect other factors *perceived* by lenders as lowering risk and justifying high debt service. We cannot make a meaningful judgment without both a model identifying borrower characteristics that enhance the probability of default given a particular debt structure *and* a model of lender behavior. Later in the chapter we provide a more detailed criticism of indicators of expropriation risk.

The purpose of this paper is therefore to present a microeconomic framework for analyzing equilibrium in international capital markets when the riskiness of foreign investment derives from the maximizing behavior of borrowers and lenders. Without attempting to specify a complete model of these markets we present some important considerations that we believe have been neglected in the literature on country risk. We hope that our discussion will stimulate a more rigorous and analytic approach to this area of study.

In principle, every conceivable investment (both real and financial) is unique in terms of characteristics such as expected profitability, safety, and liquidity. Whenever an investor can invest in more than one country, however, the issue of country risk arises. The choice of the country in which to invest affects the prospects for the investment in many ways. Thus, for analytic purposes, it makes sense to group investments by the country in which they are made. Imperfect knowledge of a country's characteristics that may affect investment outcomes is a major component of country risk. This uncertainty can usually be reduced by research. Thus, considerable resources are allocated to country risk analysis by private banks, multinational corporations, and international organizations such as the IMF. Nevertheless, even if an investor could gather and assimilate every datum relevant to an investment, much of the uncertainty associated with the nation in which an investment is made would remain.

There are at least two broad reasons why the country in which an investment is made may be of interest to an investor. First, classifying investments by country is useful in identifying a group of investments that are likely to have similar characteristics because the investments are subject to common sources of uncertainty. For instance, a country's climatic conditions may affect the productivity of a large number of agricultural investments. Or different rates of population growth may alter labor market conditions. Learning about the country then reduces the investor's subjective uncertainty about a large number of investments. This first form of country risk analysis provides information on risks that are perceived as *exogenous* to the investor's behavior.[1]

---

[1] Country risk that is solely exogenous can be analyzed within the confines of Markowitz's (1959) portfolio analysis. Country risk analysis of this form will involve identifying the means, variances, and covariances of returns on

A second reason for classifying investments by the recipient country derives from the existence of nation states. All investments within a single country share the characteristic of falling within the same government's jurisdiction. The government's policies can be decisive in determining the return on these investments. Country risk associated with government policies and political events such as war and revolution is called *sovereign* risk. Much country risk analysis thus involves forecasting policies and political developments. To some extent the policies of foreign governments and political changes abroad constitute additional forms of exogenous risk in that they are affected by factors beyond the investor's control. A major component of sovereign risk, however, is *endogenous* in that it derives from the strategic behavior of the recipient country's government toward investors. We view a government contemplating hostile acts against a foreign investor as evaluating the *economic* costs and benefits of its actions.[2] The behavior of investors will affect these costs and benefits, as well as the strategies that are optimal for the government to pursue, thus indirectly affecting the return on investments. Our analysis in this chapter focuses primarily on this second endogenous form of country risk.

In focusing on the economic aspects of country risk we treat political and cultural factors as given. In particular, we assume that recipient countries have governments that pursue a consistent set of objectives and that the populace of these countries has an observable and stable attitude toward foreigners, private property, and contracts.[3] In

---

investments in different countries, which investors will then treat as parametric. Goodman (1981) provides a recent example of this approach. When an endogenous component is recognized, however, the parameters of the asset returns can be identified only by a game-theoretic analysis of the relationship between investors and recipient country governments.

[2] A number of earlier authors (Breton 1964, Johnson 1965, and Bardhan 1967) view foreign investment as inherently offensive to domestic nationalists. This psychic commodity approach may have some validity but becomes little more than a tautology when stretched to explain why certain industries or firms and not others are objects of country actions. As we will argue throughout, economic costs and benefits do seem to affect the behavior of countries in many instances.

[3] Two departures from this viewpoint are particularly important. First, decisions may reflect the wishes of the representative citizen, but this citizen may be irrational. Dror (1971) uses the concept of a "crazy state" to characterize this situation. The case of Iran provides a partial example where the analyst's main problem is anticipating the goals of the country's behavior. Second, decisions may be the outcome of conflict or compromise among citizens with quite different goals and positions. For instance, some states

reality these factors are hard for an investor to evaluate and are subject to unpredictable changes. They thus represent important components of country risk. To some extent we believe that the economic factors we discuss help explain changes in government and social attitudes that have consequences for foreign investments, but we will not argue a position of economic determinism. Instead, we restrict ourselves to a consideration of the economic costs and benefits associated with hostile acts because this is a natural boundary for a single inquiry.

One important distinction among investments is between direct investment, implying controlling ownership of a physical investment or business abroad, and indirect or portfolio investment, usually taking the form of a loan to an agent in the country, perhaps to the government itself. In the case of direct foreign investment, investors face the possibility that the tax system or other aspects of the legal environment will change. They may, for instance, find that the host country government requires the transfer of equity to its own nationals without full compensation (indigenization programs). In the extreme, the investor may lose all control of the investment, suffering uncompensated expropriation. Indirect investments can be threatened by rescheduling, default, or outright repudiation. In the case of a direct investment or a loan denominated in the currency of the debtor, the investor also faces the risk that exchange controls imposed by the host country may prevent the conversion of foreign assets into the investor's own (or indeed a third) currency.[4]

We believe that country risk, as it applies to direct and indirect investments, involves some rather separate considerations. Nevertheless, both forms of investment can be analyzed within the same general framework. In the next section, we present a general methodology applicable to both types of investment. The third section discusses issues that are relevant to portfolio investment and the fourth section treats direct investment. The last section draws implications from our analysis for the design of public policy.

> may have political processes favoring owners of capital whereas others may be oriented toward urban workers or agriculturalists. Of particular concern are situations where the weight of different groups in decision making may shift or give rise to "voting paradoxes."
>
> 4 In focusing on country risk we shall not discuss the closely related but analytically distinct issue of currency risk, which arises when indirect investments are denominated in the currencies of different countries. Currency risk and country risk both act to reduce the mobility of funds across borders.

A framework for analyzing government policies toward foreign investment

A crucial aspect of country risk is that a country's government is a sovereign actor. Within its own territory a government, especially if it is relatively unconstrained by constitutional safeguards, has great latitude in determining the legal structure surrounding economic agreements. Governments are much more able to break contracts than are individuals operating within a given legal system. Even outside their own territories governments may have various sorts of immunity in the courts of other countries (Lillich 1965, Delupis 1973, and Levine 1977). Finally, even if a favorable judgment is secured by investors, there may be little that can be obtained from one country in the jurisdiction of another, although exceptions exist.[5]

Contrast this situation and the position of private agents experiencing bankruptcy within a domestic legal context. Legal proceedings typically strip agents of some or all of their assets if they do not meet the obligations imposed by their liabilities. In international investment, the legal penalties incumbent on agents failing to fulfill their contracted obligations are relatively poorly defined, and the ones that do exist are much more difficult to enforce.

Without a legal system to enforce contracts, investors must find other mechanisms to ensure that the profitability of their investments is not infringed by hostile governments of the recipient countries. Without any such mechanism the government would always want to assume ownership of all foreign assets. Rational foreign investors, foreseeing the absence of an adequate mechanism for repayment, will avoid the investment. Only by convincing potential investors that it will have a motive to honor contractual obligations after their assets are in place can a country attract investment.

---

[5] Despite these difficulties there are various cases where investors have been able to impose considerable costs on countries ruled in violation of contracts by another country's judicial system. Recent actions against the revolutionary regime in Iran certainly caused that country considerable trouble (Field and Adam 1980). Moran (1973, esp. p. 286) describes a number of cases where he feels successful legal action was taken against expropriating countries. In many of these cases action could be taken to prevent other businesses from purchasing raw materials from nationalized mines. He reports that Kennecott even used an unconditional guarantee embodied in its Chilean contracts to obtain writs of attachment against the jets of Lanchile when they landed in New York.

From the perspective of a period before an investment has been made, a country is likely to prefer a situation where the investment is made *and* contracts are respected to a situation of no investment. The problem is that the country may most prefer a third situation: The foreign investment takes place but the country, rather than the investor, receives its proceeds. Since the recipient's decision to honor contractual obligations is subsequent to the investment decision, a situation of perfect capital mobility, in which the real return on capital is equal in all countries and in which investment contracts are honored, could be time inconsistent (Kydland and Prescott 1977): It will seem optimal to the country before the investment is made (given the need to attract investors) but not after. Rational investors perceiving this problem will not invest and the country is left in the situation it least prefers – no foreign investment at all.

Occasionally, investors may invest knowing that time-consistent behavior on the part of the recipient will lead to a loss of control over the asset. This situation can be explained by appealing to the concept of an *obsolescing bargain:* Both parties enter into an agreement anticipating that a shift in their relative strengths will lead to a subsequent renegotiation.[6] Such situations often arise and do not imply irrational behavior. For instance, investors building a factory abroad may realize that the only protection against expropriation is their monopoly over special knowledge. It may be that as time passes this knowledge becomes available to the country, making expropriation the time-consistent strategy of the host country (i.e., the optimal strategy from that period's perspective). Investors may therefore construct smaller plants, employing more labor-intensive technologies than otherwise, to recoup costs more quickly. This behavior occurs in anticipation of the takeover and ensures that the investment is still worthwhile to investors. Any renegotiations (in this case leading to expropriation) are fully anticipated by both sides and any rhetoric merely veils this fact. We will use the term "obsolescing bargain" to denote a change over time in the shares of the country and investors in the proceeds of an investment. We assume that both sides act from the outset with full knowledge of this characteristic of the investment and that all behavior is time consistent.

A country can attract foreign investment only to the extent that it

---

[6] Much of the management literature on this subject has as its goal acquainting managers with this aspect of investment. See Vernon (1967 and 1968), Smith and Wells (1975), and Wells (1977).

can convince potential investors that it will have an incentive to allow them to extract from the country a return that is competitive with what can be earned elsewhere. Unless investors are convinced that these incentives will be strong enough to allow a transfer of capital that equates rates of return across borders, the strength of the recipient's incentives to repay will constrain the movement of capital. The weakness of a country's incentive to abstain from hostile acts against foreign investments is a distortion in the world economy in that it creates a deviation from a situation of perfect capital mobility.

Establishing mechanisms to ensure that investments are unharmed may yield further deviations from a world in which all contracts could be enforced costlessly. The recipient country has an incentive to take visible actions that would reduce its welfare should it fail to abide by contracts. (In Schelling's 1960 terminology the country may wish to provide foreign investors with a "hostage.") These actions may be costly in themselves. At the same time investors have an incentive to modify the form of their investment to make any assets they place in the foreign country less profitable to other owners. The opportunity to modify investments is greatest in the case of direct investments, but modifications also impose costs. We will provide some examples in the discussion of expropriation.

Within this extralegal context of international investment there are therefore incentives for a recipient country to avoid hostile acts. Otherwise no international investments would take place. Different types of investments are defended in different ways. Thus country risk cannot be strictly defined except with regard to a particular investment. Nevertheless, broad classes of investments naturally share common attributes that allow them to be analyzed as a group. One important partition of investments is between financial and physical investments threatened at the extreme by acts of repudiation and expropriation, respectively. Although there are similarities in the situations of these two types of investments, sufficient differences exist to justify separate treatments of each.

One particularly important factor protecting both types of investments is the recipient's incentive to maintain a reputation as a good place for future investments. This incentive may seem weak or nebulous compared to the threat of bankruptcy proceedings. As Arrow (1974) has argued, however, the desire to maintain a reputation provides the basis of much economic behavior outside the sphere we consider here. Our previous work suggests that such an incentive may allow some capital transfer but not necessarily enough to equate the marginal productivity of capital among countries.

Country risk: default and repudiation

By far the most important recent trend in private investing abroad is the rapid growth in financial lending, much of it associated with the activities of banking syndicates.[7] Long-term debt to private creditors owed by the governments of ninety-eight LDCs, or with repayment guaranteed by them, rose from $36 billion in 1971 to $269 billion in 1979.[8] Two other categories of loans, the short-term debt owed by governments or guaranteed by them and all maturities of unguaranteed debt owed by private borrowers in LDCs, have also grown rapidly. Data on these amounts are less easily available, however (BIS 1979).

Because very little of this debt consists of publicly issued bonds, information on these quantities is difficult to obtain.[9] This problem becomes more serious with regard to the terms of the loan. Even when information is available on the rate of interest, various commissions and charges are concealed (Wellons 1977).

The most difficult informational problem arises for an outside observer in ascertaining if the borrower is complying with the loan contract. Here again the fact that lending is in forms other than publicly issued bonds is crucial. Thus, for the 1930s, when widespread defaults on bonds occurred, considerable information exists (Eaton and Gersovitz 1981b). For the 1970s, however, one must rely on press reports and vague rumors. Banks may roll over loans to avoid public admission of a default. Except perhaps for North Korea, however, nothing like an outright repudiation occurred in the 1970s. Costa Rica, Gabon, Jamaica, Indonesia, Iran, Mexico, Nicaragua, Peru, Poland, Rumania, Sudan, Togo, Turkey, Zaire, and others all have posed problems of varying seriousness.[10]

---

[7] This section draws heavily on our previous work (Eaton and Gersovitz 1980, 1981a, and 1981b).

[8] The World Bank in its publication *World Debt Tables* (1981, p. xv, 1980, p. 29) reports this information on a country-by-country basis. These figures include debt outstanding and disbursed.

[9] On contrasts between bond and bank lending, see Eaton and Gersovitz (1981b, p. 14 and pp. 22–6).

[10] See, for instance, various issues of *Euromoney* and the Economist Intelligence Unit's (EIU) *Quarterly Economic Reviews* of individual countries.

*Credit constraints and potential default: a conceptual
framework*

An understanding of what prevents defaults and repudiations and
how these deterrents break down is the central goal of risk analysis
applied to financial lending. Without coercion or legal sanctions available to them, private lenders might find governments eager to borrow
so long as net flows are positive, but if net repayments are required
governments will repudiate their debts. The only retaliation open to
lenders is to refuse future loans to repudiating borrowers and, in the
case of banks, to refuse to process their trade-related transactions.

On first consideration, a refusal to lend in the future is a rather
weak penalty for a lender trying to realize a nonnegative present
value from a loan. The country already has possession of a certain
amount of funds and can be assured of a gain if it refuses repayment.
How can the lender offer the borrower an even larger gain and still
ensure that its activities are profitable to itself? A promise of a larger
future loan in return for present repayment, if kept, would seem only
to push the problem out further in time (Hellwig 1977).

In fact, the inability to borrow in the future is likely to impose
hardship on a potential defaulter for a number of reasons that we
discuss later. The costs of default will vary, of course, across countries
whereas the benefit is the ability to absorb as domestic consumption
or investment what otherwise would be transferred to foreigners as
debt service payments. The lenders must ascertain the level of debt
service obligations at which the benefits of nonpayment are likely to
exceed the costs of future exclusion from credit markets. Lenders will
not lend to the point where debt service obligations reach this level, at
least with high probability. This debt ceiling (or "country limit") provides a formal definition of the "capacity" of international capital
markets to finance a country's current account deficit, a notion frequently arising in discussions of the recycling of OPEC surpluses.

Elsewhere (Eaton and Gersovitz, 1981b) we identify four reasons
why a country may want to borrow in financial markets on a repeated
basis; each points to a cost to defaulting. First of all, borrowing allows
a country to divorce its level of consumption from its level of income
at any moment, given its level of savings. A country whose income
level varies widely is most likely to borrow for this purpose. We identify it as the *consumption motive*. By defaulting and thereby losing access
to future opportunities to borrow, a country increases the variability
in its consumption, which is costly as long as the marginal utility of
income is decreasing.

The following example, based on Eaton and Gersovitz (1981a), illustrates how the consumption motive for borrowing can sustain an equilibrium in which there is international lending with repayment. Consider a country with an income that alternates between a low and a high value indefinitely. This type of country will want to borrow in poor years. It may then be willing to repay in good years to keep open the option of borrowing yet again in future poor years when additional resources are especially valuable to it.

If the borrower's income varies in a regular and perfectly predictable way, rational and fully informed lenders will always set the credit ceiling so that it is never to a debtor's advantage to default. Although defaults will never be observed under these assumed circumstances, the *threat* of default will limit the amount that any country can be lent. If the amount a country wishes to borrow, even if it has to repay, exceeds this ceiling, the country will be credit constrained. In this case, its inability to guarantee repayment (because to repay would be time inconsistent) reduces its welfare. An increase in the variability of the country's income will increase its credit ceiling and, if it is constrained, its welfare.

If more is lent than the credit ceiling, it will always be in the country's interest to refuse repayment. Default will occur only if lenders misperceive a borrower's characteristics, for instance, the amount it has borrowed or the future path of its income. This points to an important role for the country risk analyst: understanding the resource base of a country, the sources of fluctuation in output (e.g., weather), the future productivity of public sector investments such as irrigation dams, and the sources of fluctuation in international prices for the country's output.

In actuality, since a country's income varies in an uncertain fashion, the possibility of default must be considered. Under conditions of uncertainty, a country may experience sequences of poor income performance. Debt contracted at the beginning of the sequence may then come due while low incomes persist. Other things equal, a country will be most tempted to default when income is low and the marginal utility of income is high.

If a country experiences a series of low incomes, lenders can adopt one of several responses. They can set the credit ceiling so low that the country will always choose to repay regardless of its income performance in the years when net repayment is due. In this case, it is possible that very little can be lent.

Alternatively, creditors can demand repayment after a certain number of periods, regardless of income performance and with the knowledge that a default will occur if income happens to be low on the due date. In this case, a risk premium will be charged so that the lender is indifferent between a loan to a country that may refuse repayment and a safe domestic loan. This type of arrangement characterizes the contract embodied in a publicly issued bond, where no provision is made for postponing the service of the debt if the debtor experiences a low income.

A third option for lenders is to refinance the debt if the country experiences low income, without future exclusion from borrowing. Rescheduling postpones repayment to periods when income has returned to normal levels. This policy requires that lenders have enough information to distinguish between the occurrence of low and high incomes, and between exogenous shortfalls in income and chronic economic mismanagement or other factors within the country's control that impair long-run performance. In the latter case, lenders will want to threaten an end to refinancing (rollover) of the debt and permanent exclusion from credit markets in order to force the government to change its policies and to repay its debt. This situation suggests a role for the IMF as an architect of the policy reorganization or "stabilization plan" (Srodes 1977). If lenders are unable to threaten any sanctions, the situation effectively becomes one where the country refuses to pay but is not penalized. In this case, lending becomes impossible. Thus, there is a cost to making loans in these markets associated with monitoring economic conditions in borrowing countries and the economic performance of their governments. Economies of scale in developing this type of expertise provide one justification for an IMF role.

A second reason for borrowing arises when there is a large differential between the domestic marginal product of capital and the world cost of capital. Borrowing to increase the capital stock will thus raise income above the level of debt service obligations imposed by the debt. We call this the *production or investment motive* to borrow. Countries that anticipate lucrative investment opportunities into the indefinite future, especially ones that will require increasing levels of investment, will find it desirable to retain access to international financial markets.

In the appendix to this chapter we develop a model to illustrate how the production motive for borrowing provides a mechanism to enforce repayment and establishes a debt ceiling. Many of the considerations that apply to the consumption motive are relevant here as well. Furthermore, this analysis suggests that countries with good investment opportunities and meager sources of domestic savings are likely to sustain greater levels of indebtedness. This result points to a role for the country risk analyst in evaluating the future productivity of potential capital investment projects.

We identify a third motive for borrowing as the *adjustment motive*. A country may experience sudden, unanticipated reductions in output supply. Although these may require changes in the permanent level of absorption, adjustment is likely to be less painful when it can be made slowly. Borrowing permits a smoother transition. An example of a cost imposed by a sudden adjustment of absorption is the need to abandon a project in progress. Through borrowing, a country may complete these projects even though income may have fallen drastically.

Finally, borrowing can provide liquidity to facilitate international transactions. Recent growth in the use of credit cards by individuals illustrates how a medium of exchange can take the form of a liability rather than an asset of the buyer. Individuals may find it more convenient to borrow than to run down cash reserves even if they have no desire to increase current consumption at the cost of future consumption. In a very similar way suppliers' credits serve as a medium of exchange in international markets. This reason for borrowing we call the *transactions motive*.

Countries that are excluded from international financial markets have difficulty effecting international transactions. If banks and other creditors refuse to process transfers of funds or extend credit for the imports or exports of a defaulter, the debtor may be reduced to cumbersome transaction methods and, in the extreme, to the inefficiencies of international barter. Iran in the autumn of 1979 was reported to be having this type of difficulty after banks declared its revolutionary government in default. Other factors the same, therefore, a borrower that benefits greatly from trade and that would suffer a corresponding loss from trade disruption will be allowed a high credit ceiling. This type of country is likely to have a high ratio of imports to income.[11]

As a final point we emphasize that punishing a defaulter by allowing it to borrow only at a higher interest rate afterward cannot be an adequate deterrent to default and may simply invite the country to

---

[11] Creditors may also be able to interfere directly with a borrower's trade by harassing importers or exporters in the creditors' country through the court system (Delupis 1973), but this is probably not a generally effective strategy. Creditor-country governments may also retaliate through trade embargoes.

obtain additional principal on which to default again. The higher interest, not being paid, is irrelevant. A higher interest rate on the initial loan can, however, play a role when penalties ensure that repayment will occur in at least some situations. In this case, risk-neutral lenders will set the interest rate so that the probability of repayment times the amount to be repaid just equals the gross return that can be made on a safe loan. If lenders are risk-averse, of course, the interest rate will be set at a higher rate.[12]

The effectiveness of incentives to repay: the case of Peru

Although space prohibits an analysis of the recent history of all problem borrowers, much can be learned from one case, that of Peru. This country has figured prominently during the last fifteen or so years in both disputes over expropriation and fears of default. We begin by considering Peru's more recent borrowing experience and turn in the next section to aspects of the earlier expropriation story. Both episodes illustrate the interplay between economic and political–legal aspects of country risk.[13]

Peru's long-term government-guaranteed debt to private lenders increased slowly from about $675 million in 1967 to about $725 million in 1971. In the next four years this debt more than tripled to roughly $2.3 billion by the end of 1972 (World Bank, vol. 2, 1976, p. 121, and vol. 1. 1979, p. 47). These changes occurred under a radical reformist military government in power from 1968. By 1976, Peru was in an economic crisis leading to the first of several negotiations on rescheduling.

A major cause of this situation was a series of negative shocks to Peru's trade position: Fish meal output dropped because the anchovies disappeared and widely held expectations of oil discoveries were disappointed, leaving Peru dependent on imports just as prices rose steeply and the price of Peru's copper exports dropped. Cline (1981, p. 304) estimates that these shocks accounted for 37 percent of the average current account deficit during 1974–7. Imports of military equipment, a clearly political factor, accounted for an additional 10 percent of the deficit.

---

[12] Formal empirical evidence on the existence of credit ceilings, the determinants of default probabilities, and interest rate spreads is discussed elsewhere by us (Eaton and Gersovitz 1981b, pp. 16–24 and 27–31).

[13] This account draws on Cline (1981), Derecho (1978), Downer (1980), Kuczynski (1977), Nevans (1978), and EIU (1975–81).

Several large projects proved poor investments. An $800 million pipeline was a bad choice since oil reserves were lower than expected. A $1 billion irrigation project was judged ill conceived by the World Bank and as unsuccessful by several observers subsequently, yet private bank loans were used to finance it.

The resultant economic crisis caused a new, more moderate military government to seek additional loans that the banks agreed to only after negotiating the promise of policy changes. Cline (1981, p. 306) concludes: "For reasons of data availability, technical capacity and political sensitivity, it proved impossible for the banks to enforce their lending conditions, and adverse publicity for the intervention (plus its ineffectiveness) caused the leading bankers involved to resolve that they would not become entangled in the future but would rely on the IMF as the monitoring authority." Beginning in early 1977, a series of negotiations with the IMF led to a policy package implemented in mid-1978. The next year or so saw the application of this package, a drastic fall in real incomes, political strife, and the reversal of several of the negative trade shocks. By late 1979, the government could think about prepaying some of the rescheduled debt and banks were again making medium-term loans.

Some important lessons from this experience are as follows:

1. Economic shocks and poorly chosen projects were important in precipitating the crisis.
2. Even a relatively radical regime under considerable economic stress had no desire to repudiate its debts. Indeed, it was ultimately willing to adopt an economic program proposed by outsiders rather than to forgo the opportunity for an orderly rescheduling.
3. Repayment was renegotiated between the Peruvian government and its creditors as a *group*, who acted more or less in concert.
4. The IMF has an advantage over private banks in negotiating a change in economic policy.

We offer no judgment on which economic consequences followed from the particular provisions of the plan nor whether it was appropriately designed, which are issues of some controversy.

Country risk: expropriation

The United Nations (1978, p. 277) estimates the stock of foreign direct investment in the LDCs at $33 billion in 1967 and $71 billion in 1975. Although this stock has been growing much less rapidly than the stock of debt, it still represents a very significant quantity of resources. Further, it is this type of investment rather than financial lending that is accompanied by a transfer of technology, so that it represents a contribution to host-country resources beyond an increase in real capital.[14]

In contrast to the recent experience with private debt, direct foreign investments have been subject to hostile actions by the governments of most countries. For a large sample of LDCs, Williams (1975, p. 265) estimates that about 20 percent of the value of foreign investments carried into or made during 1956–72 was expropriated without compensation in this period. Some countries (Algeria, Bangladesh, Burma, Chile, Cuba, Egypt, Iraq, and Syria) expropriated all or nearly all foreign investments, paying almost no compensation. Cuba is a striking example, expropriating $1.25 billion in assets and paying $50 million in compensation. As of 1972, it had no foreign investments at all. This case is clearly one where political factors were uppermost; small changes in the economic costs and benefits of these actions could hardly have made any difference at all. A contrasting case is that of Peru, where a radical military government took power from a civilian government precisely because the civilians were judged too lenient in their position on the expropriation of a U.S. company. Even under the new government, however, there was no policy of wholesale expropriation. The Peruvian case provides many examples where differences in the positions of individual companies led to very different fates for their investments.

Expropriation: some conceptual issues

Physical investments provide more opportunities than financial investments to alter the cost–benefit calculation of hostile governments. Perhaps as a result the prospects for an embargo of direct investments following expropriation are less. If their particular investment is very different from those that have been confiscated, potential investors may feel that the past record of a country is not relevant to their own situation. This observation is more likely to be true when expropria-

---

14 In Eaton and Gersovitz (1982) we present a number of formal models illustrating some of the points discussed in this section. Other theoretical work on this topic includes Cauas and Selowsky (1977) and Tobin (1974). These authors put special emphasis on aspects of income distribution among groups within the host country as a result of expropriation. This issue, discussed also by us in Eaton and Gersovitz (1982), is very important but has been pushed into the background in this chapter by our assumption of the representative citizen.

tions have been selective rather than across the board. In this case, vulnerable investors have little hope that their own fate will alter the host's reputation and cause the host to demur. Certainly the acrimonious expropriations undertaken by Peru did not lead private banks to withhold large loans in the early 1970s. Whatever the ability of banks to act as a cohesive group in responding to threatened defaults, they show little inclination to respond to selective expropriations. Finally, direct investment is ill suited in comparison to loans as a method of smoothing short-run variations in income or to facilitate transactions. As a consequence, investors in physical assets cannot offer a country these benefits in exchange for continued access to an investment's income.

A broad class of defenses available to the direct investor involves a cutoff of managerial expertise and skills. For instance, production may be conceived as using inputs of unskilled labor, managerially and technically skilled labor, and capital. The host may lack skilled labor and capital relative to the rest of the world. Skilled labor can be withdrawn in the event of an investment dispute; fixed capital cannot be. If the skilled labor cannot be replaced by the country, its income from the investment earned, say, by unskilled labor or collected in taxes when the investment is operated by the investor may exceed the income from seizing the plant and running it without enough skilled labor. Only as much capital as can be protected in this way will be invested if this is the sole defense. In this case the amount of foreign capital can be less than what the country would want even if it had to forswear expropriation in a binding way.

In this situation, an increase in the skill of the country's citizens makes the threat of a withdrawal of skilled labor by foreign investors less meaningful. Less foreign investment will be undertaken by investors who protect themselves with this threat. Indeed, this effect can be so strong that the contribution to the host's income of an increase in its citizens' skills could be negative. In any case the social return is almost certain to be below what is indicated by the wage differential obtained by a skilled worker. India may be an example of this phenomenon. With little capital but a large number of skilled workers, India has a great need for foreign investment but poses a particular danger to investors relying on a withdrawal of skilled labor as a defense against expropriation. These considerations also make clear that the threat of expropriation will cause foreign firms to avoid skill transfer to local nationals.

So far we have identified a defense of foreign investment as a threat to reduce factor supplies after expropriation. This is analogous to the allocative inefficiency discussed in the production efficiency literature (Forsund, Lovell, and Schmidt 1980). Another type of defense could involve the choice of a technically inefficient method of production, one which would never be efficient at *any* set of factor prices except for its use as a defense against expropriation.

To be useful as a defense, this type of distortion would have to be more damaging to a potential expropriator than to the investor. An example from a similar problem, that of firms trying to protect the products of their research and development, has been mentioned to us by Professor Stephen Magee (personal communication). Firms consciously design redundant circuits into microelectronic components. The purpose is to confuse competitors trying to steal the firm's innovations, *but* it is not a costless strategy to implement and therefore is not socially optimal. Similar options are open to foreign investors trying to ensure that an expropriating host will obtain as little as possible from possession of the investment.

There is little evidence on the exact importance of these defenses. Bradley (1977, p. 81) observes that "Third World countries are notoriously adept at locating mercenary technicians to manage expropriated properties." He concludes on the basis of a large sample of expropriations that "the company's technology must be advanced and proprietary before it can be considered a significant deterrent." But characterizing a company's technology empirically is notoriously difficult. Micallef (1981, p. 127) discusses one example of an oil company that pursued a strategy of continuously upgrading its plant even before the return on the investment justified it. By doing so the firm stayed ahead of the expertise of local engineers, though at some cost to itself. Examination of foreign investments using the techniques discussed by Forsund et al. (1980) may be useful in providing evidence on the existence of various types of technological distortions. The incidence of these distortions could then be related to the expropriation environment.

Another important defensive strategy is to locate different aspects of the production process in different countries. In the case of manufacturing investments, one option is to produce different components in different locations. This strategy will be particularly effective when the output of the industry exhibits considerable product differentiation so that components cannot easily be interchanged. Bradley (1977, p. 81) attributes the survival of Chrysler's Peruvian subsidiary to the fact that only 50 percent of the parts used in its plants were manufactured domestically, making it of little value if expropriated.

A similar but much weaker strategy involves undertaking different stages of a production process in different countries. For instance, sugarcane may be grown in one country but refined elsewhere. This strategy presupposes that there is no easily available market for the output of the early stages. Investors are in the strongest position when they are monopsonists in the next stage of production and can locate the production facilities for this stage abroad. However, this situation is rare and it will probably be possible for an expropriating host to find a market for most raw materials even if only after some initial difficulties.

Finally, we wish to emphasize that many of these distortions cannot be overcome by a management contract. This type of contract, in its purest form, is an arrangement whereby managerially or technically skilled labor is hired from abroad. It avoids the threat of expropriation by the simple solution of only providing inputs that can be withdrawn easily in the event of a dispute. This type of arrangement may overcome certain bottlenecks associated with skill shortages. It cannot, however, mitigate what we believe to be the main distinction between rich and poor countries – a large difference in the amount of physical capital per worker.

Expropriation: the case of extractive industries

Investment in extractive industries may be especially vulnerable to expropriation because it requires much expenditure in prospecting before any output takes place.[15] The findings of this activity are difficult to keep secret, especially after production is started. At this point there is very little an investor can do to prevent a host with the technical capability from taking over the find. As a consequence, companies whose technical advantage lies at the discovery stage may be reluctant to prospect widely, preferring to produce less and to protect current operations by threatening to embargo future exploration.

These difficulties in defending investments in the extractive industries suggest that an increase in the potential for expropriation can reduce the rate of extraction. This conclusion conflicts with that of Long (1975), who assumes that the probability of expropriation is exogenous. His model, however, does not incorporate the exploration process, since investors start with a fixed stock of the resource that is available to them to use as they please until expropriation occurs. Furthermore, the cost of extraction in any period is determined only

[15] Cobbe (1979) provides a detailed discussion of relations between governments and foreign investors focused entirely on the mining sector.

by the absolute amount extracted in that period. In this context investors have an incentive to get as much out of the ground as fast as possible. The longer they wait, the greater the chance that they will lose control of the resource. If, however, the threat of expropriation lowers investment in exploration or capital used in extraction, the rate of extraction may fall. Furthermore, the rate of expropriation may rise if more is invested in these two activities. Long's results depend partially upon his assumption that country behavior is exogenous. Clearly, additional theoretical research is needed to incorporate the other effects we have mentioned in a dynamic model of the type developed by Long.

These arguments suggest that the threat of expropriation may be more acute in the extractive industries than in manufacturing. If investors are rational, however, any increased vulnerability will be manifested in decreased investment and the adoption of costlier defenses. These effects are very difficult to measure, however, since one must infer the situation that would exist if expropriation could not occur. Without the ability to perform this experiment, very little can be said about the sectoral incidence of the distortions caused by a host's having the option of expropriation. The actual incidence of acts of expropriation cannot be a substitute for this type of calculation. For instance, the potential for expropriation may be so great that no investments are made. Everyone would agree that resource allocation is greatly affected yet no acts of expropriation would be observed.

Only if some event occurs that was judged unlikely at the time investments were made can the actual incidence of expropriations be an appropriate index of the inherent vulnerability of different sectors. Perhaps decolonization and the general postwar weakening of the Organization for Economic Cooperation and Development (OECD) members as political and military actors is an experiment where expropriation is first viewed as impossible and then becomes possible. This type of conjecture is, however, unlikely ever to be susceptible of meaningful testing.

Frequent expropriations are likely to occur in industries that are either subject to randomness in the factors influencing the host's decision or are characterized by the obsolescing bargain. Both cases can be illustrated using the example of a three-input production process. With regard to uncertainty, it may be unclear whether the host can acquire the specialized knowledge to run the investment. A risk-neutral investor will assess the relevant probabilities and only invest if the expected value of its profits is nonnegative. If it turns out that knowledge acquisition is easy for the host then it chooses expropriation and the investor loses; otherwise the investor earns profits above the risk-free rate.

In the case of the obsolescing bargain, however, the investor knows that the requisite expertise will be acquired by the host but that it will take time to do so. The investment is undertaken only if profits during the period of investor control provide the normal rate of return and repay capital costs. In both situations, therefore, the option of expropriation causes the high rate of return. If expropriation were impossible and the investor's industry competitive, further investments would drive down the rate of profit. Thus, high rates of return should not be interpreted as monopolistic exploitation justifying expropriation.

We do not see any particular characteristic of extractive industries leading to an expectation of frequent expropriations based either on considerations of uncertainty or the obsolescing bargain. In any case, there does not seem to be any very strong evidence for an assertion that investors in the extractive industries have suffered most from hostile acts. The imperfect evidence that exists is subject to easy misinterpretation and more documentation is clearly necessary. Using data presented by Williams (1975, Table VI) we calculate that mining and smelting and oil production and refining, taken together, had a ratio of nationalized assets from 1956–72 to all assets in 1967 of .26. All sectors other than these two had an even higher ratio of .32, whereas manufacturing had a lower ratio of .17. The same calculation using uncompensated nationalized assets in the numerator yields even more striking results of .10, .22, and .13, respectively. This second ratio is the more appropriate index of expropriation damage, and it clearly contradicts the usual assertion that extractive investments have been the most vulnerable. Especially noteworthy are the differences in the sectoral ratios of compensation paid to assets seized implicit in these ratios.

These findings must be qualified in a number of ways. First, there are difficulties involved in calculating the true value to an investor of the amount lost. There may be systematic biases across sectors in the way asset values are determined. Second, only 1967 rather than 1972 asset stock figures are available. Finally, it may be that the period since 1972 has witnessed a reversal of these findings although Kobrin's opinion (1980, fn. 36) implies that they would actually be strengthened.

Despite these difficulties in using Williams's data, other studies present even more serious problems. Bradley (1977), who shows a very high relative incidence of expropriation in the extractive industries, uses the percent of U.S. companies in the sector subjected to hostile acts as his index. The primary shortcoming of this measure is its failure to allow for intersectoral differences in compensation. As we have remarked, Williams's data show that these differences can be very important. Further, there is the possibility that expropriated investments are of a different average size than those that are untouched and that the average size of investments differs by sector. Both these problems are inherent in an acts measure rather than an assets measure of the incidence of hostile behavior by hosts.

Other problems arise with the index used by Jodice (1980, p. 182). Jodice uses the share of a sector in all acts of expropriation divided by its share in total foreign direct investment as his "vulnerability coefficient." Kobrin (1980, pp. 76–7) makes reference to this same concept. The major objection to this index can be illustrated by considering an industry with one very large investment abroad. If this investment is seized, the industry's coefficient will have a very low numerator and a high denominator yielding a low value of the coefficient. This situation is, however, hardly one of low vulnerability.

Public policy and country risk

The system we have described is characterized by an absence of enforceable contracts, by threats, and by defensive actions – all resulting in impediments to capital mobility.[16] Unable to forswear repudiation and expropriation, capital-importing countries receive less private capital than otherwise. The presumption is that capital is cheap in the rest of the world relative to its productivity in these countries. Further, the LDCs can absorb very large quantities of foreign capital relative to what they now use without appreciably affecting the stock of capital in the rest of the world or raising its cost. If this view is correct, it follows that it is the capital-importing countries and not the capital owners who lose most by the current situation. In this regard we are in disagreement with such authors as Hirschman (1969), who believes that foreign investment stifles domestic capabilities and that divestment is desirable.

One exception to our general conclusion involves situations of monopoly. If a host confronts a monopolistic investor, the option of expropriation helps strengthen the host's position. In extreme cases,

---

16 We rely on parts of our previous work (Eaton and Gersovitz, 1981b, pp. 32–6) for many of the arguments presented here. This earlier work contains citations of the exact sources of legislative acts.

it is only through threatening expropriation that the host can get anything at all from a foreign investor. A similar situation would occur with respect to repudiation if one viewed foreign lenders as effectively cartelized.

A second area of exception occurs in certain narrowly defined industries where LDCs may be important exporters. In this case, the lack of capital may limit the supply of output available to the developed countries, significantly raising prices. Indeed, these price increases may offset the decreased sales sufficiently that these LDC producers are better off. The inability of each LDC to forswear expropriation substitutes for a cartel, which the LDCs may find difficult to organize.

Although exceptions may exist to the position that the capital importers bear the brunt of the present system, we believe that this view serves as the best overall conclusion on the incidence issue. It thus follows that public policies that discourage repudiations and expropriations, and encourage foreign investments, primarily benefit the LDCs. Most public policies in this area can be classified under information provision, retaliation, or insurance.

Information provision

Because the cost of providing information is independent of the number of individuals using it, information should be provided freely. Such a rule presupposes that the cost of generating information should be publicly borne. In the international context, the natural organizations to provide information are the international institutions: the Bank for International Settlements (BIS), IMF, World Bank, and the UN.

Two broad types of information are required. First is information on the dependent variables of our discussion (amount of debt and foreign direct investment, their characteristics and the incidence of expropriations, repudiations, defaults, and other hostile acts). The information on the financial side is extensive but could be improved (BIS, 1979). It is, however, far in advance of the available information on foreign direct investments. No international organization concerns itself in a comprehensive way with this subject. Systematizing the gathering and dissemination of these data is a pressing priority. (For a survey of some data sources in this area see Kobrin 1980, Appendix 2).

The second category of information concerns the independent variables of the system – country characteristics relevant to decisions on financial and physical investments. Basic data on the situations of individual countries are disseminated by the international organizations although more work on making this information consistent across time and countries would be useful to both the country analyst and academic researcher. The World Bank performs a very valuable service by publishing many country studies. An important deficiency is in knowledge about the IMF's stabilization programs, which are largely kept secret. Reasons for some confidentiality are clear, given the sensitivity of these negotiations, but additional openness should be possible.

Retaliation

Legislation in the United States penalizes countries taking hostile actions against American companies in several ways: prohibitions of bilateral foreign aid, exclusion from the generalized system of trade preferences, and opposition by U.S. representatives to multilateral aid.

The existence of penalties activated automatically by hostile acts can play a valuable role in stabilizing international investment. If capital importers know that retaliation will occur and if the penalties are sufficiently severe, hostile acts can be deterred. In this situation investors may be better off, since they have an opportunity to invest not otherwise available. Capital importers may also be better off, since they can obtain capital that investors would not otherwise be willing to provide. In effect, the potential penalty serves as a form of collateral for an LDC that it cannot otherwise give. It may well be that the larger the penalty, the better off the capital importer.

On the other hand, there may be situations in which the capital importer's expected welfare at the time of the loan deteriorates with higher penalties. For instance, the country may be required to repay regardless of future economic conditions, which it can neither control nor foresee. In this case the option of default will have an insurance aspect, providing as it does an opportunity to lessen obligations under very bad circumstances. An increase in the penalty, therefore, may lower the country's welfare even though its credit ceiling is raised, because the probability of a large penalty curtails this insurance aspect of lending. We believe that this situation is likely to be the exception.

Penalties in this system are only as important as the resolve of the governments of rich countries to invoke them. If the welfare of both capital importers and investors actually can be improved by the existence of penalties, it is crucial that both groups perceive investor-country governments as committed to retaliation. Decision makers must realize that the failure to impose penalties may jeopardize the development prospects of poorer countries by discouraging private investment. Most analysts believe that the threat of a cutoff of foreign aid, for instance, has been generally ineffective (Olson 1975, Lipson 1976, and Kuhn 1977). It seems that this penalty has not been consistently applied and in any case requires that aid to the particular country be large. If this threat were viable, however, it suggests a multiplier effect of aid since it can facilitate private capital flows.

One possibility is to let individual LDCs agree in advance to the imposition of penalties in the event of hostile acts. In this way, they can legitimize such a mechanism and at the same time reveal the penalty level they think best for their own welfare. The Overseas Private Investment Corporation (OPIC), which is discussed in the following section, embodies the spirit of this suggestion by requiring that host governments agree to conditions for resolving disputes if they wish to be eligible for insured investments.

The international institutions can also play a role by organizing embargoes and enforcing cohesion among private investors as well as by using their political influence with the governments of investors. The IMF, for instance, has been a prominent actor in several reschedulings of bank loans.

Insurance

The Overseas Private Investment Corporation provides insurance to eligible private investors against various hostile acts (see Lipson 1978). The insurance is limited to a maximum of 75 percent of the investment. The Export–Import Bank provides similar coverage to American exporters of tangible goods. This insurance extends to financial obligations for which exports constitute security.

One difficulty with insurance schemes of this type is that the capital importer has discretion over the hostile acts. This problem of moral hazard undermines the usefulness of these institutions, encouraging hostile acts without discouraging private investment. Private investors may be less determined to embargo loans to defaulting governments or to defend themselves by other actions. Proposals to make the IMF an international lender of last resort also suffer from these same problems. These drawbacks are not as severe if the insurance is confined to unexpected and uncontrollable events such as war, revolution, or insurrection, and – more difficult to classify – natural or international events leading to poor economic performance.

The fact that OPIC offers protection only up to 75 percent of an investment provides some brake on any tendency of private investors to neglect the possibility of hostile acts. And there are administrative and transactions costs involved in obtaining compensation. Finally, and most important, OPIC can provide insurance only for investments in countries that are unlikely to act against investors and it can forbid future insured investments in any country precipitating claims, thus providing a potential penalty. For an investment in a country to be eligible for OPIC coverage, that country's government must formally agree to a number of conditions, including the recognition of OPIC as a successive claimant. Thus, OPIC provides an example of a mechanism whereby LDC governments can voluntarily increase the likelihood of a confrontation with the United States in the event that they interfere with private investments. It should be noted that OPIC concentrates on physical investments and is not at present an important insurer of financial investments.

Insurance schemes may not be a substitute for penalties, but they can complement retaliatory provisions by functioning as tripwires. For instance, by transferring the burden of default from private investors to their governments, these arrangements can strengthen the resolve of these governments to impose sanctions.

Technical appendix: time-consistent taxation and expropriation of foreign capital

In this appendix we present a simple model illustrating how time-consistent behavior on the part of borrowers interacts with the defensive strategies of investors to produce capital market imperfections. At any moment the stock of foreign physical capital invested in a host country is given. The host can, in principle, tax the income from this capital at any rate and, in the extreme, confiscate it entirely. Regardless of the host's actions, the *current* supply of capital is unaffected since it is determined by past investments. The factor constraining the host's behavior is the effect on the expectations of potential investors about the host's future behavior. This impact on its reputation may be sufficient to make favorable treatment of already invested foreign capital in the host's own interest.

In developing these ideas we make the following assumptions:

1. Domestic product in period t is a function $f(k_t)$ where k_t is the stock of capital in the country in period t. The function $f(\cdot)$ is increasing and concave.
2. The stock of capital at time t is given in that period and consists of foreign-owned capital, k_t^F, and domestic capital k_t^D so that

$$k_t = k_t^F + k_t^D \tag{A.1}$$

Capital is assumed to depreciate completely after one period.

3. The stock of domestic capital k_t^D is a constant $\bar{k}^D$, that is, $k_t^D = \bar{k}^D \; \forall \; t$

This assumption can be interpreted as meaning that the supply of domestic savings is fixed at $\bar{k}^D$ each period. For our purposes an equivalent assumption would be that the *installation* of capital requires managerial services in fixed proportion to the amount invested and that the national capacity to install capital is $\bar{k}^D$. Expropriation leads to the loss of *future* access to the installation capability of foreign firms, which otherwise would be in infinitely elastic supply to a small country. In principle, the supply of national capital need not equal the capacity to install capital, as we have assumed here for the sake of simplicity.

4. Capital can earn an after-tax rate of return r in the rest of the world.
5. In the absence of foreign investment, the marginal product of capital in the host country exceeds the rest-of-world after-tax interest rate, that is,

$$f'(\bar{k}^D) > r$$

6. Competition in domestic factor markets ensures that foreign capital earns its marginal product, $f'(k_t)$, before tax.
7. In each period t the host chooses a tax rate τ_t on foreign capital. Given k_t^F, national income in period t is

$$y_t = f(k_t) - (1 - \tau_t) f'(k_t) k_t^F \tag{A.2}$$

8. In any period t, the objective of the host country's taxation authority is the maximization of the present discounted utility of income, W,

$$W = \sum_{s=t}^{\infty} \beta^{s-t} u(y_s) \qquad \beta < 1 \tag{A.3}$$

where β is a discount factor and $u(\cdot)$ is an increasing concave function.

9. Foreign investors behave atomistically.

That is, there are a large number of foreign investors, each of whom makes a small contribution to k_{t+1} in period t in anticipation of earning an after-tax rate of return in period $t + 1$ of $(1 - \tau_{t+1}^e) f'(k_{t+1})$. Each contribution to k_{t+1} is sufficiently small to allow the investor to ignore the effect of this contribution on the aggregate level of k_{t+1}, and hence on $f'(k_{t+1})$, and on the tax rate expected to prevail in the repayment period, τ_{t+1}^e. Thus, investors make their investments taking the expected after-tax rate of return in the host country as given.

In competitive equilibrium, then, assumptions 1 and 9 together imply that

$$(1 - \tau^e_{t+1}) f'(k_{t+1}) = r \tag{A.4}$$

10. In some initial period 0, the host announces that the tax rate in each period $t \geq 0$ will be $\hat{\tau}_t$. If the host deviates from taxing at this rate in any period $s \geq 0$ investors will anticipate full expropriation ($\tau = 1$) in periods $s + i, i = 1, \ldots, \infty$

If the host deviates from its announced taxing sequence it can no longer credibly maintain a reputation. Having deviated from its announced policy a host has no incentive *not* to tax all capital in place fully, since to do otherwise will not increase its ability to attract capital in the future. If the host does decide to deviate from its announced strategy $\{\hat{\tau}_t\}$ in some period s, then it will optimally set $\tau_v = 1$, $v \geq s$; that is, it will expropriate the current capital stock and any future investment. Foreign investors, observing $\tau_s \neq \hat{\tau}_s$, will then anticipate $\tau^e_v = 1$, $v > s$; they will not invest. Thus, $k^F_v = 0$, $v > s$.[17] The present discounted utility in period s of deviating from the announced strategy, which amounts to expropriating capital in place in that period and becoming financially autarkic thereafter, is defined as W^x_s where

$$W^x_s = u[f(k_s)] + [\beta/(1 - \beta)] u[f(\bar{k}^D)] \tag{A.5}$$

For the sequence $\{\hat{\tau}_t\}$ to be credible it must satisfy the time-consistency requirement that, at each period t,

$$u[f(k_t) - (1 - \hat{\tau}_t)f'(k_t)k^F_t]$$
$$+ \sum_{s=t+1}^{\infty} \beta^{s-t}\{u[f(\hat{k}_s)] - (1 - \hat{\tau}_s)f'(\hat{k}_s)\hat{k}^F_s]\} \geq W^x_t \qquad t = 0, \ldots, \infty \tag{A.6}$$

where $\hat{k}^F_s$ is defined implicitly by the equating of the world and anticipated domestic after-tax rates of return, that is,

17 We have earlier used this type of equilibrium concept in Eaton and Gersovitz (1981a). Examples of more recent work on related topics include that by Dybvig and Spatt (1980), who apply this same equilibrium concept to examine a firm's incentive to maintain a reputation for product quality. Selten (1975) discusses this concept under the name subgame perfect equilibrium. The equilibrium is one in which an agent makes a precommitment to a certain course of action. This announcement is credible only if it is thereafter always in that agent's interest to pursue the announced course of action. Subject to this constraint the announced course of action maximizes that agent's objective function.

$$(1 - \hat{\tau}_s)\, f'(\bar{k}^D + \hat{k}_s^F) \equiv r \tag{A.7}$$

and

$$\hat{k}_s \equiv \bar{k}^D + \hat{k}_s^F \tag{A.8}$$

That is, it must be optimal in each period for the host to maintain the announced tax rate sequence rather than to expropriate the capital in place in that period and ruin its reputation as a host.

In period 0, then, the host chooses a tax rate sequence $\{\hat{\tau}_i\}$ to maximize its present discounted utility in period 0, W_0, where

$$W_0 = u[f(k_0) - (1 - \tau_0)f'(k_0)k_0^F] + \sum_{t=0}^{\infty} \beta^t\{u[f(\hat{k}_t) - (1 - \tau_t)f'(\hat{k}_t)k_t^F]\} \tag{A.9}$$

subject to the constraint (A.6). In period 0, k_0^F is exogenous. For $t > 0$ $\hat{k}_t^F$ is given by (A.7).

Differentiating W_0 with respect to τ_t, $t = 0, \ldots, \infty$, we obtain

$$\frac{dW_0}{d\tau_0} = u'(y_0)f'(k_0)k_0^F > 0 \tag{A.10a}$$

$$\frac{dW_0}{d\tau_t} = \beta^t u'(y_t)\left\{ [\tau_t f'(\hat{k}_t) - (1 - \tau_t)f'(\hat{k}_t)k_t^F]\frac{dk_t^F}{d\tau_t} \right.$$
$$\left. + f'(\hat{k}_t)k_t^F \right\} \quad t = 1, 2, \ldots \tag{A.10b}$$

To determine the effect of a change in the tax rate τ_t on k_t^F differentiate (A.7) to obtain

$$\frac{dk_t^F}{d\tau_t} = \frac{f'(\hat{k}_t)}{(1 - \tau_t)f''(\hat{k}_t)} \tag{A.7'}$$

which, of course, is negative whenever $1 > \tau_t \geq 0$
Substituting (A.7') into (A.10b) yields

$$\frac{dW_0}{d\tau_t} = u'(y_t)\frac{\beta^t \tau_t[f'(\hat{k}_t)]^2}{(1 - \tau_t)f''(\hat{k}_t)} \quad t = 1, 2, \ldots \tag{A.10b'}$$

which is negative whenever $1 > \tau_t > 0$.

Ignoring the time-consistency constraint (A.6), then, optimal policy will involve taxing initial capital fully (setting $\hat{\tau}_0 = 1$) and taxing subsequent investment not at all (setting $\hat{\tau}_t = 0$; $t = 1, 2, \ldots$); thus, a zero tax on foreign capital is optimal for a small country facing a given world cost of capital r. We denote the zero-tax capital stock as k^*, determined implicitly by:

$$f'(k^*) = r \tag{A.11}$$

Having committed itself to a zero-tax policy, if the host country decides to tax capital in any later period t it will have a national income of $f(\bar{k}^D)$ in subsequent periods while obtaining up to $f(k^*)$ in period t. For a policy of not taxing capital at all to be time consistent requires, then, from (A.6), that

$$u(y^*)/(1 - \beta) \geq u[f(k^*)] + [\beta/(1 - \beta)]\, u[f(\bar{k}^D)] \qquad (A.12)$$

where

$$y^* \equiv f(k^*) - f'(k^*)\,(k^* - \bar{k}^D)$$

If the host country is risk neutral then we may set $u(y) = y$. Multiplying (A.12) by $(1 - \beta)$ and rearranging gives

$$f'(k^*)\,(k^* - \bar{k}^D) \leq \beta[f(k^*) - f(\bar{k}^D)] \qquad (A.12')$$

Approximating $f(\bar{k}^D)$ by a second-order Taylor series around k^* and substituting the resulting expression into (A.12') yields the condition that zero taxation of capital is time consistent if and only if

$$\frac{2(1 - \beta)}{\beta} \leq (k^* - \bar{k}^D)\left[-\frac{f''(k^*)}{f'(k^*)} \right] \qquad (A.12'')$$

A host country is more likely to be capable of sustaining zero taxation of foreign capital if (1) its discount factor β is near 1; (2) the difference between the zero tax and autarkic capital stock $(k^* - k^D)$ is large; and (3) the production function is highly concave. Since, from (A.7), k^* rises as r falls, zero taxation of foreign capital is easier to sustain when the world interest rate is low.

If condition (A.12') does not obtain, then zero taxation of foreign capital is not time consistent. The constraint (A.6) is then binding. Since the constraint (A.6) takes the identical form for all periods $t > 0$ we may restrict ourselves to considering a taxation strategy that replicates itself each period, that is, in which the host announces a tax rate $\bar{\tau}$ that will apply for all periods except the initial one. To be time consistent, $\bar{\tau}$ must satisfy

$$u[f(\tilde{k}) - (1 - \bar{\tau})\,f'(\tilde{k})\,(\tilde{k} - \bar{k}^D)]/(1 - \beta) \geq u[f(\tilde{k})]$$
$$+ [\beta/(1 - \beta)]\, u[f(\bar{k}^D)] \qquad (A.13)$$

where $\tilde{k}$ is defined by

$$(1 - \bar{\tau})\,f'(\tilde{k}) = r \qquad (A.14)$$

Consider again the case of risk neutrality where $u(y) = y$. Multiplying (A.13) by $(1 - \beta)$ and rearranging gives

$$\beta[f(\tilde{k}) - f(\bar{k}^D)] \geq (1 - \bar{\tau})\,f'(\tilde{k})\,(\tilde{k} - \bar{k}^D) \qquad (A.13')$$

Substituting (A.14) makes (A.13′) become

$$\beta[f(\bar{k}) - f(\bar{k}^D)] - r(\bar{k} - \bar{k}^D) \geq 0 \tag{A.13″}$$

Define the function

$$\chi(k) \equiv \beta[f(k) - f(\bar{k}^D)] - r(k - \bar{k}^D)$$

If $\chi(k^*) \geq 0$, then zero taxation of capital is time consistent. Otherwise, the condition $\chi(k) \geq 0$ restricts the set of credible policies.

Since $\chi(\bar{k}^D) = 0$ and since $\chi''(k) < 0$, there is at most one level of capital greater than $\bar{k}^D$ that satisfies $\chi(k) = 0$. If

$$\beta f'(\bar{k}^D) - r \leq 0 \tag{A.15}$$

then foreign investment at any positive level is not sustainable by a time-consistent policy. Otherwise, some positive level of foreign investment can be sustained.

If the constraint $\chi(k) = 0$ is binding, note that (1) an increase in the discount factor β raises the maximum sustainable capital stock; (2) an increase in the world interest rate reduces the maximum sustainable capital stock; (3) an increase in the domestic capital stock $\bar{k}^D$ also lowers the maximum sustainable capital stock;[18] (4) an increase in the domestic capital stock crowds out foreign capital on a more than one-for-one basis. The reason is that an increase in $\bar{k}^D$ increases the welfare of the host country should it expropriate, reducing its incentive to abide by a given, preannounced tax rate.

Combining these results with those already reported leads to the conclusion that countries with relatively low discount rates and limited supplies of national capital are likely to treat foreign capital more favorably. Countries in which these magnitudes are *very* low will not want to tax foreign capital at all, since sustaining perfect capital mobility represents not only an optimal but also a time-consistent policy for them. Other countries, where discount rates are very high and other sources of capital are readily available, may find that full expropriation of all foreign assets is the only time-consistent policy. These countries will find themselves shut out of private international capital markets. Countries with intermediate values of β and $\bar{k}^D$ will sustain some capital mobility, but they will tax foreign capital and the domestic marginal product of capital will exceed the cost of capital to the country.

---

[18] These results follow from the fact that an increase in r and decrease in β shift the locus $\psi(k)$ downward, as does an increase in $\bar{k}^D$ if (A.15) does not obtain, so that $\bar{k} > \bar{k}^D$.

We have assumed that the production technology $f(k)$ is the same in all countries. There are, of course, differences in the endowments of other factors and in technologies. Country characteristics that augment the *future* marginal product of capital in the country, other things equal, make future access to foreign capital more desirable. Such characteristics will increase the country's ability to borrow in the present. We predict that countries that can benefit greatly in the future from foreign capital, for example, because of vast natural resources and little national ability to exploit them, can sustain larger levels of foreign investment currently.

We have treated policy toward direct foreign investment as the outcome of the maximization of a social utility function. In fact, policy is conducted by governments with objectives that can differ from those of its citizens. A new government, for example, may consider its reputation as independent of that of its predecessor. It may consequently reformulate policy toward foreign investment upon assuming power. Such a reformulation could involve treating existing foreign-owned assets as a legacy of the past and taxing them at high levels. The same government might then pursue a policy of attracting, and treating favorably, *new* foreign investment. Alternatively, a government with an uncertain future may have a higher discount rate than the representative individual and thus tax foreign assets more heavily than would be desirable from a national perspective. The bad reputation this policy creates would, with some probability, be inherited by another government and hence be of less concern to the one currently in power.

Finally, we have calculated the level of foreign investment that a country can sustain by comparing its current and future investment opportunities with its *national* capital resources. There is, however, more than one international source of capital. Some countries may continue to have access to one source even if they treat assets obtained from another source unfavorably. For example, countries that are already or willing to become members of the East bloc may be less fearful of the consequences of acting against foreign investors because they can turn to other bloc members. This phenomenon reduces the equilibrium amount of investment such countries can obtain from private capital markets.

References

Arrow, Kenneth J. *The Limits of Organization* (New York: Norton, 1974).

Bank for International Settlements (BIS). *Manual on Statistics Compiled by International Orgnizations on Countries' External Indebtedness* (Basel: 1979).

Bardhan, Pranab. "Optimum Foreign Borrowing," in Karl Shell (ed.), *Essays on the Theory of Optimal Economic Growth* (Cambridge, Mass.: MIT Press, 1967).

Bradley, David G. "Managing against Expropriation." *Harvard Business Review* vol. 55, no. 4 (1977), pp. 75–83.

Breton, Albert. "The Economics of Nationalism." *Journal of Political Economy*, vol. 74, no. 4 (1964), pp. 376–86.

Cauas, Jorge, and Selowsky, Marcelo. "Potential Distributive Effects of Nationalization Policies: The Economic Aspects," in Charles R. Frank and Richard C. Webb (eds.), *Income Distribution and Growth in Less-Developed Countries* (Washington, D.C.: Brookings Institution, 1977).

Cline, William R. "Economic Stabilization in Peru, 1975–78," in William R. Cline and Sidney Weintraub (eds.), *Economic Stabilization in Developing Countries* (Washington, D.C.: Brookings Institution, 1981).

Cobbe, James H. *Governments and Mining Companies in Developing Countries* (Boulder, Colo.: Westview, 1979).

Delupis, Ingrid. *Finance and Protection of Investments in Developing Countries* (Epping, Essex, UK: Gower, 1973).

Derecho, Stefan D. "Peru's Crisis: One Mistake after Another." *Euromoney* (June, 1978), pp. 95–6.

Downer, Steve. "Even the Anchovetas are Returning to Peru." *Euromoney* (April, 1980), pp. xi–xvi.

Dror, Yehezkel. *Crazy States: A Counterconventional Strategic Problem* (Lexington, Mass.: Heath, 1971).

Dybvig, Philip H., and Spatt, C. S. "Does It Pay to Maintain a Reputation?" *Financial Research Center Memorandum No. 32*, Princeton University (August, 1980).

Eaton, Jonathan, and Gersovitz, Mark. "LDC Participation in International Financial Markets: Debt and Reserves." *Journal of Development Economies*, vol. 7, no. 1 (1980), pp. 3–21.

"Debt with Potential Repudiation: Theoretical and Empirical Analysis." *Review of Economic Studies*, vol. 48, no. 152 (1981a), pp. 289–309.

Poor-Country Borrowing in Private Financial Markets and the Repudiation Issue (Princeton, N.J.: International Finance Section, 1981b).

"A Theory of Expropriation and Deviations from Perfect Capital Mobility." Economic Growth Center Discussion Paper no. 391. New Haven: Yale University, January 1982.

Economist Intelligence Unit (EIU). *Quarterly Economic Review of Peru, Bolivia* (London, various dates).

Field, Peter, and Adam, Nigel. "Why Did Chase Move So Fast?" *Euromoney* (January, 1980), pp. 10–25.

Forsund, Finn R., Lovell, C. A. Knox, and Schmidt, Peter. "A Survey of Frontier Production Functions and of their Relationship to Efficiency Measurement." *Journal of Econometrics*, vol. 13, no. 1 (1980), pp. 5–25.

Goodman, Laurie S. "Bank Lending to Non-Opec LDC's: Are Risks Diversifiable?" *Federal Reserve Bank of New York Bulletin*, vol. 6, no. 2 (1981), pp. 10–20.

Hellwig, Martin F. "A Model of Borrowing and Lending with Bankruptcy." *Econometrica*, vol. 45 (1977), pp. 1879–906.

Hirschman, Albert O. *How to Divest in Latin America and Why* (Princeton, N.J.: International Finance Section, 1969).

Jodice, David A. "Sources of Change in Third World Regimes for Foreign Direct Investment, 1968–1976." *International Organization*, vol. 34, no. 2 (1980), pp. 177–206.

Johnson, Harry G. "A Theoretical Model of Economic Nationalism in New and Developing Countries." *Political Science Quarterly*, vol. 80, no. 2 (1965), pp. 169–85.

Kobrin, Stephen J. "Foreign Enterprise and Forced Divestment in LDC's." *International Organization*, vol. 34, no. 1 (1980), pp. 65–88.

Kuczynski, Pedro-Pablo. "Peru Needs Truth more than Sympathy." *Euromoney* (December, 1977), pp. 73–5.

Kuhn, W. E. "The Hickenlooper Amendment as a Determinant of the Outcome of Expropriation Disputes." *The Social Science Journal*, vol. 14, no. 1 (1977), pp. 71–81.

Kydland, Richard E., and Prescott, Edward C. "Rules Rather Than Discretion: The Inconsistency of Optimal Plans." *Journal of Political Economy*, vol. 85, no. 3 (1977), pp. 513–48.

Levine, David I. "The Growing Problem of Sovereign Immunity." *Euromoney* (May, 1977), pp. 74–84.

Lillich, Richard B. *The Protection of Foreign Investment* (Syracuse, N.Y.: Syracuse University Press, 1965).

Lipson, Charles H. "Corporate Preferences and Public Policies: Foreign Aid Sanctions and Investment Protection." *World Politics*, vol. 28, no. 3 (1976), pp. 306–421.

Lipson, Charles. "The Development of Expropriation Insurance: The Role of Corporate Preferences and State Initiatives." *International Organization*, vol. 32, no. 3 (1978), pp. 351–75.

Long, Ngo Van. "Resource Extraction under the Uncertainty about Possible Nationalization." *Journal of Economic Theory*, vol. 10, no. 1 (1975), pp. 42–53.

Markowitz, Harry M. *Portfolio Selection* (New Haven, Conn.: Yale University Press, 1959).

Micallef, Joseph V. "Political Risk Assessment and the Multinational," in Richard Ensor (ed.), *Assessing Country Risk* (London: Euromoney Publications, 1981).

Moran, Theodore H. "Transnational Strategies of Protection and Defense by Multinational Corporations: Spreading the Risk and Raising the Cost for Nationalization in Natural Resources." *International Organization*, vol. 27, no. 2 (1973), pp. 273–87.

Nevans, Ronald. "Peru Crisis: Rescheduling is on the Way." *Euromoney* (March, 1978), pp. 25–6.

Olson, Richard S. "Economic Coercion in International Disputes: The United States and Peru in the IPC Expropriation Dispute of 1968–1971." *Journal of the Developing Areas*, vol. 9, no. 3 (1975), pp. 395–414.

Schelling, Thomas C. *The Strategy of Conflict* (Cambridge, Mass.: Harvard University Press, 1960).

Selten, R. "Reexamination of the Perfect Concept for Equilibrium Points in Extensive Games." *International Journal of Game Theory*, vol. 4, no. 1 (1975), pp. 25–55.

Smith, David N., and Wells, Louis T., Jr. *Negotiating Third World Mineral Agreements: Promises as Prologue* (Cambridge, Mass.: Ballinger, 1975).

Srodes, James. "Governor Wallich Wants the IMF to Advise LDC Lenders." *Euromoney* (April, 1977), pp. 24–6.

Tobin, James. "Notes on the Economic Theory of Expulsion and Expropriation." *Journal of Development Economics*, vol. 1, no. 1 (1974), pp. 7–18.

U.N. Economic and Social Council, Commission on Transnational Corporations. *Transnational Corporations in World Development* (New York: United Nations, March 20, 1978), E/C. 10/38.

Vernon, Raymond. "Long-Run Trends in Concession Contracts," in *Proceedings of the American Society of International Law* (1967), pp. 81–9.

"Conflict and Resolution Between Foreign Direct Investors, and Less Developed Countries." *Public Policy*, vol. 18 (1968), pp. 333–51.

"Foreign Enterprises and Developing Nations in the Raw Materials Industries." *American Economic Review,* vol. 60, no. 2 (1970), pp. 122–6.

Wellons, P. A. *Borrowing by Developing Countries on the Euro-Currency Market* (Paris: OECD, 1977).

Wells, Louis T. Jr. "Negotiating with Third World Governments." *Harvard Business Review,* vol. 55, no. 1 (1977), pp. 72–80.

Williams, M. L. "The Extent and Significance of the Nationalization of Foreign-Owned Assets in Developing Countries, 1956–1972." *Oxford Economic Papers,* vol. 27, no. 2 (1975), pp. 260–73.

World Bank, *World Debt Tables,* vol. 2 (1976), p. 121 and vol. 1 (1979), p. 47 (Washington, annual numbers).

CHAPTER 3

Political risk: analysis, process, and purpose

MARTIN SHUBIK

The capitalist himself is a practical man, who, it is true, does not always reflect on what he says outside his office, but who always knows what he does inside the latter.

— K. Marx *Capital*, ch. 5

What is political risk?

Political risk and international political risk

"Bet only on winners, and try to get your bets in after the horse is past the post." This is sound advice for those who like to win. The only problem is how to follow the advice.

Large firms and even private individuals face political risk in their own country by the mere fact that they exist in a political environment. Many in Hitler's Germany who ended their lives in extermination camps predicted in 1933 that they could deal with the new regime. The comings and goings of Franco, Perón, Mobutu, Amin, and many others influenced the immediate lives and fortunes of individuals and corporations far more than the fluctuations of the stock markets or the economy in general.

Ben Franklin noted that man is rarely more innocently engaged than when he is devoting his time to making money. The economic world, rough as it may be, is considerably gentler and more predictable than the world of power. And the world of politics is the world of power. Individuals and corporations who ignore economic planning and prediction may end up poorer if luck fails to smile. But those who choose to ignore the portents of change in the political environment may not survive at all, or may find themselves fortunate to be in exile.

Economic humankind lives in a society and a polity. It can ill afford to forget this simple fact of life. The Chinese curse "may you live in interesting times" is with all of us. Communication is too fast, populations too great, and weapons too fearsome to allow even the Swiss or Icelanders the luxury of ignoring the political environment.

109

Internal political risks are those run by an institution or individual due to the unforeseen actions or influence of the local political powers. They may be associated with changes in policy or parties caused by elections, public pressure, coup d'etat, revolution, or civil war.

International political risks are those generated by political entities beyond one's national jurisdiction.

The very essence of risk is dynamics and uncertainty. If the individual is certain that taxes are high and will be collected, the facts of life may be unpleasant, but there is no risk. If the policy with respect to nationalization in the next ten years has been announced and will be followed no matter who is in power, there is no risk.

Many a businessperson can find a way to survive and even prosper on what may be regarded as extremely bleak political soil as long as the rules of the game are given and one can predict that they will last.

Elementary concern for survial and viability makes it imperative to both assess political risk and protect against it. Protection may be active or passive, that is, the individual or corporation may attempt to influence the political environment or may merely react as though its actions have no outside influence. "Voice or exit," accommodation or unilateral action are choices to be faced. Literate, well-to-do individuals or very small firms may still find that the virtues of the purely competitive market apply to them. If the political situation is bad in Argentina, migrate to Australia. If expropriation in Nicaragua is intolerable or the marginal tax rate in Sweden is 102%, Canada or Costa Rica may still welcome a skilled immigrant or enterprise. But for the most part the open frontiers have gone, the system is closed, and flight now offers a viable solution to only a few.

Autarky or interconnection?

A healthy economy presupposes the rule of law. Taxes are paid, but services are rendered; contracts are honored and a stable environment is provided. But law, order, and trust at best are local growths and do not flower as well in an international setting. The future growth of international trade and commerce requires a parallel growth of international law and trust.

Table 3.1 displays a few highly aggregated figures on world trade and population. The growth is there. Furthermore, simple economic sense tells us that all nations and individuals stand to benefit from greater international trade, *all other things being equal;* but all other things are rarely, if ever, equal. Autarky and international disinvest-

Table 3.1. *World trade and population*

	1965	1970	1975	1979
World trade ($ billion 1975)	410	630	830	1,080
World population (millions)[a]	3,358	3,727	4,109	4,406

[a]Statistical Abstract of U.S., 1980.

ment are the prices that intelligent countries, firms, and individuals may all be willing to pay if the uncertainties of the international environment become too great.

Who is or should be concerned?

The actors

Before the model or the theory are the perception and the appropriate question. The need and the depth of the need, and hence the nature of the appropriate concern for political risk assessment, will vary with the different institutions and individuals. The prime groups who are or should be concerned are private citizens, banks and other financial institutions, manufacturing corporations, trading and transportation corporations, governmental agencies, government in general, and international agencies such as the World Bank.

The private citizen as an individual or even as an owner of a small business has simple and elemental concerns for both local and international political risk. They are survival, freedom, and stability. Will a totalitarian regime take over? Will civil order be maintained? Is the individual free from arbitrary arrest or confiscation of property? Can one's family survive and a reasonable living be made without harassment from the state? Are there alternative locations where opportunity is more favorable and immigration feasible? We concern ourselves no further with this important but special concern. The emphasis here is upon private or governmental economic agents who are large enough to have to consider accommodation, fight or flight, and who need to recognize consciously both the power of others and their own power. A major bank, manufacturing firm, or oil company operating in a small country cannot be apolitical no matter how much its self-image is as an economic entity passively obeying the local laws and customs and completely staying out of politics. The mere act of paying taxes and selling supplies to a regime about to fall virtually guarantees being anathema to the subsequent regime. The failure to pay taxes or sell supplies may bring repercussions from the current government whether or not it eventually falls.

Motivation

The large private financial institution or manufacturing or other business corporation is primarily an economic agent. But the large corporations and especially those engaged in international trade are not and cannot afford the luxury of regarding themselves as solely economic entities. The major firm is a social as well as an economic force. Long-term, expected, discounted profit maximization may well remain an important part of corporate goals, but it is not the only goal. An active, not reactive, recognition must be given to the firm as an agent of the international community and a promoter of international law. The larger international firms are supranational agencies. They have senior personnel of many nationalities. The responsibilities of individual citizenship must be reconciled with corporate membership.

The bank or manufacturing firm may have a major effect upon long- and short-term investment and upon the diffusion of technology and the standards of management and competition in the host country. These influences can be of social and political concern to both the host country and other countries in which the firm operates.

International trade has always been intimately related to national power. Since ancient times the trade routes were taxed and policed. The history of the Babylonian trade routes, the China trade, the Dutch East Indies Company, the Spanish trade galleons, the East India Company, the South Sea Company, and the Hudson Bay Company, for example, is the story of an intermix of governmental power and policy and individual economic enterprise.

In the modern world, although the profit-oriented corporation has emerged as an important economic form, the rise of socialist or otherwise centralized economies has placed more and more international trade into the sphere of national policy. A deal between a Soviet trade group and U.S. wheat exporters is as much a political act as it is an economic act, if not more than.

The primary economic function and motivation of the international firm must not be forgotten, but it is not enough to serve as a guide for the modern firm. The firm trading with centralized economies must seek the political support of its own government or international agencies or otherwise face an uneven contest. The goals of the

Soviet trade groups directly involve both the economic factors and political purpose of the last surviving nineteenth-century imperial colonial power.

International trade must be considered in a strategic setting. Political risk assessment by a firm not only requires an understanding of the possibilities of the occurrence of political events in general, but it also calls for an identification of political–economic forces specifically directed at the firm. Thus, the private firm engaged in international trade must consider what support its own country will provide when faced with foreign commercial state enterprises. It has been estimated that these enterprises account for over 20 percent of world sales among the 500 largest international business corporations (Lamont 1979). The problems with East–West trade and the lack of equality in the positions of state foreign trade agencies and private firms call attention to the need to know how much one's own government will help when foreign political pressure is manifested through state-owned economic enterprises.

The resources at stake

At the most elemental the key resources at stake are the very lives of the corporations and their personnel. Institutions can be and have been totally expropriated and managers can be and have been kidnapped, arrested, and killed. The veneer of international law is thin.

In essence, three types of assets are at stake in international trade: real assets, personnel, and financial assets. These categories can be broken down thus:

1. *Real assets*
   a. Institutions
   b. Fixed immovable assets
   c. Real movable assets not easily liquidated
   d. Real movable assets easily liquidated
   e. Patents and processes
2. *Personnel*
   a. Local citizens – employees
   b. Own citizens – employees
   c. Third country – employees
   d. Others
3. *Financial assets*
   a. Cash, accounts payable, prepaid taxes, other short-term loans and credit
   b. Long-term credit extensions, bonds, shares, and other financial paper

All of these can best be regarded as different types of potential hostages in the game of political–economic power. Offsetting them are the host country's assets that are located in areas where a corporation could promote retaliatory action against them.

The distinction among the assets is both quantitative and qualitative. Land cannot be moved; buildings are hard to move or to dispose of; but diamonds go across borders with ease. Oil fields are immobile, oil in the barrel somewhat less so, and some technical processes depart with the personnel.

Blood may be spilled to protect oil, but blood is still essentially thicker than oil. The moral and political problems posed in retrieving human hostages are qualitatively different from retrieving bricks and stone. A barrel of oil does not carry a passport with it as it tries to cross boundaries; people do. Bureaucratic and moral problems proliferate when the papers of employees of one nationality are in order for an evacuation, whereas others of a different nationality must be left behind because their papers are not in order.

Financial instruments are basically creatures of national law and as such the issuer may have the opportunity to use them as hostages. Anyone who holds foreign financial instruments has created potential hostages. Bearer instruments are clearly harder to control than paper with names. It is easier to freeze Iran's bank accounts than to prevent it from spending the U.S. cash it holds.

The difference in the structure of the holdings of international assets by the various concerned institutions results in distinct variations in the level of importance of political risk assessment. Before too much concern is given to how to go about assessing political risk and how accurately it can be done, the international firm needs to form a clear perception of what it really has at stake. Furthermore, it must determine how sensitive its fortunes are to changes in political climate.

The large bank deals in paper. Relatively few employees are exposed to risk and few real assets are at stake. Currency fluctuations and the exposure of short-term loans depend delicately upon day-to-day events. The actions of the central banks, the term structure of the various interest rates, and the short-term international flow of funds must be monitored continuously. This type of information is primarily economic but the boundary lines distinguishing economics and politics blur when the behavior of central banks is interpreted or an attempt is made to distinguish "flight capital" from purely economic movements of funds.

Longer-term loans to private or governmental institutions call for a greater exposure to risk. The bank can cut down on its risk by improving the accuracy of its risk assessment or by offsetting the risks by the way it structures its activities. Thus, for example, a bank can stress acting as a broker for long-term loans rather than supplying the credit itself. It may be more inclined to provide financing if international agencies are providing guarantees or if other major banks are also lending. "Misery loves company" and in finance in general it is by no means clear that more participants in a deal imply less risk per participant. The theory implicit in the notion of safety in numbers is that the individual perceptions of risk can be melded to produce a more reliable assessment than that held by the individuals. A countervailing possibility is that the perceptions of the participants are dulled when each takes as proof that the deal is good, the fact that the other is willing to participate.

For international long-term financing a bank requires a country risk assessment activity that blends the economic, bureaucratic, and political factors to produce reports and briefings that directly influence decisions on the level of exposure.

The large manufacturing firm or mining or oil company, unlike the banks, face risk in every dimension. High executives may be kidnapped and killed in Cordoba, company towns are taken over in Chuquicamata, and refineries are nationalized in Abadan and elsewhere. Tax concessions designed to attract capital investment are repudiated by new governments, and in banana republics and oil emirates with small populations and large corporations, the primary loyalties of employees and local suppliers to country or to corporation are at stake.

The large firm becomes an engine for social change or repression in a small country whether it wants to or not. The production of a labor aristocracy, the training of engineers, and the provision of hospital and other medical facilities change perceptions, expectations, and capabilities. Economic development does not take place in a vacuum; it becomes socioeconomic and sociopolitical development.

There are two forms of accounting in all societies. There are balance sheets and accounts drawn up that emphasize ownership and stocks. Then there are income statements that stress flows and "rights-to-use." When one utilizes an appropriately adjusted rights-to-use or flow accounting system the number of millionaires in the Soviet Union is not far different from the number of millionaires in the United States. The benefits to be derived from a chauffeur-driven limousine owned by the state or owned by the individual are not significantly different. There is much to be said for renting or otherwise having the right to use rather than owning. When the plumbing fails one calls the owner rather than acting as one's own janitor.

For the corporation, as for the individual, ownership is not an unmixed blessing. At the very best the corporation that owns assets abroad, in fact, owns highly exposed rights-to-use. All other things being equal the chances are good for obtaining a higher ROI (return on investment) by running a refinery or manufacturing plant owned by the host country than by owning it oneself. Furthermore, the exposure is less. When the outside firm owns a major plant abroad, the plant is a hostage in the power of the host country. When it operates the plant abroad, the hostage relationship is reversed.

The varieties of ownership, control, and rights-to-use of assets provide different ways of structuring the risk profile of a firm in a manner that not only changes the exposure of the firm as a passive entity but also changes the risk and incentive structure for the host country. In both economic and political bookkeeping both sides of the ledger are always present. In reaction to nationalization and political instability it is easy to see only the dangers of the loss of owned assets, forgetting that the running of a profitable business and the ownership of assets are not the same. Much of the success of U.S. business is based upon OPM (other peoples' money). Successful international business with gain to all can be based on other countries' assets.

These comments should not be interpreted as suggesting that the only wave of the future should be to operate in foreign locations using locally owned assets. There are many institutional forms that are each more or less viable under special circumstances. The key point being stressed is that control of assets and ownership are by no means the same, and a business opportunity that would be risky under outright ownership might be highly attractive under a different form of control.

Studies, methods, and analysis

In essence the study of political risk is the study of national and international political processes that can influence the level of risk involved in the undertakings of some entity operating in an environment sufficiently influenced by political factors that they cannot be ignored.

The assessment of risk requires the study of goals and resources in the context of uncertainty and probability. It is possible to study uncertainty and probability *in abstracto*. Thus, for example, one can invent an index measuring "propensity to have a revolution" on which, using a scale of 0–1, one offers subjective probabilities that a particular country will have a revolution within the next six months. In general, however, *it is not what the numbers are, but what the numbers mean.* The index must be set in context and appropriately interpreted. This invariably involves ad hoc considerations and considerable hand-tailoring. A revolution in country A may have completely different implications of risk than one of the same intensity in country B.

Political forecasting, contingency planning, and anticipation studies have all of the difficulties encountered in economic contingency planning and anticipation studies and more difficulties of their own. As hard as it is to construct and interpret a measure of GNP, it is far easier to do so than it is to produce a useful measure of the intensity of ideology.

Process and perception

The "squishier" the topic for investigation, the more dependent undertakings become upon correct perceptions, insight, historical understanding, and special facts, and the more valuable are "old timers," that is, people with experience and those who know the lay of the land.

But in the social sciences in general and economics in particular, the last fifty years have been the years of the methodologists and theorists. Techniques, mathematical constructs, and econometrics have displaced the essays and position papers and old-fashioned, quasi-historical, institutional studies. This change in style and emphasis clearly present in economics has made its way into political science and strategic studies. Cliometrics and polimetrics offer methodology and statistical procedures for the quantification of historical and political processes.

Are the new methodologists more or less relevant than the old hands who concentrate on war stories and "knowing their business" to the banks, corporations, governments, or revolutionaries concerned with political anticipation? The question poses a false dichotomy. But this is the dichotomy that is often presented. The choice is not between institutional understanding and theory and methodology. What is called for is an understanding of the limits and strengths of the many approaches currently available, who they were designed for, and how they can be blended together for the application at hand.

In the remainder of this section, a sketch of many of the approaches to political contingency planning is given. But before this is done a caveat must be posted: Technique biases process and mind set bends perception.

Methodologists are prone to apply methodology; old diplomats and generals tell superb war stories. Cooks in general bake better cakes than poets and poets write better verse than cooks. Organizational purpose and perception must be matched with the individual proclivities of experts to offer their general approaches as the best way to proceed.

In societies in general, and even in specific complex organizations such as large corporations, both purpose and perception emerge as parts of an ongoing process. The purposes of corporate presidents, research scientists, salespeople, typists, production engineers, lawyers, accountants, janitors, consultants, advisers, and others differ radically, but all are blended by process to provide a corporate direction.

Our current knowledge of the dynamics of goal formation is skimpy, but our perception of the differences in emphasis on goals of the various institutions of society is reasonably good. For most corporations profits still count. For political institutions power takes precedence over profits. Consulting firms are usually profit oriented, but the level of goal tension between their sales staff and their professional staff may be high.

Scientists and scholars are frequently ambivalent in their dealings with corporations and consulting firms. Large fees are usually offered in the hope of obtaining relevant advice. But relevant advice may be a product that uses the intellectual capital of a scholar rather than adding to it. In order to become a valued adviser a scholar may need to give up scholarship. Utilizing new ideas and knowledge is not the same as producing them.

The usual rationalization of scholar–advisers or scholar–consultants is that their consulting experience adds to their understanding and improves their scholarship. Up to a point this is undoubtedly true. Especially at the professional schools of law and business, a certain amount of consulting appears to broaden the professional abilities of the academic lawyer or business school professor. Yet the dangers of mixing the roles of scholarship and business were elegantly expressed by the great art dealer Gimpel, who is reputed to have commented to Berenson that he would rather be a scholarly dealer than a dealing scholar.

Forecasting, contingency planning, and anticipation

The activity of *forecasting* may be considered outside the context of a goal-oriented decision-making system. The intellectual challenge in being able to forecast accurately birthrates, the level of rainfall, the intensity of earthquakes, or the downfall of a dictatorship may be confined to scholarly pursuits. But even then attempts to derive satisfactory measures of forecasting performance call for implicit, if not explicit, recognition of the contingent features of any forecast where the contingencies arise from human or other activity. For example, the outbreak of war or the occurrence of a major earthquake or famine can influence a population forecast.

Contingency forecasting is forecasting where a single forecast is modified to account for several outside or exogenous events that are not the prime concern of the forecaster and are not explicit variables in the model. Thus, in the aforementioned instance, a contingent population forecast might be made on the contingencies of (1) no war, no famine, (2) war, and (3) famine.

It is easy for the outsider to grasp the main idea behind contingency forecasting, but in actuality there are two factors that make successful contingency forecasting difficult. In general, the selection of contingencies is highly dependent upon perception. Furthermore, although it might appear that given the existence of the high-speed digital computer one might easily be able to check many contingent combinations, in fact, at best only a handful of contingencies can be checked. (For an insightful discussion of relevance see Miller 1956.)

Contingency planning as contrasted with forecasting involves forecasting and contingency forecasting set in the context of a purposeful process. This embedding provides a new and different measure for the worth of the product of the forecasters. No longer is accuracy alone the criterion; relevance, timeliness, and the sensitivity of the system to the forecasts must all be considered.

Paradoxically, contingency planning may be easier to perform better than accurate forecasting because the specificity and purposiveness of the activity narrow down the selection of relevant contingencies and sharpen the measures of success. Contingency planning in theory is a far more general activity than forecasting; in practice, however, its goals are more narrowly limited by specific purpose.

The term "anticipation" is used in contrast with contingency planning to lay more stress on active rather than reactive planning. Forecasting and even contingency planning activities tend to stress how the outside environment influences the organization. Anticipatory studies consider action, reaction, and influence. They take into account the size and strategic influence of the firm, group, or government on its environment. The explicit recognition of one's own power and ability to influence events, whether the power is actively used or not, forces an institution to engage in anticipatory studies, net assessment, and strategic planning as a matter of necessity. The large firm in particular may begin with a self-image as an active economic entity not concerned with politics or diplomacy. But, unfortunately, its size and locations may make such a view untenable.

In summary:

> Forecasting is the prediction of specific events, all other things being equal. It may serve no other purpose than to show that it can be done.
>
> Contingency forecasting is the prediction of events contingent upon the occurrence of certain prespecified outside influencing phenomena.
>
> Contingency planning is a system-oriented activity utilizing contingency forecasting to evaluate the importance of events to a specific group or institution and to plan one's reaction.
>
> Strategic planning or anticipation is a higher level of contingency planning where the institution considers not only contingencies, but also how it actively influences them. It takes into account in its strategic plans its reactions to its environment as well as its ability to change its environment.

Advisers, briefings, newletters, situation reports, and grand tours

"There is no substitute for knowing your business. Experience counts. There are old pilots and there are bold pilots, but there are no old bold pilots." Business and bureaucratic folklore is loaded with sayings in support of the importance of experience, and the odds are that there is considerable truth in these sayings. Yet it is important to consider the degree to which experience generalizes. IBM or Royal Dutch Shell are not the State Department or the British or Dutch foreign offices. The experience of retired ambassadors, generals, newspaper correspondents, or CIA or M5 agents is not a priori transferable from a governmental to an economic institution even though the latter is concerned with the interpretation of political and diplomatic factors.

Old hands are rarely old methodologists. A Machiavelli, a Clausewitz, or a Mahan may generalize, but they are the great exceptions and not the usual or even the particularly successful practitioners. Goldhamer (1978) has written a perceptive study of the adviser to political leaders in which he considers the forms of advice given, the background of the advisers, and their role in the decision process.

The wisdom books of Aesop or La Rochefoucauld and the manuals of statecraft of Machiavelli and Richelieu have their current business equivalents in the writings of Peter Drucker and a flood of how-to books on international management. But the political adviser as educator, counselor, or "conscience of the king" is not a role that seems to be well suited to modern economic enterprises. Rather than Richelieu for life for the king, the senior partners settle for Henry Kissinger for lunch.

The knowledge of local customs, protocol, and history is of undoubted value; but not only is it important to have someone who knows the facts, one also must be able to judge their importance and be in a position to do something about them. For example, it has been suggested that General Groves had selected Kyoto as a target for the nuclear bomb but fortunately there were those who appreciated the cultural importance of Kyoto and had the power to change the target selection.

The use of ex-ambassadors, generals, and others is well established, but their value is highly dependent upon the provision of an internal corporate process that is designed to interpret and use their inputs.

In the search for knowledge and understanding, "know how" may be dominated by "know who." The British aristocracy used to send some of their members on the grand tour of Europe. The experience was in all likelihood broadening but was not unbiased. The modern version of the grand tour is the on-the-spot visit by a corporate team. It has distinct advantages. Seeing for oneself helps. Observing the problems encountered getting through the airport, getting a "feel" for the bureaucracy, the transportation system and the ambience in general can be valuable. It brings to life preliminary reports and statistics previously presented, which though intellectually appreciated were without psychological dimensions.

Offsetting the advantages of being there are the dangers of being given a biased view by those who want the business or share values that are not representative of the environment. The Shah of Iran's entourage presented a view of business opportunities in Iran different from the leading merchants of the old markets. Volition frequently beclouds perception. It is easier to see what one wants to see than what one does not wish to see.

A natural alternative or supplement to advisers and going to see for yourself is reading. Senior executives may not have time to read too much directly, but their staffs may have worked up a list of newspapers, journals, and other publications that should be scanned. Many countries have an English or other nonnational language newspaper, but if newspapers are to be checked, it is desirable to check the foreign language newspaper against those in the national language in order to form some assessment of the differences in bias.

As the recognition of the importance of political risk has grown, journals and research publications more or less oriented to the diplomatic, business, or military aspects of political risk have come into being. Publications such as *Foreign Affairs, Orbis,* or *Conflict* are available to those who study the international scene. Think tanks and consulting groups including the Brookings Institution, Rand, the Hudson Institute, and McKinsey have offered studies, books, status reports, and other forms of advice. There are now specialized publications such as *Global Political Assessment* (published twice a year by an institute at Columbia University), which specifically gives an essay-style assessment of perceived changes and trends in major international relationships followed by regional and international surveys, concluding with a discussion of trends that appear to merit special attention. The list of academic and think-tank affiliations of the board of consultants is broad. The specific purpose of the publication is to provide an interpretive survey and a highly condensed overview of international change.

Political indexes and crisis measures

The stress thus far has been upon qualitative assessment where the measures, models, and assessments are all rolled into one. The essence of advisers, essayists, old hands, and sages is that they are explicitly problem oriented and at best only implicitly methodology oriented. Their models are in the mind, and their reasons are frequently scarcely articulated.

The closer one comes to quantification, the closer the concerns of those studying the phenomena draw toward methodology. The danger increases that one may find scholars with models or theories concerned with how to fit problems to the models or theories rather than vice versa.

Formal models do not necessarily call for numerical inputs although that is frequently the case. Certain parts of economic theory have been developed based only on preference orderings rather than measures. The thoughtful book by Dahl and Tufte (1973) on size and democracy is an intermix of essay and numerical considerations in which the dimensions of size and democracy are considered and an attempt is made to characterize complexity and diversity.

Another example of an essay style congenial to some quantitative analysis is the practical handbook on coup d'etat by Edward Luttwack (1969). Here a shopping list of factors, an indication of special structures and relationships, and a smattering of a few numbers are all blended together to produce a highly persuasive picture of the constellation of conditions propitious for a coup d'etat.

Moving further in the direction of measurement with the intent of producing indexes of international tension and change has been the work exemplified by Quincy Wright (1942), Lewis Richardson (1960a), and more recently, Rummel (1966). Richardson's two works, *Statistics of Deadly Quarrels* (1960a) and *Arms and Insecurity* (1960b), show his basic concern for the marriage of measurement and theory. In the former, he began with commentary on the literary use of mathematics, discussed the interaction of many causes, and then gave a plan for the collection of information characterizing wars and other deadly quarrels. Richardson suggested that "the magnitude of a fatal quarrel is defined to be the logarithm to the base ten of the number of people who died because of that quarrel" (1960a, p. 6). Why this measure, as opposed to, say, the square root of the number dead together with some weighting of the wounded? One has to start somewhere and Richardson was aware of the difficulties in characterizing and gathering information. For example, he asked if small fatal quarrels form a class apart from large ones. In order to consider this, he looked at East African slave raiding, homicide in India, banditry in Manchukuo, and gang activities in Chicago. He concluded that there is enough similarity to include small as well as large quarrels.

Many criticisms can be made of Richardson's methodology, but setting aside any technical critique or detailed scrutiny of a particular measure one can ask the more general and important question, namely, what was the purpose to be served by these measures? Richardson was a Quaker, a pacifist, and a Fellow of the Royal Society. He believed in the use of scientific methods to help illustrate the causes of war and other forms of violence so that these studies might be used in the prevention of violence. He also, as a theorist, suggested several dynamic processes that could be studied mathematically and that required for empirical validation the type of data he was proposing. His contributions must be regarded as being primarily to methodology and theory. He raised and tried to formalize important questions concerning conflict, and he suggested explicit models. But there is little if any evidence that this work actually provides an empirically verifiable dynamics of conflict.

Work on the dimensions of conflict behavior continued as is evinced by Rummel's (1966) consideration of twelve measures of domestic conflict for 118 countries, including internal warfare, turmoil, rioting, and terrorism. Data for the international comparisons come from sources such as *Keesing's Contemporary Archives, The New International Yearbook,* and for more economically oriented factors, publications of the United Nations and the World Bank.

Especially in urban and development economics there has been a recognition that economic statistics are not enough (Adeleman and Morris 1967). Concern for the quality of life and how to measure it and a desire for the development of social indicators has called not merely for new measures but for new concepts as well (Bauer 1966). Neoclassical economics has been virtually of no use in predicting technological or social changes that have had profound effects on societies and their economies.

Social scientists and international bureaucrats have a natural tendency to indulge in general international and cross-cultural comparisons. But preliminary scholarly research and useful indexes for policy makers are far from each other. It would be nice to have trustworthy single numbers (or even vectors) to measure the relative levels of democracy and political freedom in all countries, the levels of economic development, the degree of pollution, the propensity to make war, the propensity for other violence, the propensity to innovate, the quality of life, and so forth. Any honest attempt to construct such measures, if published with sufficient qualifications, may help to sweeten the intuitions of those who see the measures. But at this time there are no data bases that do more than sweeten the intuition. The actual underlying processes being represented are too complex for the level of generalization implicit in most international indicators. Whether life is better for the average individual in the United States or Haiti is probably reasonably well reflected in the comparisons of international GNP figures; such figures do not tell us much about the quality of life comparisons among the United States, Sweden, Canada, Japan, New Zealand, or Iceland.

We may suspect that the level of democracy in Switzerland is higher than in Argentina, but unfortunately the ten, twenty, or thirty factors that may go into making up a democratic rule index are not culture or context free. Thus, the significance of suicide or homocide levels or of arrest without warrant cannot be judged by the numerical data alone. Cultural, historical, and societal corrections will be called for if the data are to be used as a basis for policy.

Political science is at that stage in its development when research in index construction and theory building offers much promise. The data banks arising from such activities and the measures suggested by the scholars can be of some limited use to individuals with operating problems if they are interpreted with care and if the general indexes are considered within the context of the specific problem at hand.

There are only around 150 countries in the world and most problems facing international agencies or corporations involve only a handful of countries. Even twenty countries is a number small enough that it is possible to maintain special information on each that can be used to interpret and correct or modify any overall comparative indexes.

The strategic audit and net assessment

Much of economic and bureaucratic analysis is at best only implicitly competitive. It tends to be introspective or a "one-person" analysis. Explicit competitors are replaced by abstractions such as the market, or behavioral assumptions concerning the reaction of others. Oligopoly theory or the study of competition among the few is more explicitly strategic. Military and diplomatic analyses are also strategic, the latter being more concerned with cooperative solutions than the former. Political analysis is also explicitly strategic; policy, to be successful, cannot be merely reactive. Intentions and capabilities must be taken into account. Moves must be planned and countermoves must be assessed and evaluated.

Few, if any, strategists or planners are in a position to calculate complex chains of action and reaction. A move, countermove, and possibly, a counter-countermove are about as far as any strategic planning goes. Too many possibilities and too many intangibles can intervene, which makes it hardly worthwhile to calculate many complex chains of hypothetical events. Sun Tzu observed that a good general makes many calculations; his advice, given 2,500 years ago, is still relevant to good strategic planning. How many alternatives one considers in the calculations is to a great extent a matter of judgment and art, dependent upon an understanding of the specific task at hand.

Both at the level of scholarship and the carrying out of national or corporate policy, there has been a growth in concern for explicit strategic analysis. The methods of game theory are devoted to the study of explicit goal-oriented strategic behavior. The growth of corporate planning and defense planning has seen the stress placed upon active policies designed to exert control over the environment rather than reactive moves based upon ad hoc adjustments to the environment.

The military has long been concerned with the evaluation of both the capabilities and intentions of all parties to a potential conflict. The term "net assessment" has been used for the overall evaluation of own and enemy capabilities but, as it is with international economic and political comparisons, so it is with international military comparisons. Here lists of weapons, forces, or other resources provide basic and valuable information, but they must be interpreted in the appropriate context. The modeling methods suggested by the theory of games provide a guide for viewing the environment in a manner that is explicitly strategic.

Without going into detail a checklist is presented for modeling oneself and the environment as parts of a strategic game. The major headings are (1) scope, (2) time frame, (3) description of the players or strategic actors, (4) rules of the game and scope of choice, (5) payoffs and goals, and (6) behavioral assumptions. Each of these is split into many subcategories, the description of which is given elsewhere (Shubik, in press). Here the concern is with considering the style, strengths, and weaknesses of this type of approach rather than the specifics of technique. Strategic analysis can only be utilized successfully if it is integrated into the policy formation and execution system of the organization using the analysis.

It is relatively easy for outside scholars or advisers to devise a checklist for a strategic audit, but the successful use of such a list depends upon avoiding a delegated and almost automated response used in many organizations to generate answers to routine or imposed requests for information. The goals of most large organizations at any point in time are at best only partially known. They are usually set by a complex ongoing internal and external adjustment process. They are intimately related to both the volition and perceptions of management and others. A key ingredient in strategic planning is to have at least a reasonable knowledge of corporate or other institutional goals.

Forecasting, the generation of indexes, and even, to some extent, assessment activities can take place with little concern for use or purpose. Strategic planning is of little value without a sense of institutional purpose. Furthermore, the evaluation of risk of all varieties depends upon purpose.

The methods of strategy are discussed by military writers such as Sun Tzu, Clausewitz, Mahan, and others. The formal construction of models of strategic conflict has come about more recently with the development of operations research in general and game theory in particular. The key difference between the writings of the great strategic thinkers and those with a more mathematical bent and more formal models is that the former stressed *social process* whereas the latter tend to stress methodology.

Clausewitz (1968, p. 203) noted: "We say therefore War belongs not to the province of Arts and Sciences, but to the province of social life . . . It would be better, instead of comparing it with any Art, to liken it to business competition, which is also a conflict of human interests and activities; and it is still more like State policy, which again, on its part, may be looked upon as a kind of business competition on a great scale."

Modern strategic analysis calls for informal and formal models. Purpose must be understood before risk can be evaluated, but to be of value, strategic audits, checklists, scenarios, or models must be part of a social process and not isolated exercises in methodology.

Delphi techniques, scenarios, games, and simulations

The Delphi technique was originally proposed by two senior Rand Corporation researchers, Norman Dalkey and Olaf Helmer. In essence, they were concerned with the possibilities for the formal pooling of expertise. Dalkey's interests were directed more to formal experimentation than to broad operational forecasting (Dalkey 1969), whereas Helmer was cautiously in support of application to predictions by groups of experts to items such as the introduction of new technology. The Institute for the Future, the nonprofit organization of which he was a founder, utilized Delphi studies for predictions.

In essence, a Delphi study is a controlled feedback questionnaire. A group of experts is selected and each, without knowing the identity of the others, answers a comprehensive questionnaire concerning the assessment of and predictions about a set of developments. The data from the first round are processed and given back to the participants, who then have the opportunity to change their views, given that they have seen the predictions of their peer group. The argument in favor of a Delphi study in contrast with, say, a brainstorming session, is that social pressures and groupthink behavior are avoided (Janis 1972).

There are several problems with Delphi. In particular, the quality of the results is presumed to depend upon the quality and number of experts used. It is possible that pooling can result in a pooling of ignorance or bias rather than knowledge or extra insight. Briefly, the problems with a Delphi study for political risk assessment are as follows:

1. Difficulties in the design of questionnaire and specification of the dimensions of the measures
2. Problems in the selection and availability of a pool of experts
3. Control and motivation of the experts
4. Interpretation and utilization of results

The first difficulty has already been noted in the discussion of political indexes and measures. Concepts such as propensity to revolt are difficult to formalize, but they may appeal to the intuition as being the right sort of concepts when political risk is contemplated.

Relative to the importance of the problem, the supply of political experts is relatively sparse. They consist of a selection of the old hands, noted earlier, and some academics.

For Delphi studies in general there have been considerable problems in motivating the experts once they have been found. A full-time company employee or an intensely used and well-paid consultant may well take both the time and care called for to provide serious answers to a Delphi questionnaire. For a corporation or other goal-oriented institution, it is difficult to motivate outside experts sufficiently and to communicate to them the operational context within which the questions are being asked.

Experts, when predicting the future, are frequently making implicit guesses about economic, social, or political acceptance of things that already exist. For example, the question in 1980 of when the home computer market would take off is qualitatively different from the question in 1890 of when atomic power would be available. In the first instance both the theory and technology already exist, and social acceptance and economy are the problems; in the 1890s, neither the basic science nor the technology were available.

For a Delphi study to be usefully interpretable the qualifying assumptions of the experts must be made known. In the study of forecasting of all varieties by Ascher it was suggested that the key feature in accurate forecasting was the selection of core assumptions and that pertinent insights into the process were of considerably higher worth than sophisticated data processing (Ascher 1978; see also Kobrin 1981).

In summary, hard sociopsychological evidence for or against the Delphi method as a scientific tool is not conclusive. Delphi questionnaires are relatively cheap, easy to understand, and highly attractive to those who like a "quick fix." If used intelligently and not oversold, a case can be made that if a company or institution is sophisticated enough to believe that it is asking the right questions, a Delphi is a relatively cheap additional check upon answers it may have obtained in a different manner.

Scenarios, games, and simulations are closely related but different devices whose use was to a great extent pioneered by the military, but they have been utilized for other purposes, in particular, for the study of international relations and for the modeling of global political–economic systems.

War gaming as a formally recognized technique dates back to the efforts of von Reisswitz in the Prussian army in 1824, although military interest in formal training and operational exercises predates von Reisswitz considerably (Shubik 1975, ch. 12). Before any war game or field exercise can be carried out, the context must be set. The act of setting the context or delineating the rules of the game in and of itself calls for planning, data gathering, and isolation of relevant questions and factors that may be of considerable value. It may well be that most of the value to be derived from a war game can be derived from writing the scenario or scenarios without ever actually playing the game.

The art of scenario writing calls for a high level of imagination and synthesis (DeLeon 1975). The setting of the stage for the action calls for a qualitative feel for the whole. In the United States the better war game scenario writers have been military historians or those well read in history.

Closer to our concern with political risk than most war games is the political–military exercise. This free-form exercise is originally attributed to Herbert Goldhamer and Hans Speier of the Rand Corporation (Goldhamer and Speier 1959). The purpose of this type of game is to explore the actions and reactions of the interacting groups of several countries in a situation that might or might not lead to war. For example, a scenario might begin in 1984 with a Lybian-, Syrian-, and Iraqi-backed uprising in Saudi Arabia and the Egyptians having announced intentions to send troops to help restore order. The situation at the start has to be described both qualitatively and quantitatively for the major parties. Thus, logistic facts and the sociopolitical ambience of Egypt, the United States, Israel, Jordan, Syria, the Soviet Union, and others must be supplied.

The different countries may be broadly divided into two blocks whose actions are selected by two teams and a residual whose actions are set by the referee group. The game in general will be played by two teams composed of operating personnel, with some experts and advisers, and a third refereeing team composed primarily of experts whose job it is to question the plausibility and assess the impact of the suggested moves and to evaluate challenges concerning the feasibility and relevance of the scenario.

A corporation concerned with international operations could game them in a manner akin to the political military exercise, but to do so would require not only the cooperation, attention, and enthusiasm of many senior executives, but also the writing of the appropriate scenarios, which in turn calls for a planning staff capable of both quantification and context description.

The possession of a planning staff capable of generating scenarios is a necessary prior condition for successful gaming. Such a staff may generate scenarios as part of its planning activities without using them for gaming. Several corporations, in particular, Royal Dutch Shell, have utilized scenario construction as a way to consider sociopolitical and geopolitical factors. The next step, namely, actual gaming, does not yet appear to have been taken. This is not particularly surprising as even gaming research for the study of international business and international politics is relatively new and fraught with difficulties. Furthermore, the type of tradition in the military that leads to any colonel's accepting as a matter of course that, at staff college or at some other time in his career, he will be exposed to a gaming exercise does not hold for middle and upper corporate executives.

Strategic games and simulations have been used by the military for several purposes, such as the examination of force structure and doctrine. In business and government their usage has been somewhat limited. A simulation is a model in which some real system is usually represented by a computer program that, when run, generates hypothetical histories of the behavior of the system. Different histories will be generated by changing the initial conditions. Thus, in theory, contingency planning can be performed by asking a series of "what-if" questions through changing parameters or parts of the program. In practice, it is extremely difficult to build good simulations of squishy systems.

A game differs from a simulation in that live players, rather than computer instructions, provide decisions in an interactive environment. A game such as the political–military exercise may not even utilize a computer simulation at all; it may be played in a loosely structured environment calling for judgment to determine how it should progress.

Large-scale econometric models utilized as simulations have come into their own in the past twenty years. Models involving several hundred equations portraying the aggregate behavior of consumers, the banking system, the labor force, and many other features of the economy are estimated. Although the first attempts at large-scale macroeconometric modeling came into being as a natural outgrowth of the development of macroeconomic theory, the commercial possibilities of such work have been realized by firms such as Chase Econometrics, DRI, and Wharton Econometrics. By expanding specific segments, for example, the aircraft industry, it is possible to trace through what-if answers to questions such as how the aircraft industry will be influenced by changes in the Department of Defense budget or new depreciation allowances and so forth.

As integrated data organizing, planning, and accounting devices the models have been useful. However, their track record appears to be highly dependent upon the length of time selected for the forecast and how fortunate the assumptions were that other factors did not matter (Ascher 1978).

The original economic models were primarily one-country models with possibly an international trade sector and only economic and some socioeconomic factors modeled explicitly. More recently a need has been recognized for exploring international trade in more detail. There has also been a recognition of the desirability of exploring social and political factors. Project LINK (Hickman and Klein 1979), the Bariloche model (Herrera et al. 1976), WIM (Hughes 1980), FUGI (Kaya and Onishi 1977), and World 3 (Meadows et al. 1974) are representative of the various simulation approaches to international, but primarily economic, modeling. Over the past few years, the International Institute for Applied Systems Analysis has sponsored a series of conferences on these projects in world or global modeling.

The main thrust of LINK is the short-term study of international economic growth and development via interlinked econometric models. The Bariloche model involves the long-term projection of demographic growth and basic needs utilizing a mathematical model and employing dynamic optimization methods. The World Integrated Model (WIM) of Mesarovic and Pestel and others and the World 3 model of Forrester, Meadows, and others are systems engineering oriented. The Future of Global Interdependence (FUGI) is essentially a macroeconomic model interlinked with an input–output structure.

The time horizon of economic or business forecasts that can be made on the safe assumption that all political and social factors are constant or otherwise irrelevant is, at best, small. Corporate planning needs, especially with regard to investment, require the consideration of time periods in which politics and society count. National planning needs go well beyond mere economic prediction.

Starting with the pioneering work of Guetzkow and Noel, political scientists have experimented with mixed political, economic, and military models (Guetzkow and Valadez 1981). These efforts include INS, IPS, NIC, WPS, and GLOBUS as well as projects at the Soviet All Union Institute of Systems Sciences. International Simulation (INS) began as a gaming exercise in political science and social psychology played by teams using both numerical and verbal or written inputs (such as newsletters or broadcasts) (Guetzkow 1959). The countries had internal and external decision makers and in the course of play, as certain configurations of indexes exceeded specified values, internal revolt or war could break out. International Process Simulation (IPS) is a live player–machine game derived from INS with the same level of time horizon of five to ten years (Smoker 1970). Nations in Conflict (NIC) is a completely computerized long-term simulation of international alliances and conflicts (Choucri and North 1975). World Politics Simulation (WPS) is an all-computer simulation concerned with retrospective validation stressing a cybernetics and artificial intelligence approach to the modeling of political and diplomatic behavior (Bennett and Alker 1977). Generating Long-term Options by Using Simulation (GLOBUS) is a simulation intermixing economic political and social process (Bremer and Cusack 1981).

All of these political science oriented models must be regarded as preliminary academic attempts to go beyond the use of taxonomies and lists of indicators interwoven only in essay context. Even all of the basically economic models noted have limited application. They were designed primarily for two purposes, either as part of a basic research program or to aid national or international macroeconomic policy. The large econometric models need special sections or other modifications to be of value at the corporate level.

Political risk assessment in the firm

In the previous section a brief overview of the state of the art in political and political–economic analysis and prediction was given. Many of the methods and studies are not particularly intended for goal-oriented risk analysis by any specific institution. Here our concern is specifically directed to risk analysis in a corporate context.

Prior to considering the context of political risk assessment in the corporation, an essential distinction among the following four terms must be made: (1) objective probability, (2) subjective probability, (3) uncertainty, and (4) risk.

Objective probability: The probabilities we can attach to a random event generated by a phenomenon producing outcomes with a known frequency are called objective probabilities. The classic examples are the probabilities of heads or tails appearing in the toss of a fair coin, or the number 26 appearing in the spin of an honest roulette wheel.

Subjective probability: A prior or subjective assessment of probabilities attached to events for which no underlying initial experiment or direct frequency interpretation can be given is a subjective probability. The assignment of subjective probabilities can come about casually or after much thought, research, and calculation. Rummel and Heenan (1978) choose to call thought-about subjective probabilities "objective." This is contrary to virtually all current usage and can be dangerously misleading.

Uncertainty: The term "uncertainty" is used by those who argue that there are unknown situations where no objective probabilities exist and where, furthermore, observers cannot meaningfully assign subjective probabilities as they do not have a sufficiently developed cognitive map.

Humans tend to break up their perceptions of an uncertain environment into checklists of items. If the lists are known and believed and the items are clearly defined, probability assessments may be made with a certain amount of ease. If individuals cannot even comfortably characterize the uncertain environment, they are not in a position to assign even subjective probabilities with any confidence.

This is not the place to indulge in a philosophical discussion of the basis of probability theory; for that, readers are referred to a sample of writings ranging from a text on data analysis in politics to a broad philosophical discourse on uncertainty in human affairs, in general, and political economy, in particular (Knight 1921, Feller 1950, Savage 1954, Raiffa and Schlaifer 1961, Shackle 1969, Tufte 1974).

In essence, there are those who argue that if we are pushed to do so and take sufficient care, we can give betting odds on anything. After all, in essence any investment is a bet. There are, however, several other schools of thought, including economists and psychologists who argue that although it may be true that you can force individuals to take bets on anything, such as whether the Soviets will invade Poland, or whether one of the next three presidents of the United States will be assassinated in office, the betting will not represent the outcome of a consistent, coherent process of probability evaluation. In other words, individuals can be forced into naming probabilities but whether such an exercise is of use in estimating political, societal, or many other events is doubtful.

Risk: Risk is a value assessment of the importance of uncertainty to the concerned corporation or other agency. The point stressed here is that risk is only defined in the context of a specific goal structure. It cannot be assessed independently from purpose. Probabilities or the possibility of the occurrence of an event exist independent of purpose. The risk to an individual given that something occurs depends upon that individual's goals and resources.

The context of corporate political risk assessment

The large international corporation is a goal-oriented bureaucracy. At any particular point in time its goals are not completely known even to its members. Goal formation is part of an ongoing internal and external bargaining process involving perception and ethical considerations. In quiet times, more or less simple rules of thumb are sufficient to avoid many of the problems involved in acting with only partially perceived and changing goals. As a first-order approximation the corporation may take as its goal some form of profit maximization, qualified by taking no more than "reasonable" risk and being a "good corporate" citizen. If the line executives are able to communicate with staff planners to the point that they share a more or less coherent comprehension of what constitutes reasonable risk and good corporate citizenship, then the assessments obtained by any or all of the methods suggested in the discussion of studies, methods, and analysis can be translated into operational evaluations of risk to the corporation, and management can adjust its risk profile accordingly.

When the organization is far flung and the environment volatile the problems of risk assessment become more managerial for the single reason that all the techniques for probability or possibility evaluation of events have remained the same but the dangers have increased.

At a more specific level several critical features of management are directly relevant to how risk will or should be assessed:

1. The dangers of groupthink in assessment (Janis 1972)
2. The differences in perceptive bias of managers of different nationalities (Laurent 1980)
3. The clash between national and corporate loyalties
4. The biases in risk assessment caused by using accounting data prepared for one purpose, for another purpose
5. Corporate distinction between disastrous risk and acceptable risk

What can be done?

Utilizing the foregoing observations, nine operational questions are posed and answered.

1. What is a useful framework in which to conceptualize political risk?
2. To what extent can political developments be predicted?
3. Can political risk be defined except in regard to a particular loan activity or investment?
4. What techniques, theories, or methods should be used to study political risk?
5. What research needs to be done and who should do it?
6. What range of hazards should be viewed as the outcome of a political process? Should political risk analysis comprehend discontinuous events such as civil disorder, expropriation, and war, as well as the more gradual changes in climate leading to variations in price controls, taxes, and other operating constraints?
7. To what extent is political risk diversifiable?
8. Where are the major possibilities in the improvement of political risk assessment?
9. How should assessments of political risk be integrated into the decision-making process?

1. The framework for the large corporation or agency must be strategic and anticipatory, active and not merely reactive. Individual goals and strategic scope must be compared directly with the goals and power of those who control the environment in which the firm operates.

Risk is associated with the expected worth of policies in the face of uncertain outcomes; it is not merely a probability measure on the uncertainty of an outcome without reference to goals and policy.

2. In general, most political developments are harder to predict than economic developments. The state of the art is less developed than in economics and even the track record of economic prediction is not particularly good.

3. Political risk can only be defined with respect to goals and policies. This contrasts with estimates of the probability of the occurrence of political events that can be defined independently from a passive observer's goals.

4. Essentially all of the approaches noted in the discussion of studies, methods, and analysis are worth considering. There does not appear to be a clearly best way to study political risk at this time. A coordination of the different approaches helps to "keep the game honest." It is important to contrast numerical and nonnumerical approaches.

5. The techniques for modeling, scenario writing, index construction, and testing, data bank building, and simulation at the level of corporate planning all could use considerable further research work. Much of this work is best done at universities, possibly in long-term collaboration with corporate planning groups.

Much of the academic work in political science is devoted to the development of indexes for use in general prediction rather than for specific risk assessment. As such, the work is relevant to the long-term development of risk assessment methods but is one step removed.

Basic research on how well experts perform using Delphi methods, on subjective probability assessment, and on individual and fiduciary risk (i.e., risking someone else's money or life) behavior is woefully small and is needed by society as a whole. The locus of such work is primarily in the academic setting of a university, business school, or research institute. The immediate operational value to corporate decision making is probably slight but the longer-term value is high.

6. Political risk analysis should encompass the study of violent and sudden as well as gradual political change. There appears to be a fundamental difference between high-probability, low-downside events, and low-probability, high-downside events. With the latter, survival may be at stake. A key task of good corporate strategic planning is to avoid major disasters. Frequently, one must try to predict not only a low-probability event, but also how a radical political change will influence the firm. There were those who correctly assessed Castro's chances for overthrowing Batista, but they totally misestimated the chances of doing business with Castro and left themselves unduly exposed.

7. Political risk is as diversifiable as geopolitical and economic realities let it be. If a firm's only business is platinum, it has few choices. If a bank operates on a worldwide basis there are enough countries and financial institutions around to enable it to spread its risks. In essence, the nature of political uncertainty is such that outside insurance markets must be highly imperfect (basically because of the type of uncertainty, the size of the exposure, and the uniqueness of the phenomena), and the costs of laying off political risk for a manufacturing firm with high overseas investment are high, involving the structuring of joint ventures with local participation and other detailed ad hoc schemes for sharing risk or minimizing exposure.

8. The major possibilities for improving political risk assessment are probably in the internal organization of corporate strategic planning staff and in the design of the procedures whereby the planning and assessment are utilized. In particular, at the very least it is important

that both quantitative and nonquantitative procedures are utilized in concert and are integrated.

9. Assessments of political risk should be integrated as closely as possible into the decision-making process. Briefing sessions, the visit by outside experts, and even the country report run the danger of becoming part of the ritual or even entertainment if no decisions are to be made.

Whether it is the country risk committee of a bank or an investment committee for a manufacturing firm, the more the process is designed for briefings tied in directly to the decision making, the better will be the communication concerning goals and strategies and the more chances are improved for a better translation of the perception of political uncertainty into the relevant assessment of political risk.

References

Adelman, I., and C. T. Morris (1967). *Society, Politics and Economic Development.* Baltimore, Md.: Johns Hopkins University Press.

Ascher, W. (1978). *Forecasting: An Appraisal for Policy-Makers and Planners.* Baltimore, Md.: Johns Hopkins University Press.

Bauer, R. A. (1966). *Social Indicators.* Cambridge, Mass.: MIT Press.

Bennett, J. P., and Hayward R. Alker (1977). "When National Security Policies Bred Collective Insecurity: The War of the Pacific in a World Politics Simulation," in Karl Deutsch, Bruno Fritsch, Helio Jaguaribe, and Andrei Markovits (eds.), *Problems of World Modeling: Political and Social Implications.* Cambridge, Mass.: Ballinger, pp. 215–99.

Bremer, Stuart A., and Thomas R. Cusack (1981). *The National Macro-economic Framework of the GLOBUS Model.* Publication Series of the International Institute for Comparative Research, Science Center, Berlin, IIVG/dp., pp. 81–106.

Choucri, Nazli, and Robert C. North (1975). *Nations in Conflict: National Growth and International Violence.* Cambridge, Mass.: MIT Press.

Clausewitz, Carl von. (1968). *On War.* (Original in German, 1832; translation Pelican Classics) London: Penguin Books.

Dahl, R. A., and E. R. Tufte (1973). *Size and Democracy.* Stanford, Calif.: Stanford University Press.

Dalkey, N. C. *The Delphi Method: An Experimental Study of Group Opinion.* Santa Monica, Calif.: Rand RM-5888-PR, June 1969.

DeLeon, P. (1975). "Scenario Designs: An Overview." *Simulation and Games,* 6, pp. 39–60.

Feller, W. (1950). *Probability Theory and its Applications.* New York: Wiley.

Goldhamer, H. (1978). *The Adviser.* New York: Elsevier.

Goldhamer, H., and H. Speier (1959). "Some Observations on Political Gaming." *World Politics,* 12, pp. 71–83.

Guetzkow, H. (1959). "A Use of Simulation in the Study of Internation Relations." *Behavioral Science,* 4(3), pp. 183–91.

Guetzkow, H., and J. J. Valadez (1981). "Substantive Outcomes: Simulated International Processes vis-à-vis International Relations Theory," in H. Guetzkow and J. J.

Valadez (eds.), *Simulated International Processes: Theories and Research in Global Modeling.* Beverly Hills, Calif.: Sage.

Herrera, A., H. D. Scolnik, G. Chichilnisky, G. C. Gallopin, J. E. Hardoy, D. Mosrovich, E. Oteiza, G. L. deRomero Brest, C. E. Suarez, and L. Talavera (1976). *Catastrophe or New Society? A Latin American World Model.* Ottawa: International Development Research.

Hickman, B. G., and L. R. Klein (1979). "A Decade of Research by Project LINK." *Social Science Research Council Items,* 33(3–4), pp. 49–56.

Hughes, B. B. (1980). *World Modeling: The Mesarovic-Pestel World Model in the Context of Its Contemporaries.* Lexington, Mass.: Heath.

Janis, I. (1972). *Victims of Groupthink.* Boston: Houghton Mifflin.

Kaya, Y., and A. Onishi (1977). "Report on Project FUGI: Future of Global Interdependence." Tokyo: Nippon Institute for Research Advancement.

Knight, F. (1921). *Risk Uncertainty and Profit.* Boston: Houghton Mifflin.

Kobrin, S. J. (1981). "Political Assessment by International Firms: Models or Methodologies?" *Journal of Policy Modeling,* 3(2), 251–70.

Lamont, D. F. (1979). *Foreign State Enterprises, A Threat to American Business.* New York: Basic Books.

Laurent, A. (1980). "Once a Frenchman Always a Frenchman." *International Management,* June 1980, p. 45.

Luttwack, E. (1969). *Coup d,État.* New York: Knopf.

Meadows, D. L., W. W. Behrens III, D. H. Meadows, R. F. Naill, J. Randers, and E. K. O. Zahn (1974). *Dynamics of Growth in a Finite World.* Cambridge, Mass.: Wright-Allen Press.

Miller, G. (1956). "The Magical Number Seven Plus or Minus Two." *Psychological Review,* 63, pp. 81–97.

Raiffa, H., and R. Schlaifer (1961). *Applied Statistical Decision Theory.* Cambridge, Mass.: Harvard University Press.

Richardson, L. F. (1960a). *Statistics of Deadly Quarrels.* Chicago: Quadrangle Books. (1960b). *Arms and Insecurity.* Chicago: Quadrangle Books.

Rummel, R. J.(1966). "Dimensions of Conflict Behavior Within Nations 1946–59." *Journal of Conflict Resolution,* 10(1), pp. 65–73.

Rummel, R. J., and D. A. Heenan (1978). "How Multinationals Analyze Political Risk." *Harvard Business Review,* January/February, pp. 67–76.

Savage, L. J. (1954). *The Foundations of Statistics.* New York: Wiley.

Shackle, G. L. S. (1969). *Decision, Order and Time in Human Affairs,* 2nd ed. Cambridge: Cambridge University Press.

Shubik, M. (1975). *Games for Society, Business and War.* Amsterdam: Elsevier. (in press). "Game Theory: The Language of Strategy?" in M. Shubik (ed.), *The Mathematics of Conflict.* Amsterdam: North Holland.

Smoker, P. L. (1970). "International Relations Simulation." *Peace Research Reviews,* 3(6), 1–84.

Tufte, E. R. (1974). *Data Analysis for Politics and Policy.* Englewood Cliffs, N.J.: Prentice-Hall.

Wright, Quincy (1942). *A Study of War.* Chicago: University of Chicago Press.

CHAPTER 4

Country risk: social and cultural aspects

JOHN DUNN

Mr. Macquedy: Then, sir, I presume you set no value on the right principles of rent, profit, wages, and currency?

The Rev. Dr. Folliott: My principles, sir, in these things are, to take as much as I can get, and to pay no more than I can help. These are every man's principles, whether they be the right principles or no. There, sir, is political economy in a nutshell.

Mr. Macquedy: The principles, sir, which regulate production and consumption, are independent of the will of any individual as to giving or taking, and do not lie in a nutshell by any means.

Thomas Love Peacock, *Crotchet Castle*, ch. 2, "The March of Mind"

The growing importance of country risk

Among the components of what bankers and corporate investors now analyze as "country risk," the categories of political and social or cultural risk are of special interest for any social or political theorist. Country risk in the first instance may be seen simply as a type of risk faced by an international capital investment, loan, or export sale, not because of the properties of the factor markets concerned or the capacity to pay or repay of the foreign borrower or buyer, but because of the character of social and political relations in the country in question and because of the implications this character may have for the possibility of the expropriation of the investment, default on the loan, or more or less protracted failure to pay for the export (Kern 1981, p. 76). Social and cultural risk may be contrasted with economic or political risk as representing that set of hazards for lenders, investors, or exporters that arises from the fact that human beings are not merely economic agents in institutionalized political settings but also social and cultural creatures.

The growing salience of country risk in the thinking of bankers and

I am very grateful to the editor and to Michael Cook, Geoffrey Hawthorn, Michael Ignatieff, and Quentin Skinner for their generous help in emending the first draft of this chapter.

businesspeople is a product of the drastic changes in the shape of the world economy since the end of World War II and of the particularly turbulent conditions that have prevailed since the OPEC price increases of 1973. These changes can be traced in virtually any measure of the degree of foreign trade exposure of the advanced capitalist economies (Bergsten, Horst, and Moran 1978, pp. 7–15) and come out particularly vividly, for example, in the growth of the proportion of the U.S. domestic market in manufactures accounted for by large-scale firms (now virtually all multinational in scope) from 17 percent in 1950 to 42 percent in 1967 and 62 percent in 1974 (Vernon 1977, p. 13) or in the increase in the percentage of patents issued to foreigners, for example, from 13 percent in 1955 in the United States to over 30 percent in 1972 (Vernon 1977, p. 7). The rapidity of modern communications, the rapid growth in the scale of international exchanges, and the greatly increased complexity and instability of the environment in which investment decisions are made have compelled a more explicit awareness of political and social factors. The growing importance, especially since 1973, of the less-developed countries in sustaining the export industries of Europe, the United States, and Japan in conditions of recession (Brandt 1980, pp. 70–1) and the greatly increased loan exposure of international banks in these countries (Angelini, Eng, and Lees 1979, Eaton and Gersovitz 1981), which has been necessary to sustain this pattern of exports (Kern 1981, p. 77), have focused attention especially on the non–oil exporters among the less-developed countries. (The impact of the recession on the growth rates of these countries appears to have been less than in the case of either the industrialized countries or the members of OPEC itself [Kern 1981, p. 77]). In response to this experience, and perhaps especially in response to the Iranian revolution (Kern 1981, p. 79), it now seems quite natural to a banker to recommend in assessing longer-term risks, particularly of default on a loan, the use of a country risk matrix that allocates almost half the numerical assessment of risk to political or strategic factors (Kern 1981, pp. 78–80).

Distinguishing political from social and cultural risk

The division between political risk and social or cultural risk is arbitrary. The distinction, that is to say, may be clumsy or illuminating. It cannot be true or false. For analytical purposes, it is useful to take it as the distinction between hazards that follow directly from the purposes of an incumbent government and any reasonably predictable constitutional successor and hazards that follow, by a necessarily less direct path, from the beliefs, values, and attitudes of a population at large. Social and cultural risk is risk threatened by the as yet politically inefficacious, that is, the political risk of the temporarily politically impotent – a form of involuntarily delayed gratification. (Where social and cultural risk is effectively actualized, as, for example, in extralegal interventions by factory work forces in Chile during the presidency of Allende [Kobrin 1980, pp. 84–5] or in the occupation of foreign-owned farms or factories in Portugal, it becomes effective essentially because it is accepted and protected by the forces of coercion of an incumbent government and ceases to be so as soon as these forces intervene to reverse it.) The analytical distinction between political and social risk is thus partly one of time horizon. (Imminent social and cultural risk is risk on the very point of becoming political risk.) It is also partly one of organizational specificity and hence of practical tractability. The assessment of political risk falls within the field of what Jon Elster refers to as "routine politics" (Elster 1978, ch. 3, esp. pp. 50–1). In effect, it can be seen essentially as a competitive game played by an investor, lender, or (less plausibly) exporter against a single rationally acting other player, namely, the foreign state in question; and calculation of advantage within it would be strongly analogous to market calculations.

Social and cultural risk, by contrast, is necessarily organizationally diffuse. It consists in a set of actual and potential responses that have not yet been synthesized (and that may well never become synthesized) into a single rational actor and that, in consequence, permit neither the eliciting of common interests through negotiation nor the securing of firm instrumental advantage through skillful competitive play. Political risk is no doubt increasingly an investor's or banker's headache. But social or cultural risk is closer to being their nightmare. (Because social and cultural risk is less immediate than political risk, it is unlikely to apply to export payments and it is particularly likely to apply to long-term investments, though present levels of international indebtedness of less-developed countries may well in due course cause it to apply equally obviously also to international loans. See especially Eaton and Gersovitz [1981].)

This contrast as it stands is obviously oversimple. In practice, the transition from social or cultural risk is neither neat nor sudden. Given the political circumstances that have prevailed and the political traditions that have developed since World War II, social or cultural risk in even the most effectively repressive of capitalist societies is unlikely to remain entirely organizationally inchoate for very long (Dunn 1980, ch. 9). We know much less, at least outside Poland and

142   **John Dunn**

Czechoslovakia, about the form that social and cultural risk takes within Communist countries. The Polish case certainly suggests that an accurate assessment of such risk may be of urgent importance for Western bankers and businesspeople (Rupnik 1979).

Semiorganized social and cultural risks, in the form of small-scale terrorist organizations or, still more, in the form of an organized revolutionary movement, are more elusive competitors than an incumbent government. (They are so, not least, because incumbent governments necessarily have such strong views of the types of contact or relations that foreign interests may have with them.) But in the case, for example, of the kidnapping of corporation executives for ransom, the nature of the competitive game is extremely clear. An instructive example of the transfer of (*economic*) risk in such cases is the insuring of executives against the risk of ransom payments. In reported instances, where premiums per year per executive insured amount to one-tenth of the maximum ransom sum for which they are insured, the level of social and cultural risk would appear to be high (Krogh 1979, p. 128). Where terrorists are especially gifted and committed to their activities, as in West Germany some years ago, they can no doubt, at least for a time, impose insurance hazards of this scale even where they are themselves socially rather isolated. But most effective terrorist activity over long periods of time is restricted to settings in which there is strong communal solidarity: the Catholic population of Northern Ireland, the Palestinian diaspora, incipiently the black communities in the Union of South Africa. An intermediate case, at present largely confined to domestic personnel, would be the activities of the Red Brigades in Italy.

Other forms of "social" or "cultural" risk sometimes mentioned include ethnic, tribal, or communal animosities and particular local traditions of organized labor. Communal riots and, more extremely, civil war (Stremlau 1977) can hardly expedite most business transactions (though they no doubt gratify manufacturers of arms and police apparatus), and it is no doubt exceedingly trying to have to deal with labor organizations that are culturally more militant or work forces less cooperative than those to be found in one's home market.[1] But it is analytically uneconomical to consider the control and costing of labor as an external and political element in determining a productive

[1] For helpful, brief critiques of interpretations of work force attitudes in purely cultural terms that bring out the complicated historical interplay between work structure, political experience, and consciousness, see Mann 1973 and Ingham 1974.

investment, and it is hard, outside Uganda and Ruanda, and perhaps Nigeria, to believe that tribal or communal strife has yet made a large difference over several years to the profitability of many foreign investments or even to the repayment of many loans.

On the whole it is likely to be more illuminating not to attempt a shapeless but exhaustive inventory of all the social or cultural factors that may possibly already have given or should, in future, give bankers or businesspeople a sleepless night or two, but to try instead to bring into focus just what in a society or culture is likely to menace the property rights of foreign lenders or investors. If political risk, at its simplest, is the more or less effective encroachment by foreign governments on the profit margins of an investor, social or cultural risk is perhaps, prototypically, the rising impatience of a population in the face of a government that it perceives to be serving not its interests but rather those of foreign investors or foreign governments.

Response to political risk: intellectual and practical

There has been some recent study of how investors do in fact respond to what political scientists believe to be semibehavioral measures of political risk. The results are predictably inconclusive (Thunell 1977), and even if they were clearer and the measures themselves were more convincing it is not obvious what implications they would have for how investors have good reason to respond to such indexes. In fact, one of the main theses I wish to advance is that investors would be unwise to waste their time in inspecting such indexes at all. Contrast, for example, Jodice (1980) or, more cautiously, Rummel and Heenan (1978).

There have also been some distinctly more illuminating studies of the incidence of forced divestment of American investment in foreign countries (Kobrin 1980, Jodice 1980[2]). These confirm, unsurprisingly, that forced divestment, more generally, and expropriation, in particular, both actions that can only be performed by governments, have in fact been implemented in a rational and discriminating manner. Following the logic of the "obsolescing bargain," the terms on which it initially appears attractive to a host country to acquire a foreign investment, together with its organizational linkages and technological knowledge, become in many cases steadily less attractive to the recipient (Vernon 1977, pp. 151, 172, Bergsten et al. 1978, pp.

[2] Dr. Jodice has since taken up a post with the Office of Analytical Methods of the Central Intelligence Agency (Jodice 1980, p. 178).

130–40, Kobrin 1980, p. 70), producing "a shift in power from multi-nationals to home countries which is cumulative, irreversible and speeding up all the time" (Bergsten et al., cited in Kobrin 1980, p. 70). Forced divestment has markedly accelerated over the period from 1960 to 1976 (Kobrin 1980, p. 73, Jodice 1980, pp. 180, 182, 186, but cf. Sigmund 1980). In the case of most countries it has concentrated especially on extractive, utility, banking, and insurance sectors (Bradley 1977, p. 79; Kobrin 1980, p. 78; but cf. Eaton and Gersovitz, this volume), though in the five countries that between 1970 and 1976 took over an especially large number of foreign firms (Algeria, Chile, Peru, Ethiopia, and Tanzania), the largest portion of the takeovers came in the manufacturing and trading sectors. The industries in which forced divestment has been least frequent – drugs, chemicals, and plastics (Kobrin 1980, p. 83) – all tend to have very high research and development expenditures and to be globally integrated, whereas those in which it has been most frequent tend to have low research and development expenditures and to display low international integration. Forced divestment has increased in frequency and scale, and it has been selective, even at the level of firms. What this pattern reflects is a change in the balance of power, following a change in the balance of perceived advantage in a competitive game (Kobrin 1980, pp. 85–6, Jodice 1980, pp. 180, 194, 202). There is some residual vagueness as to how to model each of the players in this game. Partly this reflects awareness of what each player is like in actuality. Governments are plural entities and their members have many purposes besides that of maximizing the gross national product of the countries they govern. Multinational corporations are at least equally plural entities, the components of which baffle academic analysts as to the real objects of their allegiance (cf. Vernon 1977) and which, like governments, certainly act as they do partly because of their organizational characteristics. If what was in question here was the historical explanation of particular investment decisions it might be appropriate to apply, as Thunell does (1977, ch. 2), the contrasting models of Graham Allison – rational actor, organizational process, and bureaucratic politics – to see which best captures the historical *explicandum*. But risk analysis is part of the theory of rational choice, and in order to appear within that theory at all investors and lenders must be represented as rational actors. The question is not what they are like or what, consequently, they are likely in practice to do, but rather what they have good reason to do. And, in effect, the first thing they have good reason to do in confronting political risk is to get themselves together as rational actors, to identify goals, and to get their organizational processes and bureaucratic politics sufficiently under control to enable themselves to operate as though they in fact are rational actors.

Because social and cultural risk is organizationally diffuse in its form and necessarily holistic in its consequential impact, it is impossible in principle to calculate its probability with any accuracy. But, if it cannot be accurately predicted, and if the pragmatics of what to do about it are thus, in theory, rather simple, this does not imply any necessary obstruction to an understanding of its nature. All that can be done about it, offsetting loss of profit by "insurance," is to pass on as much as possible of the expected risk to a third party or set of parties, while passing on as little as possible of the expected profit. (If the analysis offered here is valid, it follows that actuarially sound insurance cannot in principle be written for such risks, though governments may nevertheless elect to provide cover against them.) This, of course, is a familiar and intricate competitive game, and all its interest lies in a type of detailed knowledge of particular cases that, at least outside business schools, academic commentators virtually never possess, except in severely retrospective circumstances. And since the expected risk cannot in principle be predicted with any accuracy, the only additional clear consideration (one of sophomoric simplicity) is that in international transactions there are no countries at all in which social and cultural country risk is zero. Any countries of standardly high profitability are especially unlikely to display zero social and cultural risk.

The desirability of transferring risk was already apparent to a (deservedly) politically vulnerable American copper company in Chile as early as the mid-1960s (Moran 1973). The arrangements under which the Kennecott Copper Corporation sold a 51 percent interest in its huge El Teniente mine to the Chilean government in return for $80 million, a management contract, and a cut in its tax rate, financed a vast expansion of the mine through loans from the Export–Import Bank and the Chilean Copper Corporation, secured an insurance guarantee of the sale price from the American Agency for International Development (together with a Chilean government guarantee of both sale price and Export–Import Bank loan, justiciable under the law of the state of New York), and raised additional funds for the mine expansion by writing long-term contracts for its output with European and Asian customers and selling collection rights on these to consortia of European and Japanese banks, were impressively complex and single-minded (Moran 1973, pp. 278–9). As Robert Haldeman, the executive vice-president of Kennecott's Chilean operations, put it: "The aim of these arrangements is to insure that nobody expropriates Kennecott without upsetting relations to customers, creditors and governments on three continents." The aim was successfully realized and Kennecott was handsomely rewarded for its interim stewardship and very adequately compensated, despite prior pledges – "Ni un centavo" (Moran 1973, p. 282) – when President Allende expropriated the mine. Unsurprisingly, these arrangements set a fashion (Moran 1973, pp. 284–7). (For further discussion of the defensive strategies open to multinational corporations in the face of these risks, see Bradley 1977, Stoever 1979, Newman 1979, and Doz and Prahalad 1980.)

Understanding the nature of social and cultural risk

The transferring of political risk is a relatively urgent objective for a prudent investor or banker. But, since the time scale of social or cultural risk is in general less importunate, in its case there is much to be said for the attempt to minimize the risk in the first place. The attempt to understand the nature of social and cultural risk should be a helpful prelude to this attempt. Two reasonably well-demarcated problems in academic social and political theory bear directly on the understanding of social and cultural risk. The first is the problem of explaining the incidence of revolution. (This is unsurprising since, on the analysis offered here, the completed trajectory of a revolution is the quintessence of actualized social and cultural risk.) The second is the less well-defined problem of identifying just what in social, cultural, and political terms makes capitalist production and the patterns of exchange it generates viable at all.

Explaining revolutions: problems of method

The explanation of revolution is instructive because it has proved so elusive, and because in recent years some of the main obstacles to it have become distinctly clearer. The most influential American approaches to the explanation of revolution, the Parsonian structural functionalist analysis, with its strong emphasis on cultural factors, associated particularly with the work of Chalmers Johnson (Johnson 1964, 1966, but cf. 1973), and the more explicitly psychological approach of Ted Gurr, centering on the concept of relative deprivation (Gurr 1970), have made an extremely unimpressive contribution to the understanding of the phenomena with which they have been concerned. The broader school of comparative politics with which Gurr's work is associated, which seeks to construct indexes of the political vulnerability of societies by the increasingly grandiose computation of social and political indicators, has continued to thrive (Gurr 1970, 1973, Hudson 1971, Markus and Nesvold 1972). It would be silly to deny that graphic presentation even of the inherently vague information deployed in these calculations may be of some help in focusing the judgment of potential investors who initially know nothing of the political and social relations of a particular country (Rummel and Heenan 1978), though, as with the more comprehensive assessments of country risk favored by some bankers (Nagy 1978, p. 141), the interpretation of the implications of the results is best left to someone who already knows a great deal about the particular country in question. (For an attempt to draw inferences from an even less promising tradition in American political science, see Green 1974).

But the "induction by brute force" approach adopted, with its quasi-magical aping of the routines of natural science and its innocent faith that the deficiencies of the information handled will come out in the wash, through the vigor of the computational techniques employed, has highly insecure theoretical foundations. There are a number of different objections to such "kitchen blender" approaches to social and political analysis. The most important of these, the objection to the implied natural science ontology of human beings, is far more important in relation to social and political scientists than it is likely to prove in relation to bankers or corporate investors. For example, bankers (unlike social scientists) are no doubt rather well aware when they construct models of country risk that they are attempting to improve and clarify their judgment, not playing at natural science on especially refractory materials. One basis of the natural science paradigm is a very soggy conception of the relations between the categories of action and those of behavior and a wholly inadequate grasp of the obstruction that cultural differentiation poses for any accurate translation from the former into the latter (MacIntyre 1971, ch. 22, Dunn 1980, ch. 5). The unpredictability of political action (which is what is especially crucial in explaining the incidence of revolution) is probably only a blatant instance of what is true of virtually any human performance of much interest (MacIntyre 1973, 1981). But in the context of revolutions it is an eminently pragmatic, and not merely a logical, consideration. The most impressive explanatory study of revolutions has been holistic and structural in ambition (Skocpol 1979), but even this has so far been explanatory within rather strict limits and has neither shown, nor perhaps could in principle show, much capacity to integrate cultural factors or strategic skill and nerve into its explanations (Dunn 1972, 1980, ch. 9, 1982a). (Culture is perhaps an unwisely broad term to employ. In this context it certainly should not be read in the idiom of 1960s "modernization" theory, as the infliction of Western conceptions of existential and practical rationality on the hapless inhabitants of the less-developed countries.)

In the explanation of revolutions, the key cultural consideration resides in the evaluative, and still more, the causal, beliefs of candidates for political leadership (Dunn 1980, ch. 9; 1982a). Because of the intrinsically competitive character of political action (the prevalence of opponents, not the absence of authentically shared interests and commitments), the causal beliefs both of potential revolutionaries and of incumbent governments play a strongly dynamic role in revolutionary process and guarantee a persisting gap between inductive extrapolation from past conflict and the character and outcome of future conflicts. Equally importantly – and usually somewhat in advance of changes in the causal beliefs of agents – shifts in the ecological context of revolutionary or counterrevolutionary action alter the prospective outcomes of identical initiatives or responses (Dunn 1980, ch. 9). This point has a direct relevance to the assessment of political risk (and a somewhat more tangential bearing on the assessment of social and cultural risk also). Precisely because of the ecological changes in international trade that have shifted the balance of advantage from multinationals toward host countries in the exploitation of natural resources over the last two decades, any assessment of political risk inferred by induction from the levels prevailing in the early 1960s to levels likely to prevail in the early 1970s would have sharply underestimated the anticipated extent of expropriation.

A further consideration, this time drawn from the structural analysis of revolutionary potentiality (Skocpol and Trimberger 1977–8, Skocpol 1979), is the degree to which the weight of social and cultural risk will depend not simply on the characteristics of class relations within a particular national society but at least equally crucially on the precise character and organizational structure of the nation state concerned and on the balance of external pressures and supports – economic, political, ideological, and military – to which this is subjected. At either of these levels of specificity, assessment by induction from episodes of behavior will necessarily be far less illuminating than assessment founded upon the attempt to grasp the internal and external dynamics to which a particular national society is exposed.

Why is capitalist production possible: a key question, feebly answered

The second main problem in social and political theory directly relevant to the assessment of social and cultural risk is the analysis of the social, cultural, and political preconditions for capitalist production and the patterns of exchange this generates. There has been much recent writing on the political aspects of this topic (Alavi 1972, O'Connor 1973, Poulantzas 1973, 1974, Habermas 1976, Miliband 1977, Dunn 1978, Holloway and Picciotto 1978, Therborn 1978, Wright 1978, Skocpol 1980, Urry 1981), but it has yet to make an explanatory contribution of much power. In relation to social and cultural risk it is likely to be more helpful to focus explicitly on the intrinsic moral vulnerability of capitalism. Moreover, it is worth emphasizing that, in terms of social visibility, this is a genuine perceptual property of capitalist relations of production, which certainly does *not* depend on the (hazardous) judgment that a superior socioeconomic order, "socialism," is waiting everywhere (or anywhere) in the wings to replace it on stage. There is some evidence, too, that this property is especially hard for Americans (in contrast with the inhabitants of most countries in the world) to perceive. To a degree thus far unique in world history, and one clearly dependent on distinctive geographical and historical endowments, the United States has been a society ideologically integrated in the endorsement of capitalist relations of production (Hartz 1955). By contrast, Great Britain, for example, as Professor Hayek (1978) has long complained, has historically responded to capitalist production relations with what (in Hayek's eyes) are essentially primitive moral sentiments, evoked by perceptions of distributive injustice, that, when they enter into democratic politics, devastate the capacity of the market to maximize economic welfare. (Hayek himself, appropriately, draws the conclusion that majoritarian democracy based on universal adult suffrage is, against Engels, a somewhat unsuitable political shell for the reproduction of capitalist relations of production, though in the United States he would presumably be compelled to admit that it is still not doing too badly.) The significance of the moral vulnerability of capitalism, in the end of decisively *political* importance, is still very poorly understood and its implications are still being actively explored in practice (Dunn 1979). The potential range of these political implications is, of course, restricted by the vulnerabilities of precapitalist production relations and, more crucially, by those of other existing states that entitle themselves "socialist." But it is unlikely to be necessary, to an American audience, to emphasize these latter vulnerabilities, even if the intricate politics of the Polish crisis serve to underline the point that social and cultural risk as a practical concern for bankers and investors is far from being a prerogative of capitalist societies.

What is probably the most sustained, imaginative, and illuminating consideration of the construction and reconstruction, over the last three centuries, of a culture capable of facilitating capitalist production relations has been produced in recent decades by socialist (and, in many cases, Marxist) historians of the British Isles (Tawney 1912, 1938, Hobsbawm 1959, 1962, 1967, Thompson 1963, 1971, 1975, Hill 1964, 1972, Hay, Linebaugh, and Thompson 1975, Stedman Jones 1976, and Foster 1977). But, in part because of its political orientation, this historiography has failed to show at all clearly the interrelations between the political construction, through a legal order and public apparatus of coercion, of the space within which this culture evolved and the evolution of the culture itself. In some ways the relation appears more clearly, if more abstractly, in the powerful account of the preconditions for the flourishing of what they called a "commercial society" set out by the great Scottish social theorists of the eighteenth century and most particularly by David Hume (1911) and Adam Smith (1976) (see also Forbes 1975, Winch 1978). The relations between effective governmental power, the predictable guarantee of private property, and the dynamic productivity of the "system of natural liberty" and justice sketched in the *Wealth of Nations* were strongly emphasized by Hume and Smith themselves and the contrasts drawn, as they had been by Montesquieu, with the disincentive effects of arbitrary or despotic rule. Neither Hume nor Smith understood very well the potential ideological fragility of the new order (Dunn 1983), but they did see with exemplary precision the direct dependence of this order upon both secure rights of property and a government with the capacity to defend these effectively against challenge.

Comparable historical studies of the cultural incorporation of the industrial working class in Western European countries other than Great Britain for the most part have been less illuminating (but cf. Moore 1978, and more abstractly, 1966). But the political implications of the structural and temporal differences in such incorporation have recently been emphasized by sociologists (Giddens 1973, Mann 1973) and ought perhaps to be apparent to any reader of regular newspaper reports on the politics of, for example, France, Italy, Spain, West Germany, Holland, or Portugal. It is because of how they are educated, by their experiences domestically and at work, to see and feel about their position in society – because of the culture into which they are inducted – that groups of workers or voters adopt and sustain the political tastes and allegiances they hold.

Extranational guarantees for property rights

The creation and maintenance of effective guarantees for the forms of private property required by capitalist production has proved historically to be difficult enough even within a given national society. But it is, naturally, a decidedly harder task internationally than it is domestically (Sigmund 1980, pp. 34, 327–8). The quite conscious equation of extending nineteenth-century Western European conceptions of property with the prerequisites for expanding international commerce and spreading civilization itself has been effectively emphasized by recent economic historians (Hopkins 1980). As the British consul, Brand, put it in April 1860, in a letter to Lord John Russell, not long before the annexation of Lagos: "The increase of trade and civilised ideas and European interests and habits demand that there should be such an administration of Government as to give efficient protection to property," while at this point in Lagos there was "no effective protection of property, no mode of enforcing the payment of debts applicable to Europeans" (Hopkins 1980, p. 788). A month later, he wrote again: "Year after year a feeling of insecurity is raised in the minds of those who have property exposed here, and their plans for turning that property to best account are upset by doubts as to the amount and certainty of the protection they have to expect" (Hopkins 1980, p. 788). The issue of the sanctity of contracts (Vernon 1977, p. 151, Bergsten et al. 1978, pp. 381–95) and the absence of effective guarantees for the payment of debts or the protection of property held by Americans in foreign countries remains an urgent preoccupation for the American government (Baklanoff 1975, pp. vi, 15, 21, 113, Sigmund 1980) as it does for American multinational corporations. The clear relation between this preoccupation in 1860 and the establishment of formal colonial rule over Lagos brings out very well how colonial rule was a natural and, for a time, an economical successor to the more erratic techniques epitomized in Lord Palmerston's slogan: "Half-civilised governments require a dressing down every eight to ten years" (Hopkins 1980, p. 795). The ending of colonial rule in the aftermath of World War II, an uneven and in some cases a painful process, was a product of the discovery, both by colonial powers and by political entrepreneurs in colonial territories that the balance of economic advantage in policing a congenial property law within an alien society had always been extremely narrow and that in the geopolitical context after 1945, it could be dependably reversed by political and military action (Dunn 1980, ch. 9). Marxist theories of imperialism have not been very cogent in detail (Kemp 1967, Owen and Sutcliffe 1972, Barratt Brown 1974, Wallerstein 1974, Brewer 1980, but cf. Cohen 1974, Warren 1980, Zolberg 1981), but they have certainly focused on a political phenomenon of massive dimensions – the expansion and contraction of formal and informal empire by capitalist powers – and there is no reason to believe their central explanatory intuition to be mistaken. The ebb of colonial power has created much, though not, of course, all, of the political frame in which the more politically vulnerable components of modern international trade occur. It certainly (Jodice 1980, p. 180) offers part of the explanation of why expropriation of foreign enterprises is more frequent than it used to be. But, seen in broader persepctive, what it principally highlights is the underlying continuity across the entire era of colonial rule and the direct connections between the preoccupations of Palmerston and those, for example, of President Nixon.

It is worth emphasizing how much easier it proved in colonial territories to devise and extend a congenial set of property rights (Hopkins 1980, Dunn and Robertson 1973, ch. 3) than it was to establish a culture that fully endorsed the legitimacy of these rights (Scott 1976) in the case of indigenes, let alone in the case of foreign corporate interests. Indeed, in any society the blend of voluntary choice and experienced constraint that is central to capitalist production will be perceived and understood as it is, in part because of the objective character of the exchange relations in question, but also in part because of the beliefs and attitudes – the culture – of the population. Even in the ideological haven of the United States there exist, at least among the intelligentsia, the most profound and irresolvable clashes of intuition on the relation between property entitlements and social justice (Rawls 1973, Nozick 1974, MacIntyre 1981, ch. 17). The cultural attitude broadly christened "economic nationalism" (cf. Johnson 1968) may well often misdirect its holders as to which economic arrangements do and do not maximize the welfare of a given national population. But it is best understood in itself not as a belief about the causal preconditions for maximizing domestic welfare but rather as a resolute refusal to regard particular internationally extended property rights as compatible with the requirements of distributive justice and a consequent refusal to regard them as genuine rights, *entitlements*, at all.

The incidence of expropriation

In this perspective we may consider briefly the record of large-scale expropriations of American or European assets in the present century and attempt to draw a broad moral. It would not be easy to compile a reasonably full list of such expropriations (Robock 1971, p. 13, Knudsen 1974, Baklanoff 1975, Jodice 1980, Kobrin 1980, p. 87, Sigmund 1980, pp. 36–9), let alone one that showed the relative scale of each instance in constant prices. But some of the major instances can be located readily enough: Russia after 1917, Mexico in the late 1930s, Eastern Europe and China after 1945, Vietnam, Algeria, Cuba, Chile under the presidency of Salvador Allende, Angola, and perhaps now, Iran. A number of features stand out in any such list. One is the close connection between large-scale expropriation (and more particularly of explicit confiscation with no compensation at all) and the occurrence of anticapitalist or anticolonial revolution. Three factors loom especially large in this particular set of revolutions: world war, decolonization, and an intimate and acute hostility toward the United States on the part of a number of countries on its more or less immediate periphery. (Iran, of course, stands at some distance from all three.) The relation of world war and a coerced decolonization to revolution is not particularly puzzling (Skocpol and Trimberger 1977–78, Dunn 1980). But the contrasts between Mexico, Cuba, and Chile, on the one hand (Baklanoff 1975, Sigmund 1980), and much of the rest of Latin America, on the other, may be a good deal harder to draw persuasively, though in the case of Mexico (Ashby 1967, Reynolds 1970, ch. 6) and still more of Cuba (Smith 1960, O'Connor 1970, Dunn 1972, ch. 8, Baklanoff 1975, pp. 15, 21, Dominguez 1978) the intensity of the hostility at least is far from puzzling. A government that gives its subjects less reason to see it as representing their interests than as protecting the property rights of foreigners (colonial governments are an extreme example) can expect little allegiance from its subjects (Dunn 1980, ch. 7, esp. pp. 195–205). What is especially important in the instance of Iran is its demonstration of the capacity of a government to cast itself in this way as a catspaw of foreign interests on the basis of an altogether more distant and historically shallower relationship and of the devastating impact of this identification upon its viability as a government.

The changing ecology of international capitalist enterprise

The morals to be drawn from these considerations can be summarized crudely in five points. First, the ecology within which domestic governmental power is exercised and foreign property rights are or are not protected has been changed sharply by the outward geographical pressure of capital from the most advanced industrial societies. This may yet prove to be of major importance for the security of foreign property rights even within some parts of Western Europe. Second, the same ecology has been altered in addition by a real shift of mutual advantage within investment bargaining (Bergsten et al. 1978, Newman 1979, Stoever 1979). Third, it has been further altered by the political apprehension of this shift in advantage within incumbent governments and among the ranks of immediate contenders for governmental power. (It is an important qualification to the second and third points that an unintended consequence of LDC government action that is rational in relation to each individual investment may be an increasing subsequent exclusion from international capital markets; Sigmund 1980, Eaton and Gersovitz, this volume). Fourth, it has been altered still further by the changing pattern of international conflict, the sharp shift in external aid and coercive threat produced by the Russian and Chinese revolutions, and the intricate competitive fields that have emerged from these changes. A clear example of the consequences of this shift is the increasing difficulty faced by the U.S. government in resisting the expropriation of American assets and in enforcing the payment of prompt, effective, and adequate compensation where this has already taken place. This weakness is neatly epitomized by the fact that the famous Hickenlooper amendment has virtually never in fact been applied in the case of an expropriated American investment (Moran 1973, Baklanoff 1975, Vernon 1977, Bergsten et al. 1978). (Of course, as the fate of President Allende showed, the United States government and even individual American multinational corporations do have the capacity on occasion to intervene quite effectively by less formal means on the political margin.) Fifth, and more speculatively, there is perhaps also reason to regard this ecology as being changed still further by present (and, prospectively, by future) levels of popular political participation and response. Even the least politically sophisticated of populations in the last quarter of the twentieth century can expect to encounter a variety of agencies competing to interpret to them the political possibilities open to them. Some of these agencies may be a little surprising to Western social scientists (mullahs, for example). But their cultural idiosyncrasies will not necessarily preclude their exercising dramatic power, at least of a negative kind.

This is a very simple picture. Insofar as it is accurate, it should certainly discourage the attempt to predict the course of future political struggles by simple induction from past political struggles. But it should also, in compensation, help to bring out the logic through which these struggles have been and are being transformed. In terms of this logic, it seems likely that social and cultural risk will be maximized in the face of repressive governments (correctly) perceived by their subjects as tied to the protection of foreign economic interests; lands, for example, too fit for American investors to do business in. Such societies are societies of standing social and cultural risk, even if the risk happens for a time to be kept under control by skillful and ruthless repression and capable management of the economy. A tentative list of such societies might include South Africa, Indonesia, Chile today, South Korea, perhaps Argentina and Brazil, possibly in the end, Egypt.

Iran: a case study in social and cultural risk

The case of Iran is illuminating in this context not because of the direct damage it has inflicted on Western economic interests (which, at least until the release of the American embassy hostages, must in comparative terms have been decisively less than the damage it inflicted on Iranian economic interests), but because of the drastic reversal of any rational assessment of the political risks of dealing with the Pahlavi monarchy that its occurrence represented (see, e.g., the assessment of a bitter left-wing critic of the Shah's regime given in the first edition of Halliday 1979). What exactly made this reversal possible, and how far does it support or impugn the preceding characterization of social and cultural risk?

Two points in particular stand out. The first is the astonishing extent to which the Shah's regime in its last eighteen months contrived to unite against itself the most heterogeneous social and political forces (Sullivan 1980, Arjomand 1981b), casting itself as the deadly enemy of Iranians of every class and ethnic grouping, across virtually the entire continuum of cultural and political allegiance in a highly differentiated and segmented society. Such patterns of projective identification, positive and negative, have long been identified as the essence of revolutionary process (Marx 1964, p. 56).[3] The second

---

[3] "For *one* class to represent the whole of society, another class must concentrate in itself all the evils of society, a particular class must embody and represent a general obstacle and limitation. A particular social sphere must be regarded as the *notorious crime* of the whole society, so that emancipation from this sphere appears as a general emancipation." The class terminology does not fit the Iranian case very happily, but the dynamics of the judgments in question are difficult to miss.

point, more distinctively, is the very close link that the Iranian revolutionaries (and the Ayatollah Khomeini, in particular) have seen throughout between their hostility to the Shah and their hostility to the United States of America. When in late June 1981 (*Times* [London], June 30, 1981) the headquarters of the Islamic Republican Party was bombed in Tehran with heavy loss of life in the course of the persistent internecine feuds that have dogged the country since the Shah's overthrow, the party's response took the form of yet another broadcast attack on the United States, the "Great Satan," presenting the attack as the opening of "a new chapter in the history of struggles by the Islamic nation against the criminal America," warning America and Israel that the Iranian revolution would not lose heart in the face of the assassination since, "you, revolutionary people, have already identified yours and God's friends and enemies and have already declared, within the framework of this revolutionary recognition, your war on the side of the oppressed people." To be identified so crisply as the enemies of God and to be incorporated into what is on occasion an authentically paranoid vision, in a setting where the practical political implications are so disastrous for American interests, is perhaps at present the epitome of cultural risk for Americans (Lenczowski 1979). More domestically, of course, it had possessed very similar resonances for the Shah himself, who attributed the demonstrations scornfully, as late as June 1978, to "a lot of mullahs pining for the seventh century" (Graham 1979, p. 230).

America as the Great Satan

The first of these points, in retrospect, is not especially difficult to explain, though there do not appear to have been any publicly announced assessments of Iran that to any degree foresaw it. Indeed, there is ample evidence that neither American intelligence analysts (Ledeen and Lewis 1980) nor even Russian strategists (Halliday 1979) had much inkling of its likelihood. The second point is in some ways more intricate and, for present purposes, perhaps also more important. The extent of hatred for the United States felt by urban Iranians is quite remarkable, and the cultural style of Khomeini's version of Twelver Shi'ite Islam is sufficiently startling to Western eyes to be readily mistaken for a form of collective derangement. But it would be an error to see the hatred as a simple product of misinformation and the religious sensibility as a medium of learning that virtually guarantees that the benign intentions of the United States will fail to

secure accurate understanding. It is, for instance, exceedingly unlikely that the sentiments of the majority of the Tehran or Shiraz
population would be much mollified if they were more extensively
and precisely informed about the conflicts prevailing within the U.S.
administration in the years of the Shah's fall (Lenczowski 1979, Ledeen and Lewis 1980, Sullivan 1980). Nor is it likely that they would
share the Shah's view (and that of some of the tougher American
participants or academic analysts) that his eventual fall is to be attributed, first, to the vagaries of President Carter's enthusiasm for
human rights, and second, to the President's incapacity to make up
his mind and act firmly in situations of crisis. The American involvement with the Shah's regime was as busy and intimate as ever in these
years, though it was certainly also strikingly ineffective. Throughout
his reign the Shah had owed much to the United States, first for
persuading the Russians at the end of World War II to return the
entire territory of Iran to his rule and to withdraw their support from
the left-wing regimes that had been established under their aegis in
northern parts of the country, and later in 1953 for aiding the coup
that brought down the nationalist government of Dr. Mossadegh and
enabled the Shah to return from a humiliating exile. For the last
decade of his reign, and most decisively after the OPEC price increases of 1973, the Shah had become a very important ally indeed,
the world's largest purchaser of American armaments, a formidable
military force in the troubled Persian Gulf area, and a key bulwark
against Russian advance toward the Gulf oil fields.

To be sure, this is not to say that the Shah was simply an American
puppet. The leading role he played in the early stages of the OPEC
cartel in forcing up the price of oil, for example, was strongly opposed to American interests. But the directness of the links between
Iran and the Pahlavi regime in 1977 was apparent enough in the
country itself, with 40,000 American military and air force personnel
or engineers and businesspeople permanently stationed in a small
number of centers in the country and making their presence very
blatantly felt (Lenczowski 1979, p. 807). It was thus a very natural
assumption in the crisis of 1978–9 that the Iranian army, with its
extensive American training and massive endowment of American
matériel, could be trusted to serve as an instrument for implementing
American purposes in the country. One does not have to be a Twelver
Shi'ite waiting for the Hidden Imam, or even a militant member of
Solidarity, to find this sort of calm expectation that a national army
will serve as the agency for another nation's purposes (Ledeen and
Lewis 1980, Sullivan 1980) startlingly offensive.

Cultural risk incarnate: the role of the ulama

One way of seeing the vulnerability of the Shah's situation in 1978–9 is thus in terms of a widening gap between a state very weakly articulated with the remainder of Iranian society (Mahdavy 1970, Halliday 1979, ch. 2–4) and very closely tied to a foreign power, and a society with very little temptation to see this state as serving its own interests and with strong reasons, even in terms of day-to-day experience, for viewing it as the tool of a foreign power. The eventual mechanics of this state's breakdown appear to have been fairly simple: massive street demonstrations in the face of an increasingly irresolute army, many of the units of which were composed largely of conscripts, followed by sharp and well-coordinated strikes by the modern industrial labor force, especially in the oil fields (Graham 1979, pp. 235–7, Halliday 1979, pp. 317–18, Arjomand 1981b, p. 306). The missing link between the fairly palpable odiousness of the Shah's regime by 1977 and the scale of popular action, culminating in the largest urban demonstration in history in Tehran, was the very practical and historically tenacious union between the urban merchants and artisans of the bazaar and the Shi'ite ulama (Arjomand 1981b).

This alliance was an old one, older by far than the Pahlavi dynasty itself. The relations between its two partners (and their subordinate components) and the two Pahlavi monarchs changed through time. But over the decade and a half since the early 1960s, they had both simplified and deteriorated (Graham 1979, Walton 1980, Arjomand 1981b). The bazaar communities had benefited rather little from the grandiose ventures of the oil boom, and in Tehran they had suffered in some respects from the urban property boom and redevelopment plans this promoted. At least since 1963, the ulama had been treated by the Shah with a mixture of hostility and contempt, despite the very real services some of them had rendered him in his coup of 1953 (Cottam 1979, pp. 155–6), and their economic position and cultural influence had been frontally attacked in a number of ways. In 1964, Richard Cottam estimated that it was "most unlikely that religious influence in Iranian nationalism will ever again reach the proportions it exercised in 1951–52" (Cottam 1979, p. 156). In the late 1960s, Professor Nikki Keddie offered an equally low assessment of their political prospects: "Given the continued growth of government power, and the expansion of the army, the bureaucracy, and of secular education, even in the villages, it appears probable that the political power of the ulama will continue to decline as it has in the past century . . . They now appear at most able to modify or delay certain government policies and not strongly to influence their basic thrust and direction" (Keddie 1972, p. 229). Writing in the same volume, Hamid Algar, the leading historian of the nineteenth-century ulama (Algar 1969), observed more forcefully that, "it would be rash to predict the progressive disintegration of the political role of the ulama. Despite all the inroads of the modern age, the Iranian national consciousness still remains wedded to Shi'i Islam, and when the integrity of the nation is held to be threatened by internal autocracy and foreign hegemony, protests in religious terms will continue to be voiced, and the appeals of men such as Āyatullah Khumaynī to be widely heeded" (Algar 1972, p. 255).

The position the ulama hold in Iran differs markedly from that which they occupy in most Islamic societies (Algar 1969, Keddie 1972, Akhavi 1980, Arjomand 1981a,b). Under the Qajar monarchy it involved a relatively clear separation both of functions and of powers, made possible by the possession of an independent economic base. Most of the major elements of this base were removed from the ulama's control through the Shah's land reform of the 1960s and the secularization of education and assumption of control over religious endowments and the judicial process by both of the Pahlavis. But, although this certainly had the effect of counterposing the ulama sharply to the Shah's regime, the enforced independence was sustained by the final source of economic support open to the ulama, namely, the receipt of voluntary taxes on behalf of the Hidden Imam. In the comparative affluence induced by petrodollars, this autonomous source of funds proved to be quite handsome (Arjomand 1981b, p. 300). The combination of independence from the state and existing organizational capacity has in several instances enabled Islamic religious groupings in other settings in recent decades to act as effective agencies for political representation in societies that are largely devoid of other forms of politically effective representation. (A particularly striking instance is the Mouride brotherhood in Senegal; Cruise O'Brien 1971, 1977). In Iran the links with the bazaar, the possession of an external linkage with the Shi'ite center in Iraq at Najaf, and above all, in the demographic avalanche of the late 1960s and 1970s in Tehran, the vast proliferation of local religious associations among the urban population, old and new (Arjomand 1981b, pp. 310–13) made the mullahs uniquely capable of organizing and sustaining effective political opposition in the face of a savage, but by 1977, increasingly irresolute, autocracy.

It is clear, too, that the struggle against the Shah evoked some of the deepest themes in Iranian religious culture and that it resonated

compellingly with the idiosyncratic emotional tone of Twelver
Shi'ism, with its intense feeling for the pathos of suffering and the
dignity of the struggle against tyranny and injustice even – or perhaps especially – when the struggle was beyond hope (Algar 1972,
Thaiss 1972). The dramas of the 1960s and 1970s were interpreted
with as much assurance and effect by the ulama to their audiences
through scriptural types (the martyrdom at Karbalā of the Imam
Husayn and the tyranny of the Umayyad caliph Yazid) as they might
have been by the Puritan giants in seventeenth-century New England.
The affective dynamics of this vivid religiosity, with its sadomasochis-
tic obsession with pain, certainly has more potential for mustering
crowds to serve as machine gun fodder than a short course in the
theory of surplus value. But its instrumental political utility in 1978
and 1979 should not be allowed to obscure its true nature. Weirdly, in
our time, it was quite literally the stuff of which martyrs are made,
and it was the glad acceptance of martyrdom, the eagerness to die on
the machine guns of a heavily armed modern army, that, for the first
time since the revolutions of 1848[4], saw the army of a modern state in
peacetime and without effective external threats crumble before the
uprising of the *menu peuple* of the cities. Twelver Shi'ism is not likely to
thrive as a late twentieth-century doctrine of state. But, even in the
1960s, at the time when opposition to the Shah's regime was at its
most desperate and least effective, it gave a memorable depth of
purpose to the resistance against oppression. "We cry today because
we don't want to give up to tyranny. We beat our heads and our chests
because we don't want to go under the pressure of dictatorship or
accept coercion . . . We have been crying for 1,000 years, it doesn't
matter if we cry for another 10 million in order to bring justice against
tyranny. I cannot laugh so long as tyranny *is* ruling. I cry in order to
resist . . . We [ulama] are trying to make justice popular among society, and to prevent cruelty and tyranny . . . We are crying because
justice is gone" (Thaiss 1972, p. 365).

Cultural risk actualized: the fall of the Pahlavi dynasty

It is clear, too, that the Shah's regime was a singularly felicitous object
for this particular brand of odium. The chaos unleashed in the pe-

---

[4] Compare the assessment by Frederick Engels in 1895 of the implications of
change in military technology for the prospects of urban risings (Engels
1958, pp. 130–4). For a useful study of Engels's thinking on this topic, see
Berger 1977.

trodollar boom of the mid-1970s was indisputably a product of *folie de grandeur* (Graham 1979, Walton 1980). The intimate links with the United States gave rich support to the perennial ulama claim, from the Tobacco Protest of 1891–2 to the struggle against Anglo-Iranian in the early 1950s, to defend the economic interests as well as the cultural integrity of Iran against the foreign infidel. The capitulatory regime that governed the legal status of American servicemen in Iran (Pfau 1974) was one of the main targets of Khomeini's 1963 attacks on the Shah (Algar 1972), and the links between American and Israeli advisers and the secret police (SAVAK) aroused particular hatred. In the face of the misery of urban Tehran by 1977, with its millions of uprooted peasants scrabbling for a place in the slackening construction boom, its soaring inflation and inexorably rising sewage levels, the antics of the tiny band of favored beneficiaries of the oil money were egregiously obtrusive. A $15 million exact reproduction of the Petit Trianon in downtown Tehran (Graham 1979, p. 48) and the $100 million Gulf playground island of Kish, bewilderingly owned largely by SAVAK (Graham 1979, p. 161), when set beside the savage repressions of the preceding decade and a half, signified a regime and social order bizarrely compounded of folly and vice. No doubt the Shah need not have fallen. He might have spent the first flood of petrodollars altogether more prudently. He might have been far less brutal in earlier years or more decisively brutal in 1977, more inhibited by concern for human rights in the 1960s and less harried by Carter's State Department at the beginning of the latter's presidency. The Shah might certainly have been retired more gracefully and replaced by a regime that initially gave better protection to American interests (Ledeen and Lewis 1980, Sullivan 1980). But what is certain is the rich abundance of reasons why he stood in danger of falling, the sheer volume of social and cultural risk that he had succeeded in amassing.

Social and cultural risk as deserved odium

At the center of social and cultural risk is deserved odium.[5] This insight will not necessarily enable an investor over a particular time span to guess the risks of expropriation with much accuracy. The

---

5 With the essential proviso that attribution of responsibility is characteristically collective between enterprises of common national derivation, deserved odium is a necessary condition for high social and cultural risk. It is not, of course, a sufficient condition for such risk to be actualized.

width of the gap between rich and poor in a society, for example, may not prove a good predictor of the probability of unheaval over a given period (Rummel and Heenan 1978). What this would show, if it were definitely true, is that over that time span, social and cultural risk would be something investors could have afforded to ignore. It certainly does not and cannot show that they will be well advised to ignore such risk in the future over any equivalent length of time, let alone forever. Inductive political science on a scientistic model is a more or less amusing academic game. But history goes on.

It is difficult in principle to integrate assessments of social and cultural risk into the decision-making processes of lenders or investors. Apart from avoiding foreign investment and taking very low profits – to be enviable it is necessary to be successful – there is probably nothing that can be done literally to *minimize* exposure to social and cultural risk. And even this strategy would not necessarily minimize the risks of, for example, British or Italian investors. Any country from which there occurs a massive flight of capital in the face of political crisis is judged by some of its inhabitants to be decidedly riskier[6] than some other countries of which they are not nationals. Country risk begins at home.

But what can be done, and what, in the longer run at least, banks and the more ambitious internationally investing institutions have every reason to try to do is to understand the nature of social and cultural risk. Once this has been understood it can be assessed casually through regular reading of good newspapers and, less casually, by the protracted and culturally attentive study of particular countries.

The appropriate response of an investor, exporter, or even, in some cases, a lender to the social and cultural risk that their action will be perceived (and responded to) as odious by some large portion of the population of the country with which they are dealing is not the construction of a numerical model but, rather, the choice of an idiom of prudence. At the most morally disabused level, the rational response is to extract profits over a very short time horizon (to operate on a "get it while you can" basis, as many American firms quite explicitly did in Iran; Halliday 1979, p. 156). This style is against the long-term interest of capitalist producers as a whole (and, more distressingly, it may well imperil many features that have been closely associated hitherto in fortunate countries with capitalist production: constitutionally elected representative governments, civil rights, cultural freedoms, etc.). But there is no reason why it should not often be

---

[6] It has been estimated that $100 million per month of private capital was leaving Iran in the period 1975–8 (Graham 1979, p. 199).

economically optimal for an individual firm. A less short-term and morally crass idiom of prudence would require looking at an investment area, borrower, or trading partner as elements of a real society and noting the broad incidence of foreign economic relations upon that society through time.

All economic transactions take place in real social settings. High profitability in a corrupt, repressive, and disorganized society signifies high cultural and social risk though, of course, high profitability in a particular investment that is simply the outcome of the application of high intelligence does not necessarily imply high social risk. Low profitability in an honest, efficient, and free society (where such are to be found) may not represent an enticing investment opportunity, but it does signal very low social and cultural risk. The essence of the relation is far from mysterious. Very broadly, investors, lenders, and exporters can expect to face the risks they *collectively* deserve. The best recipe for assessing the social and cultural risks you will face (or are facing) is to ascertain what in practice you will be (or are already) doing, that is, what the loan you make or the production in which you engage will bring about (or has already brought about) in the setting for which it is destined. It is advisable, too, to keep a weather eye open for what your compatriots are doing, since the attribution of responsibility is so likely to be collective.

Culture is not the superstitious beliefs and attitudes of alien populations. It is the medium through which men and women interpret and respond to what is done to them. What social and cultural risk means for bankers or investors is that in the end they may have to pay a price for not knowing (or not caring) what they are doing.

References

Akhavi, S. *Religion and Politics in Contemporary Iran.* Albany: State University of New York Press, 1980.

Alavi, Hamza. "The State in Post-Colonial Societies: Pakistan and Bangladesh," *New Left Review*, 74, July–August 1972, 58–81.

Algar, Hamid. *Religion and State in Iran: The Role of the Ulama in the Qajar Period.* Berkeley: University of California Press, 1969.

"The Oppositional Role of the Ulama in Twentieth-Century Iran," in Keddie (ed.), *Scholars, Saints, and Sufis.* Berkeley: University of California Press, 1972, 231–55.

Allison, Graham T. *Essence of Decision: Explaining the Cuban Missile Crisis.* Boston: Little, Brown, 1971.

Angelini, Anthony, Maximo Eng, and Francis A. Lees. *International Lending, Risk and the Euromarkets.* London: Macmillan, 1979.

Arjomand, Said Amir. "The Shi'ite Hierocracy and the State in Pre-modern Iran: 1785–1890." *Archives Européennes de Sociologie*, 22, 1, 1981a, 40–78.

"Shi'ite Islam and the Revolution in Iran." *Government and Opposition*, 16, 3, Summer 1981b, 292–316.

Ashby, Joe C. *Organized Labor and the Mexican Revolution under Lázaro Cárdenas.* Chapel Hill: University of North Carolina Press, 1967.

Ashraf, Ahmad. "Obstacles to the Development of a Bourgeoisie in Iran," in M. A. Cook (ed.), *Studies in the Economic History of the Middle East.* Oxford University Press, 1970, 308–22.

Baklanoff, Eric N. *Expropriation of U.S. Investments in Cuba, Mexico, and Chile.* New York: Praeger 1975.

Barratt Brown, Michael. *The Economics of Imperialism.* London: Penguin Books, 1974.

Berger, Martin. *Engels, Armies and Revolution; The Revolutionary Tactics of Classical Marxism.* Hamden, Conn.: Archon Books, 1977.

Bergsten, T. Fred, Thomas Horst, and Theodore H. Moran. *American Multinationals and American Interests.* Washington, D.C. The Brookings Institution, 1978.

Bradley, David G. "Managing against Expropriation." *Harvard Business Review,* 55, 4, July–August 1977, 75–83.

Brandt, W. et al. *North-South: A Programme for Survival.* London: Pan Books, 1980.

Brewer, Anthony. *Marxist Theories of Imperialism: A Critical Survey.* London: Routledge & Kegan Paul, 1980.

Cohen, Benjamin J. *The Question of Imperialism: The Political Economy of Dominance and Dependence.* London: Macmillan, 1974.

Cottam, Richard W. *Nationalism in Iran,* 2nd ed. Pittsburgh: University of Pittsburgh Press, 1979.

Cruise O'Brien, Donal. *The Mourides of Senegal: The Political and Economic Organization of an Islamic Brotherhood.* Oxford University Press, 1971.

"A Versatile Charisma: the Mouride Brotherhood 1967–1975." *Archives Européennes de Sociologie,* 18, 1, 1977, 84–106.

Dominguez, Jorge I. *Cuba: Order and Revolution.* Cambridge, Mass.: Harvard University Press (Belknap Press), 1978.

Doz, Yves, and C. K. Prahalad. "How MNCs Cope with Host Government Intervention." *Harvard Business Review,* 58, 2, March–April 1980, 149–57.

Dunn, John. *Modern Revolutions.* Cambridge: Cambridge University Press, 1972.

(ed.) *West African States: Failure and Promise.* Cambridge: Cambridge University Press, 1978.

Western Political Theory in the Face of the Future. Cambridge: Cambridge University Press, 1979.

Political Obligation in its Historical Context. Cambridge: Cambridge University Press, 1980.

"Understanding Revolutions." *Ethics,* 92, 2, January, 1982a, 299–315.

"From Applied Theology to Social Analysis: The Break Between John Locke and the Scottish Enlightenment," in Istvan Hont and Michael Ignatieff (eds.), *Wealth and Virtue: Political Economy and the Scottish Enlightenment.* Cambridge: Cambridge University Press, 1983.

Dunn, John, and A. F. Robertson. *Dependence and Opportunity: Political Change in Ahafo.* Cambridge: Cambridge University Press, 1973.

Eaton, Jonathan, and Mark Gersovitz. *Poor-Country Borrowing in Private Financial Markets and the Repudiation Issue.* Princeton Studies in International Finance, 47, June 1981.

Elster, Jon. *Logic and Society.* New York: Wiley, 1978.

Engels, Frederick. "Introduction" (1895) to Karl Marx, *The Class Struggles in France from 1848 to 1850,* in Karl Marx and Frederick Engels, *Selected Works,* vol. 1. Moscow: Foreign Languages Publishing House, 1958, 118–38.

Forbes, Duncan. *Hume's Philosophical Politics.* Cambridge: Cambridge University Press, 1975.

Foster, John. *Class Struggle and the Industrial Revolution.* London: Methuen & Co., 1977.

Giddens, Anthony. *The Class Structure of the Advanced Societies.* London: Hutchinson & Co., 1973.

Graham, Robert. *Iran: The Illusion of Power,* 2nd ed. London: Croom Helm, 1979.

Green, Robert T. "Political Structures as a Predictor of Radical Political Change." *Columbia Journal of World Business,* 9, 1, Spring 1974, 28–36.

Gurr, Ted. *Why Men Rebel.* Princeton: Princeton University Press, 1970.

"The Revolution-Social-Change Nexus; Some Old Theories and New Hypotheses." *Comparative Politics,* 5, 3, April 1973, 359–92.

Habermas, Jürgen. *Legitimation Crisis,* trans. T. McCarthy. London: Heinemann Educational Books, 1976.

Halliday, Fred. *Iran: Dictatorship and Development,* 2nd ed. London: Penguin Books 1979.

Hartz, Louis. *The Liberal Tradition in America.* New York: Harcourt Brace & World, 1955.

Hay, Douglas, Peter Linebaugh, and E. P. Thompson (eds.). *Albion's Fatal Tree.* London: Allen Lane, 1975.

Hayek, F. A. *New Studies in Philosophy, Politics, Economics and the History of Ideas.* London: Routledge & Kegan Paul, 1978.

Hill, Christopher. *Society and Puritanism in Pre-revolutionary England.* London: Secker & Warburg, 1964.

The World Turned Upside Down. London: Temple Smith, 1972.

Hobsbawm, Eric. *Primitive Rebels.* Manchester: Manchester University Press, 1959.

The Age of Revolution 1789–1848. London: Weidenfeld & Nicolson, 1962.

Labouring Men: Studies in the History of Labour. Garden City, N.Y.: Anchor Books, 1967.

Holloway, John, and Sol Picciotto (eds.). *State and Capital: A Marxist Debate.* London: Edward Arnold, 1978.

Hopkins, Anthony G. "Property Rights and Empire Building: Britain's Annexation of Lagos, 1861." *Journal of Economic History,* 40, 4, December 1980, 777–98.

Hudson, Michael C. "Political Protest and Power Transfers in Crisis Periods." *Comparative Political Studies,* 4, 3, October 1971, 259–94.

Hume, David. *A Treatise of Human Nature,* 2 vols. London: J. M. Dent & Son, 1911.

Ingham, Geoffrey K. *Strikes and Industrial Conflict: Britain and Scandinavia.* London: Macmillan, 1974.

Jodice, David A. "Sources of Change in Third World Regimes for Foreign Direct Investment 1968–1976." *International Organization,* 34, 2, Spring 1980, 177–206.

Johnson, Chalmers. *Revolution and the Social System.* Stanford, Calif.: Hoover Institution Press, 1964.

Revolutionary Change. London: Athlone Press, 1966.

Autopsy on People's War. Berkeley: University of California Press, 1973.

Johnson, Harry G. "A Theoretical Model of Economic Nationalism in New and Developing States," in H. G. Johnson (ed.), *Economic Nationalism in Old and New States.* London: Allen & Unwin, 1968, 1–16.

Keddie, Nikki R. "The Roots of the Ulama's Power in Modern Iran," in Keddie (ed.), *Scholars, Saints and Sufis.* Berkeley: University of California Press, 1972, 211–29.

Kemp, Tom. *Theories of Imperialism.* London: Dennis Dobson, 1967.

Kern, David. "The Evaluation of Country Risk and Economic Potential." *Journal of the Institute of Bankers,* 102, 3, July 1981, 76–80.

Knudsen, Harald. *Expropriation of Foreign Private Investment in Latin America*. Bergen: Universitetsforlaget, 1974.

Kobrin, Stephen J. "Foreign Enterprise and Forced Divestment in the LDCs." *International Organization*, 34, 1, Winter 1980, 65–88.

Krogh, Harold C. "Guarantees against Loss to Transnational Corporations." *Annals of the American Academy of Political and Social Science*, 443, May 1979, 117–28.

Ledeen, Michael A., and William H. Lewis, "Carter and the Fall of the Shah: The Inside Story." *The Washington Quarterly*, Spring 1980, 3–40.

Lenczowski, George. "The Arc of Crisis: Its Central Sector." *Foreign Affairs*, 57, 4, Spring 1979, 796–820.

MacIntyre, Alasdair. *Against the Self-Images of the Age*. London: Duckworth, 1971.

    "Ideology, Social Science and Revolution." *Comparative Politics*, 5, 3, April 1973, 321–42.

    After Virtue: A Study in Moral Theory. London: Duckworth, 1981.

Mahdavy, Hossein. "Patterns and Problems of Economic Development in Rentier States: The Case of Iran," in M. A. Cook (ed.), *Studies in the Economic History of the Middle East*. Oxford University Press, 1970, 428–67.

Mann, Michael. *Consciousness and Action in the Western Working Class*. London: Macmillan, 1973.

Markus, Gregory B., and Betty A. Nesvold. "Governmental Coerciveness and Political Instability: An Exploratory Study of Cross-national Patterns." *Comparative Political Studies*, 5, 2, July 1972, 231–44.

Marx, Karl. "Contribution to the Critique of Hegel's Philosophy of Right: Introduction," in Karl Marx, *Early Writings*, trans. and ed. T. B. Bottomore. New York: McGraw-Hill, 1964, 41–59.

Miliband, Ralph. *Marxism and Politics*. Oxford University Press, 1977.

Moore, Barrington. *Social Origins of Dictatorship and Democracy*. Boston: Beacon Press, 1966.

    Injustice. London: Macmillan, 1978.

Moran, Theodore H. "Transnational Strategies of Protection and Defense by Multinational Corporations: Spreading the Risk and Raising the Cost of Nationalization in Natural Resources." *International Organization*, 27, 2, Spring 1973, 273–87.

Nagy, P. "Quantifying Country Risk: A System Developed by Economists at the Bank of Montreal." *Columbia Journal of World Business*, 13, 3, Fall 1978, 135–47.

Newman, William H. "Adapting Transnational Corporate Management to National Interests." *Columbia Journal of World Business*, 14, 2, Summer 1979, 82–8.

Nozick, Robert. *Anarchy, State, and Utopia*. Oxford: Blackwell Publisher, 1974.

O'Connor, James. *The Origins of Socialism in Cuba*. Ithaca, N.Y.: Cornell University Press, 1970.

    The Fiscal Crisis of the State. New York: St. Martins Press, 1973.

Owen, Roger, and Bob Sutcliffe (eds.), *Studies in the Theory of Imperialism*. London: Longman, 1972.

Pfau, Richard. "The Legal Status of American Forces in Iran." *Middle East Journal*, 28, 2, Spring 1974, 141–53.

Poulantzas, Nicos. *Political Power and Social Classes*, trans. T. O'Hagan. London: New Left Books, 1973.

    Fascism and Dictatorship, trans. Judith White. London: New Left Books, 1974.

    "The Capitalist State: A Reply to Miliband and Laclau." *New Left Review*, 95, January–February 1976, 62–83.

Rawls, John. *A Theory of Justice*. Oxford University Press, 1973.

Reynolds, Clark W. *The Mexican Economy: Twentieth Century Structure and Growth.* New Haven, Conn.: Yale University Press, 1970.

Robock, Stefan H. "Political Risk: Identification and Assessment." *Columbia Journal of World Business,* 6, 4, July–August 1971, 6–20.

Rummel, R. J., and David A. Heenan, "How Multinationals Analyze Political Risk." *Harvard Business Review,* 56, 1, January–February 1978, 67–76.

Rupnik, Jacques. "Dissent in Poland 1966–78: The End of Revisionism and the Rebirth of Civil Society," in Rudolf L. Tökes (ed.), *Opposition in Eastern Europe.* London: Macmillan, 1979, 60–112.

Scott, James C. *The Moral Economy of the Peasant: Rebellion and Subsistence in Southeast Asia.* New Haven, Conn.: Yale University Press, 1976.

Sigmund, Paul E. *Multinationals in Latin America: The Politics of Nationalism.* Madison: University of Wisconsin Press, 1980.

Skocpol, Theda. *States and Social Revolutions.* Cambridge: Cambridge University Press, 1979.

"Political Response to Capitalist Crisis: Neo-Marxist Theories of the State and the Case of the New Deal." *Politics and Society,* 10, 2, 1980, 155–202.

Skocpol, Theda, and Ellen K. Trimberger. "Revolutions and the World-Historical Development of Capitalism." *Berkeley Journal of Sociology,* 22, 1977–78, 101–13.

Smith, Adam. *An Inquiry into the Nature and Causes of the Wealth of Nations,* ed. R. H. Campbell and A. S. Skinner, 2 vols. Oxford: Clarendon Press, 1976.

Smith, Robert F. *The United States and Cuba: Business and Diplomacy, 1917–1960.* New York: Bookman Associates, 1960.

Stedman Jones, Gareth. *Outcast London: A Study of the Relationship Between Classes in Victorian Society.* London: Penguin Books, 1976.

Stoever, William A. "Renegotiations: The Cutting Edge of Relations between MNCs and LDCs." *Columbia Journal of World Business,* 14, 1, Spring 1979, 5–14.

Stremlau, John J. *The International Politics of the Nigerian Civil War 1967–1970.* Princeton, N.J.: Princeton University Press, 1977.

Sullivan, William H. "Dateline Iran: The Road not Taken." *Foreign Policy,* 40, Fall 1980, 175–86.

Tawney, R. H. *The Agrarian Problem in the Sixteenth Century.* London: Longman & Co., 1912.

Religion and the Rise of Capitalism. London: Penguin Books, 1938.

Thaiss, Gustav. "Religious Symbolism and Social Change: The Drama of Husain," in Nikki R. Keddie (ed.), *Scholars, Saints and Sufis.* Berkeley: University of California Press, 1972, 349–66.

Therborn, Göran. *What Does the Ruling Class Do When It Rules?* London: New Left Books, 1978.

Thompson, E. P. *The Making of the English Working Class.* London: Gollancz, 1963.

"The Moral Economy of the English Crowd in the Eighteenth Century." *Past and Present,* 50, February 1971, 76–136.

Whigs and Hunters: The Origin of the Black Act. London: Allen Lane, 1975.

Thunell, Lars H. *Political Risks in International Business: Investment Behavior of Multinational Corporations.* New York: Praeger, 1977.

Urry, John. *The Anatomy of Capitalist Societies.* London: Macmillan, 1981.

Vernon, Raymond. *Storm over the Multinationals.* London: Macmillan, 1977.

Wallerstein, Immanuel. *The Modern World-System.* New York: Academic Press, 1974.

Walton, Thomas H. "Economic Development and Revolutionary Upheavals in Iran." *Cambridge Journal of Economics,* 4, 3, September 1980, 271–92.

Warren, Bill. *Imperialism: Pioneer of Capitalism,* ed. John Sender. London: New Left Books, 1980.

Winch, Donald. *Adam Smith's Politics.* Cambridge: Cambridge University Press, 1978.

Wright, Erik Olin. *Class, Crisis and the State.* London: New Left Books, 1978.

Zolberg, Aristide R. "Origins of the Modern World System: A Missing Link." *World Politics,* 33, 2, January 1981, 253–81.

Perspective: The risks of lending to developing countries

HELEN HUGHES

To be sustained, capital flows must move funds from those with a high marginal propensity to save to investors with high marginal returns on capital. This is obviously the underlying rationale of current capital flows from capital-rich, high-income countries to low-income, capital-poor, developing countries.

International capital flows are as old as nations. Some lending across national borders has always had higher risk elements than some domestic lending: For some of the lenders and intermediaries involved, such risks made lending very profitable, but others, of course, suffered losses.

It was widely argued when the flow of commercial capital to developing countries began again after World War II that investing in developing countries was very risky. The developing countries' outlook was very uncertain, many were ideologically opposed to private foreign capital inflows, and it was feared that political instability would diminish rather than expand further investment opportunities. Expropriation (the nationalization of direct investment without compensation) and repudiation (the cancellation of debt) were feared. A broad network of public insurance and guarantees therefore began to be laid down by both the industrial and developing countries to stimulate capital flows.

More than thirty years later it is not at all clear that lending to developing countries is, on the whole, unduly risky, or that it is riskier than lending to other countries or than domestic lending.[1] It is also

[1] Developing countries are not a homogeneous group, but represent a spectrum ranging from very poor and slowly growing countries to those that are catching up with the industrial countries in both productivity and living standards. Some of the rapidly growing countries have, moreover, graduated from the very poorest categories.

not clear that "managing" risks entailed in international capital flows reduces the costs of borrowing and increases the profits of lending.

Commercial bank flows to developing countries should not be viewed in isolation but as part of a stream of capital that has changed its composition with changes in capital markets and the developing countries' progress. Capital flows overall have not only steadily increased in volume (in real terms) during the past thirty years, but have also become diversified in form, expanding from direct investment by transnational corporations to suppliers' credits, bank flows, bond issues, and portfolio investment. In the late 1940s, capital flows to developing countries were mainly in the form of grants or concessional loans from official sources. These expanded as more countries became independent (often merely involving a switch from colonial to aid budgets) and as industrial countries became more aware of the developing countries' needs and of the potentially high economic and political returns on aid. Few developing countries were creditworthy for flows from private sources. The initial private flows were therefore predominantly project related, taking the form of direct private investment by transnational corporations. The mineral-rich and more advanced and rapidly growing developing countries, however, also began to have access to suppliers' credits in the 1950s, and by the mid-1970s, untied bank lending began to flow, and some developing countries even began to borrow from the bond market.

Supported first by industrial countries' savings surpluses, and then by liquidity engendered by the Middle Eastern petroleum exporters' savings, bank lending increased considerably in the 1970s (Table 1, this chapter). The costs of borrowing from banks fell markedly in the mid-1970s as a result, as interest rates dropped and even became negative in real terms. Borrowing from banks also gave developing countries freedom from the ties associated with aid flows, equity investment, and suppliers' credits. Thus, although total capital flow increases remained fairly stable, moving commensurately with the developing countries' domestic and export growth, there was a marked switch from equity and suppliers' credit to bank borrowing.[2] Direct private investment continued to expand in the 1970s at more than 3 percent a year in real terms as it had in the 1960s, but bank

---

[2] This also suited the lenders. Whereas dividends earned on equity were taxable as profits, interest payments on loans were deductible from profits as costs. These issues were particularly important in mineral investment, where the switch from equity to bank borrowing was also associated with resource ownership questions.

Table 1. *Composition of net annual capital flows*
to developing countries, 1960–2 and 1978–80 (in percent)

	1960–2	1978–80
Official development assistance	59	34
Official nonconcessional	7	13
Private nonconcessional	34	53
Direct investment	(20)	(14)
Export credits	(7)	(13)
Financial flows	(7)	(26)
U.S.$ billion	9	84
U.S.$ billion in 1980 dollars	30	92

Note: The figures for 1978–80 cover flows from OPEC and the centrally planned economies as well as from the Development Assistance Committee and India, Ireland, Israel, Luxembourg, Spain, and Yugoslavia.
Source: OECD, *Development Cooperation* Paris, 1968–80.

lending grew faster until 1978–9. The transfer of income from lenders to borrowers could not go on forever. Interest rates began to reflect inflation expectations, rising steeply in real terms from negative to a three or four positive percentage points. Although management and other front-end fees fell somewhat, offsetting the interest rate increases, the real cost of borrowing rose sharply. The aftermath of the 1979–80 petroleum price increases also made borrowers cautious and selective. They again switched among borrowing instruments, moving back to trade-related suppliers' credits (which became more highly subsidized in the renewal of mercantilism that marked the reaction to the petroleum price increases), and to direct private investment, which became cheaper in relative terms as interest rates rose. The volume of direct investment flows to developing countries thus doubled between 1978 and 1981.

The arguments for public insurance against the risks of lending to developing countries

A large part of the risk of lending across international borders, as in lending within a country, is associated with judgments about an entrepreneur's or government's ability to invest the borrowed funds profitably.[3] This type of risk clearly should not be "managed." Countries that have attempted to reduce or eliminate business risks by economy-wide and detailed (rather than broadly indicative target) planning have performed much worse than market economies that rely on entrepreneurs' individual reactions to uncertainty through risk taking to shake out inefficient performers. Investors and financial intermediaries such as banks are entrepreneurs whose profits must be related to their judgments about borrowers' economic and political acumen if lending is to be efficient. It is true that a private enterprise may cease to be profitable or may not be able to remit capital service payments abroad, if major political changes take place. A government enterprise may depend on the retention of political power for its profitability. A borrowing government may be thrown out of power and replaced by one that will repudiate its predecessor's debts. But in practice all these have occurred in industrial countries during the last thirty years (directly or through policies leading to inflation) as well as in developing countries.

Many of the arguments for the public insurance of the risk of lending to developing countries by industrial countries turn out to be specious. Thus it is often argued that lending should be publicly insured because the information about developing countries is poorer than that about industrial countries. But the remedy for this problem is not risk insurance but rather the improvement of the flow of information about developing countries.

Another group of arguments suggests that commercial capital flows are a form of aid to developing countries. It is said that insurance or guarantees benefit developing countries by lowering the cost of borrowing, at least to the extent that the lending countries bear the cost. They are said to encourage flows that would otherwise not take place. But these arguments do not take the potential costs of the "moral hazard" inherent in such insurance into account (Arrow 1974). Mixed aid–profit transactions often lead to a backlash of bad political relations with the recipient countries. Aid and commercial capital flows are complementary and can be mutually supportive, but they should be kept distinct for the most part.

A mercantilist subsidy argument, much in vogue again in response to the aftermath of the 1978–9 petroleum price increase induced

---

[3] Even if a government borrows in the short run for reasons of balance-of-payments management, direct consumption, and so on, the funds usually have an investment impact on the economy; in the longer run, borrowing must clearly be for investment if capital flows are to be sustained.

recession in industrial countries, is that private investment or bank lending is necessary to support the industrial country's exports, so that public insurance is needed as aid to the private sector in industrial countries. The long-term costs of such policies are too well known, and were too well demonstrated in the 1930s, to need repetition.

The valid case for public insurance or guarantees against the risks of lending to developing countries is concerned with three principal issues. The first is the difficulty of legally recovering losses abroad that may be more easily recoverable in a national framework (see Eaton and Gersovitz, this volume). The second concerns the additional political instability associated with the very condition of underdevelopment. The third is concerned with the public planning and ownership and the concomitant tendencies to expropriation and repudiation that are inherent in the current ideological tendencies of a number of developing countries. The first of these is associated with all lending abroad, and the importance of the latter two appears to be declining as more developing countries become more mature and as more move to market-oriented development strategies.

Valid or not, the arguments for risk reduction have been instrumental in the establishment of a very considerable insurance or risk management network by both industrial and developing countries. Most industrial countries provide insurance to their nationals for direct investment in, and trade-related and other banking flows to, developing countries. In addition, a considerable proportion of lending is guaranteed de jure or de facto through parent corporations for buyers' credits and loans to subsidiaries and associated corporations in developing countries.

It has also been argued that on the developing country side, government guarantees can stimulate and support foreign investment and borrowing abroad. Developing countries therefore typically give assurance of protection for private investment against expropriation without compensation and other risks,[4] and guarantee bank borrowing, often not only for public, but also for private borrowers. More than 75 percent of debt owed by developing countries to private lenders is covered by such guarantees.[5]

---

[4] The vast literature on every aspect of this subject is so well known that it does not need repetition here. For a fairly recent survey see Billerbeck and Yasugi (1979).

[5] The proportion of the remaining 25 percent or so of debt owed to private lenders covered by the industrial countries' or parent corporation guarantees is not known, but it is substantial.

Additional protection for investors and lenders is provided through the International Monetary Fund's and World Bank's "good housekeeping" functions. These institutions' dialogues with developing countries provide a flow of background information about the countries' state of economic health. At the margin they indicate when a country is in difficulties by withdrawing their support.

Implicit political guarantees are also a factor in risk management. Even tenuous political guarantees have encouraged lending to some developing (and to centrally planned) countries. In a number of cases they have been so strong that commercial banks continued their lending activities even after the International Monetary Fund considered it unwise for countries to borrow further.

Many international attempts have also been made to diminish the risks of investing in developing countries by establishing codes of conduct for lenders and borrowers. A number of initiatives on these lines have taken place, and they have probably had some "conscience raising" effects in indicating how good practice by borrowers and lenders can improve the investment and lending climate. The attempts have, however, failed to produce generally accepted rules because such rules are even less enforceable internationally than within countries. Only the market system with its rewards in the form of profits and sanctions in the form of losses (and, ultimately, bankruptcy) appears to be able to protect lender and borrower alike.

The growth of commercial capital flows to developing countries is strong evidence of the limited deterrent of country risk overall. In real terms, moreover, the cost of borrowing has varied considerably by investing and lending instrument, and by individual project as well as by country over the past thirty years. General experience suggests that normal business and economic considerations dominate over country risk by a considerable margin in setting the costs of borrowing. It also appears that country risks – commercial or political – have in fact been no greater overall in developing than in industrial (market economy) countries. On the contrary, it seems that, on balance, investment in, and lending to, developing countries had been more profitable for the lenders than similar domestic transactions. This, no doubt, reflects that the high overall productivity of capital in rapidly developing countries is the fundamental reason for the capital flows, although the existence of mineral and monopolistic rents is sometimes also important.

The reduction of country risk (and its effect on lending profits and borrowing costs) through public measures is difficult to evaluate. Any assessment of insurance guarantee schemes would have to include the cost of premiums and the payments that have to be made if the insurance is called up. If insurance is public, or if guarantees are given and claims are made against them, the costs have to be borne by the tax payers. The insurance or guarantee becomes a free good to the borrower and lender, exacerbating the moral hazard inherent in any insurance situation. Measuring what total charges (interest rates, front-end fees, maturity term, etc.) would have been without insurance (or guarantees) would be beset by such difficulties that it has thus far not been attempted.

Whether insurance and guarantee measures have reduced the countries' cost of borrowing overall is thus moot. Developing countries have clearly benefited in the short run, for example, from the availability of low-cost suppliers' credits.[6] Public risk management may have benefits, but it also has costs. At the margin lenders and borrowers have no doubt been less prudent than they would have been without insurance and guarantees. Real and apocryphal stories of borrowing and lending for "white elephants" abound. Some private lenders have experienced losses, although most private loans have been rescheduled quite profitably. The borrowing countries have met the extra costs involved. Where the loans were to public borrowers, rescheduling has often meant that the taxpayers in the lending country have had to meet the costs caused by the inappropriateness of the borrowing, particularly where debts have been "forgiven" as a part of an aid package. Fortunately, lending that has run into difficulties has only involved a small proportion, certainly less than 10 percent, of total private capital flows to developing countries. It does, however, account for most of the debt problem countries.

Lending to developing countries as a source of risk to international capital markets

Lending to developing countries has been perceived to create risks for the international (and principal national) financial systems. It has been argued for almost ten years that there is a danger of a "domino" pattern in developing country debt difficulties, and that this will lead

---

6 In addition, subsidized suppliers' credits also make it difficult for the newly industrializing countries to compete in international markets. They have to borrow abroad to match industrial country subsidies to be able to export capital goods.

to crises and repudiations. An alternative or complementary scenario sees an impending threat in a similar sequential failure of banks.

It is by definition true that, having gained access to capital markets, the developing countries have acquired debt liabilities. The question that should be asked is whether these debts are excessive in relation to the productivity (in social as well as financial terms) of the projects that have been financed, and the national income growth of the countries concerned.[7] This is the "solvency" equivalent of a private enterprise's borrowing (Aliber 1980). It has, of course, been greatly eased by inflation, which transferred income from lenders (particularly the petroleum-rich countries) to borrowers.

A second legitimate question relates to the management of the debt and its servicing, and associated balance of payments issues. This relates to "liquidity" considerations. The initial reaction to accelerated inflation in the 1970s in allowing interest rates (and other costs of borrowing) to lag behind inflation gave developing countries a breathing space in debt management. The shift to positive interest rates at the end of the 1970s led to a buildup of interest rate obligations for the early 1980s, but these are stabilizing and will decline if inflation drops. The private market's development of refinancing arrangements has made the maturity terms of debts of less concern than they often were on official loans. The continuing growth of exports (including service as well as merchandise exports and bolstered by workers' remittances) has meant that debt service obligations could be met; that is, countries that grew rapidly with strong export growth could borrow. The middle-income countries account for more than 90 percent of developing-country commercial debt, and this debt is highly concentrated with twelve countries accounting for more than two-thirds of total private debt. With the exception of Turkey, these are all countries that either have rich mineral resources or that have grown rapidly because of sensible domestic policies.

Thus, although the developing countries' debt has been increasing – they owed about $500 billion at the end of 1981 – for developing countries as a group as well as for the principal borrowers, a crisis is not likely. The ratios of debt to exports and to GNP naturally in-

---

[7] Projects with high financial but low social returns, and countries with inappropriate economic policies (that result in low social marginal productivity of capital) can often attract foreign capital in the short run. Projects and policies must, however, be soundly based; that is, the marginal productivity of investment must be high in private and social terms, if countries want to continue to grow and thus to borrow over the long run.

Table 2. *Developing country debt and debt service indicators, 1970–80 (in percent)*

Indicators	1970	1977	1978	1979	1980[c]
Debt/GNP	15	22	23	23	22
Debt/exports	98	102	111	99	100
Debt/reserves	321	274	274	220	232
Debt–service ratio[a]	12	15	19	18	18
Interest–service ratio	4	5	6	6	8
Capital–service ratio[b]	18	16	20	21	19
Total debt (U.S. billion)	61	256	319	372	427

Note: Includes all developing countries except (1) the capital surplus petroleum exporters, and (2) countries for which reliable time series data are not available (Afghanistan, Bahrain, Burundi, Comoros, Guinea, Iran, Iraq, Lebanon, Lesotho, Maldives, and South Africa). Indicators are total developing country debt to total GNP, exports, and reserves of all developing countries.
[a] Redemption and interest payments as percentages of merchandise exports, nonfactor service receipts, and factor services (including emigrant remittances and other private transfers) earnings.
[b] The debt–service ratio plus profits and dividends (including profits on direct investment) in the numerator.
[c] Estimated.
Source: World Bank, *World Debt Tables*, 1981.

creased in the 1970s as the developing countries' access to capital markets improved, but they are still relatively low. Debt–reserve ratios have been falling as large borrowers have increased their reserve levels to add flexibility to their debt management capacity. Debt–service ratios have risen, but this in part reflects the shift from direct to indirect financing. The interest–service ratio is still low for most countries and overall. Capital–service ratios that include direct investment service payments have remained stable (Table 2, this chapter).

Countries that have run into severe debt servicing problems are not large borrowers. Their debt crises are signs of general economic management problems that lead to low returns on investment and balance-of-payments difficulties. Most of the large borrowers have gained access to international capital markets because of their domestic growth, their export performance, and their management of reserves and other aspects of the balance of payments. Over several years even relatively high debt–service ratios of 30 percent and more are manageable. Countries such as Canada and Australia had higher rates of borrowing and higher debt–service ratios in the late nineteenth and early twentieth centuries than most developing countries have now.

The banks operating in the international sphere have also been sound on the whole. The developing countries accounted for about half of all international borrowing in the late 1970s, and on these flows losses have been negligible and profits as already indicated, correspondingly, higher than on domestic lending. If private deposits are included together with official reserves, developing countries also have considerable assets – about equal to their debt – in industrial countries. Private and public interests in developing countries thus have a stake in the stability of the international financial system. The threat to international financial stability must in any case be seen in context. Lending to developing countries still accounts for less than 10 percent of the total lending activities of the industrial countries, principally because the developing countries' absorptive capacity for commercial capital is limited by their growth capacity. It is likely to prove more useful to borrowers and lenders alike to stimulate that growth by recovery in the industrial countries and by continuing liberal trading conditions than by attempts to manage international risk.

References

Aliber, Robert. "A Conceptual Approach to the Analysis of External Debt of the Developing Countries." World Bank Staff Working Paper no. 421, October 1980.

Arrow, Kenneth J. "Uncertainty and the Welfare Economics of Medical Care" and "The Economics of Moral Hazard; Further Comments," in *Essays in the Theory of Risk Bearing*. Oxford: North-Holland, 1974.

Billerbeck, K., and Y. Yasugi. "Private Direct Foreign Investment in Developing Countries." World Bank Staff Working Paper no. 348, July 1979.

World Bank, *World Debt Tables*. Washington, D.C.: 1981.

Perspective: Country risk, a banker's view

RIMMER DE VRIES

My task is to reconcile the academic and practical views. The academic speakers have emphasized the growing economic and political risks, and Helen Hughes says the amount of risk is highly exaggerated or at least is not enough to get too excited about. Let me say this: My own instinct is that there is a considerably higher risk today than ten or twenty years ago. Twenty years ago, we were in the fixed exchange rate system. We had low rates of inflation and low interest rates, which were fairly stable, and we were lending mainly to industrial countries whose balances of payments were in reasonably good condition and who had also fairly good adjustment policies.

Today, we have very volatile exchange rates, very high rates of inflation, and an international lending system that is much larger and more widespread than ten years ago.

When preparing these comments, I asked my management whether we had higher risks now than a decade ago. The answer was yes, but not in the sense that we as economists would think. From a bank's balance sheet and profit and loss account, the risks in the past decade have been in the area of interest rates and exchange rates. The impact on the banks' earnings of these variations in exchange and interest rates has been far greater than the risks associated with international lending. I should add that corporate management is spending a great deal more time on weighing exchange and interest rate risks than on determining country risk. Historically, the losses in the area of sovereign lending have been remarkably small.

I would like to comment briefly on three points: Why have the banks been so relaxed about country risk? Are the banks underestimating country risk? What are the lessons and conclusions we can derive from our experience?

That the banks are quite relaxed in the field of international lending is very clear from the loans they have been willing to make. For example, since 1975–9, bank loans to Brazil have risen 30 percent per annum, and even last year it has continued to go up by 20 percent. In Argentina, the rate of increase of international bank lending, based on data compiled by the BIS, is close to 50 percent per annum. For Korea this growth figure is about 40 percent. Loans to Chile have been rising at an annual rate in excess of 50 percent. For the Philippines international lending growth is around 30 percent. In the case of Mexico it was about 25 percent, but more recently it is close to 40 percent.

In fact, international lending has the highest rate of growth to those countries where banks have the largest amount of loans outstanding, resulting in considerable concentration of loans. About six or seven countries have received the bulk of international bank loans. However, there are very few countries where loans have grown at an annual rate of less than 15 percent: El Salvador, Sri Lanka, South Africa, China, Peru, and India are examples. This rate is a sort of yardstick because bank capital is estimated to rise by about 15 percent per annum.

Why are the banks so relaxed about international lending? In the first place, as Helen Hughes has indeed indicated, the concentration of risk is very diffused. There are only two countries, Mexico and Brazil, where the concentration of lending exposure is about 10 percent of total international loans. This figure is difficult to compute, but if one subtracts loans to money center countries such as Great Britain, Singapore, Hong Kong, and so on from total international loans, one has a fairly clean base of country loans from which loans to individual countries can be measured. Next to Brazil and Mexico, banks have about 5 percent of their loans concentrated in about three countries: Argentina, Venezuela, and Korea. Loans to other countries amount to about 1 or 2 percent of their total foreign loans, or substantially less than that. The concentration has been reduced in recent years despite the very rapid lending I just referred to. The expansion of loans to Brazil has been less fast than to other countries. Brazil, for instance, used to have about 12 percent of bank loans but now it is about 9–10 percent. In the case of Mexico, it used to be 11 percent, and now it is also about 9 percent.

A very interesting phenomenon is the entry of new banks, particularly the Arab banks. Today about a third of Eurocurrency loans are managed by Arab banks, compared with virtually none a few years ago. Of course, the new entrants are not only Arab banks but also French, Dutch, or German banks, who have been lagging in participation in international lending. All this helps reduce the loan concentration of *individual* banks. If more banks enter the system and bring in sizable capital, there is more distribution of lending risk.

Furthermore, the rate of international loan expansion has been falling. The rate of growth of the banks' international claims used to be about 35 percent per annum, but now it is closer to 18 percent. These figures refer to global international lending and are not confined to LDCs. They also include countries such as Yugoslavia, Denmark, and other smaller industrial countries that are heavy borrowers, as well as Eastern European nations. There is a definite slowdown, albeit from an increasingly higher basis. Despite the slowing down in the rate of growth of international lending, the absolute amount of net new loans may still be the same; but the relative growth is more significant in this inflationary, dynamic world. The slowdown can also be observed as one looks at the ratio of lending to exports, which has come down from 50 percent to 20 percent in the last half decade. All these numbers are in the right direction.

It should also be stressed that the IMF has played a constructive role in difficult circumstances. It has come to the rescue in Turkey,

Zaire, Peru, Jamaica, and other countries. The IMF presence and role underpin confidence, just as a steady local central bank strengthens the domestic monetary system. The Fund can help individual countries in correcting policies and making them ready again for the private markets. I am very glad to see that the Reagan administration, despite criticism of international institutions, is still very much supportive of the IMF's role.

The most important factor in international lending proceeding as smoothly as it has is the fact that the adjustment mechanism works. If one looks back at the past ten years, the countries about which the banks have had to worry the most have done very well. About ten years ago, U.S. banks were told not to lend to Italy. U.S. supervisory authorities seriously questioned the soundness of Italian loans. The banks were told to worry about Italy. They also were told by just about everybody to worry about Brazil. Over ten years ago they used to worry all the time about Japan, which experienced recurring balance-of-payments problems and was one of the countries of high risk. This episode, I am sure, has long been forgotten. There were other countries, such as Korea, Indonesia, and Denmark. In retrospect all these countries have performed very well. They have adjusted well if one looks at economic growth, at export growth, at their oil consumption imports, and at their current accounts, their real effective exchange rates, and their real interest rates.

If one reviews these factors in some key problem countries one has to conclude that countries can and do adjust. Take Brazil, for example, which has a very impressive record. Economic growth, which many experts believed could not go below 5 percent, has fallen from the traditional 7–8 percent to 0. Export growth last year was 32 percent. This year this may still be close to 20 percent. Imports are being cut back to a 4.5 percent growth rate. Oil imports have been growing barely at 1 percent in the last couple of years. Oil consumption as a percentage of GNP has fallen by 5 percent. The current account, excluding oil and interest payments, has moved from about $.5 billion surplus in 1979 to almost $3 billion surplus in 1981. These are formidable indicators of domestic adjustment. Brazil's real effective exchange rate, difficult as it may be to compute, is also very competitive.

I can go through very similar numbers for Korea or Denmark. Denmark, for instance, maintained a 2 percent rate of growth during 1974–9, but this year it has decreased to −1 percent. Its oil imports have fallen nearly 15 percent, and its current account, excluding oil and interest, has moved from a $2 billion surplus to close to $5 billion surplus in 1981. This country has also gone through a period of significant domestic adjustment. Korea has improved its current account, excluding oil and interest, from a $1 billion surplus in 1979 to a $7 billion surplus in 1981. When we look at some of these significant indicators of domestic and external management, including export promotion, oil consumption, and exchange and interest rate policies, it is not surprising that those countries that have adjusted the best also have received the most loans.

A word should be added about OPEC. We remember how gloomy many analysts were in 1974 about the surplus, and yet it disappeared in about three years. Again, when the problems in Iran began and oil prices surged, as well as the OPEC surplus, analysts became very pessimistic. The OPEC surplus reached more than $110 billion in 1980 and most of us were more skeptical than ever that it would fall drastically. Nevertheless, the OPEC surplus is now projected to amount to only $60 billion in 1981 and is projected to fall to a very low level next year.

The reason for this enormous drop, of course, is all very familiar. Consumption is down sharply because of higher prices and the use of alternative energy resources. Oil production is rising steadily outside the OPEC area so that OPEC's share of total world oil consumption is cut to less than half from about two-thirds a few years ago. Barring supply interruptions due to political disturbances, there is no doubt in my mind that the OPEC surplus again will disappear. All this is to underscore that markets and prices work very effectively.

These are some of the reasons why banks are fairly relaxed about country risk. Yet, there are substantial risks in the international area, and some banks perhaps underestimate them. I will list a couple. First of all, there is the oil factor. There is the risk of political instability in the Middle East, which could lead again to a surge in oil prices. The Middle East is a very volatile area and it is probably fairly safe to assume that at some time in the future there will again be some political shock there. In the absence of such shocks, oil prices are likely to drop in real terms, which could pose serious balance-of-payments problems for a number of oil-exporting countries.

Among the areas of adjustment in which many less-developed countries seem to lag the most is conservation of energy. Anyone who travels to less-developed countries experiences the high degree of subsidization, particularly in the energy field. This applies to countries with or without adequate domestic energy output. Brazil is the outstanding example of a country that has made strong progress in this area. Interestingly, oil demand in the industrial countries as a whole is projected to decline over the next few years. In contrast, oil demand in the less-developed countries still may be growing at around 4.5 percent per annum; without Brazil, the growth could be in excess of 5 percent. In the OPEC countries, of course, oil demand growth is even much larger than that.

The second area of concern involves interest cost on the high debts. Banks are praying for lower interest rates, but these do not seem to come down a great deal. They remain high even in a time of recession. If Henry Kaufman's expectations of record high interest rates come true, many countries would face serious balance-of-payments financing difficulties.

Brazil and Mexico, which have the largest amount of debt outstanding, will be affected the most by higher interest rates. If interest rates in this country remain high while the industrial countries are in a recession, the less-developed countries have a double risk as their export markets are adversely affected. Right now countries such as Chile, Peru, and Bolivia are beginning to feel the impact of lower prices for their exports. The export earnings of these countries already are significantly down. I stress these risks because, although these countries do quite well in the areas of adjustment under their control, such as exchange rate policy, domestic interest rate policy, domestic growth, and export policy, they can be seriously affected by factors outside their control such as interest payments on their loans and the developments in their export markets. In the North–South dialogue, these issues figure significantly and could lead to confrontation between borrowing countries and lenders.

Further, there are the political factors, which as a rule are far more serious than economic factors when evaluating country risk. In Poland, Iran, and Nicaragua, where groups outside the government suddenly emerged and took effective control, the economic situation deteriorated rapidly and created, in a short time span, serious debt payment problems. Country risk analyses in banks do not sufficiently take into account political risk. This again is evident in recent developments in the COMECON countries.

A word about bank capital–asset ratios is in order. Authorities in many countries do not pay much attention to bank capital, but in the United States they do. Even though the rate of growth of international bank lending has come down, it is still well above the increase in bank capital. Capital–asset ratios have undergone a steady erosion. A recent issue of the Federal Reserve *Bulletin* contains interesting data in this respect and reflects a worrisome, certainly not a complacent point of view. The restoration of capital–asset ratios has been a desire on the part of the Federal Reserve and some other central banks in

Europe for some time. One of the suggestions currently being made is that the banks should make reserves against loans that are being rescheduled. I do not know whether this is possible or can be enforced, but it reflects a desire to obtain greater discipline and caution in international lending. If there is some penalty associated with reschedulings, then banks may be more cautious in granting international loans.

What are some of the major conclusions?

In the first place the most important factor to watch is a country's domestic economic management – the whole range of domestic economic policies, the quality of economic management, and its political influence. Brazil is a good example; so is Turkey, now in the throes of severe adjustment, with the full backing of the political leadership.

Second, if economic policies and economic development strategy have been poor for a long time, the allocation of resources has been misdirected, agriculture has been neglected, exports have been discouraged partly because of a wrong exchange rate policy, and so forth, it will take a long time to correct and adjust the situation. It will not be enough to put a new team in place, but a period of several years of perseverance is needed to restore a country's creditworthiness. Turkey, again, is a good example.

Third, as pointed out, the highest risks appear to be political and cultural, which can affect a country very *suddenly* in contrast to the *slow* erosion of creditworthiness stemming from economic factors. In this context of the sudden deterioration of creditworthiness, one should particularly be concerned about short-term debt. In general, one should be more careful in the extension of short-term debt. There is also a tendency among lenders to shift from long-term credit to short-term maturities if risks are deemed to increase. I do not believe this to be good practice. If a country's credit is bad, it applies to both long-term and short-term credit. In fact, the shrinking of long-term credit in favor of short-term credit may precipitate a debt crisis.

Fourth, the IMF can play a very important role in helping to manage international credit risk. It can help countries with serious balance-of-payments problems to develop policies that will enable them to find their way back to the private credit markets. But probably more important than that, the Fund can help the markets by providing essential data and information necessary for the market to assess credit risk and to make sound loans. The Fund should improve its data in areas essential for banks to assess country risk such as government budgets, real exchange rates, real interest rates, and short-term debt, including intercompany debt. After all, the private markets have provided and will continue to provide the market with information to help it make better judgments to the benefit of borrowers and lenders alike.

Perspective: Managing country risk for a manufacturing corporation

JOHN T. REID

Any analysis of the management of risk, be it personal risk or business risk, fire, flood, famine – or even country risk – can be of only academic interest without affirmative answers to the following questions:

> Will such analysis allow predictions concerning the future?
> Will such predictions be sufficiently credible, accurate, and time specific (and different from conventional wisdom) to stimulate decision makers to take actions to avoid these risks?
> Are there any such actions that can be taken in a cost-efficient manner?

From the point of view of a direct foreign investor, operating a manufacturing/marketing business in a market, it can be advanced, as at least one credible thesis that:

> Country risk is not significantly different in kind from any other home market business risk.
> Meaningful country-risk-oriented decisions can only be made at time of initial investment or subsequent major investment or divestment decision points.
> Such investors probably operate with far fewer degrees of operational freedom to minimize country risk (again, once they are fully operational) than is generally supposed.

Against this background, it would not be surprising if at least some of us in the corporate world were tempted to answer in a generally reserved vein to the foregoing three questions, when they are posed in connection with country risk analyses and the management of such risk.

Although the chapters by Eaton and Gersovitz, Shubik, and Dunn have offered much that is interesting, much that is entertaining, and much that seems obvious once stated, it must be questioned whether they – and the burgeoning industry of country risk analysis that has sprung up in the recent years – have added much that is truly actionable for the already committed foreign direct investor. It is from the perspective of the concrete-in-the-ground, ongoing, operational today and tomorrow, often unglamorous, but finally necessary, commercial enterprise that the preceding and following comments are offered.

That perspective is important. Other chapters have wisely differentiated between the "actors" in the country risk equation and at other points noted differences in leverage between investors and the country. Different types of investors have different leverages and exposures, not only between themselves but also at different times in the lives of their investments. We can consider a list from bankers and suppliers of various financial services, through contractors, importers, and exporters, to extractive industries and other direct foreign investors. The flexibility to leave ("ability to flee," as Shubik puts it) decreases, and the commitment to stay, and (necessarily) ride out the storms of actual occurrences and impacts of risks, increases down the list. In part, this is due to the threat of retaliation from the world banking community if one of its own is violated versus the minimal backup accorded a single industrial corporation. In part, it is due to the obvious liquidity, flexibility, and mobility of financial versus "real" assets. And in part, it is due to the recognition of the balance of need between country and foreign investor in bidding for the service and requiring and wanting recompense and growth in such recompense for those services. That balance can change as a country develops its own expertise, as its policies change to allow competition against its own expertise, or as its overall economic policies change. Different leverages between host country and foreign investors, therefore, will change with time.

Time will also have differential effects on different "actors," depending on the presumed length of time for which the investment will be exposed. A bank loan will have a finite period to repayment. An export item is for a fixed period of outstandings. Contractors will reckon their transformation period and risk exposure when they attempt to lock in their contract price – and risk. An extractive industry is obviously location bound and immobile and may have leverage in time only so long as it commands technology or marketing outlets. Manufacturers–marketers, also, are in for the long term, and this perspective affects all their decisions and their abilities to react to, or plan for, risk. It also sets them apart from many of the others on the list of foreign investors. Decision-making executives for a foreign-invested manufacturing and marketing operation are in, or contemplate entering, a market for one reason, that is, to achieve potential sales and profits in that market. True, they always have the option, at a cost, to withdraw from the market. But if they do withdraw, they have given up on that piece of business, and on its growth, which had been in their long-term growth plan. They also have the option, at a lesser and "only" opportunity cost, of reducing their future investment plans and cutting their current operations and exposure, hoping for better times in the future. As a prime alternative, however, they also have the option of trying to make the best utilization of whatever resources they have already committed, of improving their performance and developing their franchise, and of strengthening their current base in order to weather whatever risks may eventuate.

It must be recognized, however, that their abilities to so utilize their resources in the face of country (business) risks are not unlimited. Basic business fundamentals suggest that inventories and receivables should always be as low as possible; in uncertain times they will not be adding extra personnel or approving new spending programs, and they will always be pursuing cost improvement programs. They must, however, also carry out the plans of action to achieve their planned profits and growth. What magical strategies then, what actionable events, are truly available that can be turned on and off at will? Very few!

The probability of being able to successfully predict all major risks, especially along with their timing, is small. The possibility of being able to divest ahead of them is low. The chance of being able to predict, to divest, and then to reenter and reinvest is likely to be minimal. Even where such in-and-out possibilities are actuals, such as in the stock market, history suggests few consistent winners. Long-term trends, however, can be assessed and predicted; long-term directions can be estimated. An assessment of future trends of a host government's policies, for instance, will be most important in deciding whether to invest in a country or not. But once the investment is made, those same trends must be consigned to the potentially serious, probably not urgent (because timing of impact is not predictable), and ultimately nonactionable areas of concern. Once investment is made the leverage is weighted to the host country. Once commitment is contracted, the focus shifts to operational tactics and skills and, except for the degree of future investment or a cataclysmic divestment, shifts away from investment determination. Theoretically, all investments are reversible (at a cost) at all times. In fact, however, most investments in operating assets are made to be continued and can be protected against risk within only rather narrow bounds.

Thus, the foreign direct investor, once the investment is committed and the concrete is poured, is at the whimsy of the foreign power – the sovereign government – and its leverage and degrees of freedom to operate may be severely limited. For, as noted elsewhere in this volume, the government is sovereign. Much as the halls of international conferences may ring with the excoriation of the "all powerful MNCs who are raping the [particularly LDC] foreign markets," the reality in the marketplace – which is, after all, where production and economic growth will take place, rather than in those conferences – is that international trade takes place on the basis of a wager or, more properly, an equation, between host country and MNC. The host country wagers it will gain more than it loses by allowing foreigners in (by "selling" access to its market in the case of manufacturing and marketing operations) and the MNCs or other foreign agents wager that they will produce gains in excess of the costs, difficulties, regulations, duties, taxes, and "risk" that operating in such markets will entail (i.e., the costs of "buying" access into the market). The big wild card for the MNC is the assumption that the sovereign government will not exercise its power to alter the rules of the wager, that is, will not unilaterally alter the structure of the macroeconomic environment.

There is, however, another big and obvious difference: Results achieved from the MNCs operations will be accounted for in foreign exchange, with effects both on continuing operations (translations at new exchange rates) and one-time balance sheet impacts. Yet many of the very government-induced changes in economic structure that can introduce risk to operations will, themselves, also produce changes in the relative foreign exchange rates. There is the potential for a "double whammy." Thus, in considering the management of country risk we see that we must focus on the government-induced changes in the environment and their effects on business operations and on their effects on its measurement in foreign exchange – the unit important to the investor. We come back, therefore, to the rather obvious, but intrinsic difference between investing in a home market and a foreign one, namely, the possible effects of exogenous actions by a sovereign government.

And those actions will be based, as expounded on at length in the chapter by Dunn (this volume) on all the social, cultural, economic (and precursor political) chance and pure personal leader factors that have shaped those governments. They will also be based on the current pressures, including the impact of strong local competitors whose claims may be strong on current politicians even when their isolationist aims may be antithetical to the country's aims of economic growth or of social equity in participation in such growth.

The actors are defined. Timings and different leverages of their actions are noted, government's sovereignty underlined, and foreign exchange introduced. But what, really, is the risk that might ensue from operation in foreign countries? Here we must pause, if belatedly, to define the risk we intend to manage. If risk can be defined as a deviation from expectations, then managing such risks must focus on avoiding, minimizing, or insuring against such deviations. But if country risks are the direct result of sovereign country government actions, or inactions when things get out of hand, then the only time at which a manufacturing and marketing MNC might hope to affect those risks would be at the initiation of the investment. Some concessions might then be obtained, some laws interpreted, and some guarantees obtained or perhaps some promises of stability. Or, ultimately, a negative decision – that is, to not invest – might be made. But governments fall, contracts are broken, the rule of law is somewhat less than universal and, as Shubik notes (this volume), the rule of international law is rather thin. Expectations may not be achieved. Predictions may fall short. Risks are actualized.

But is this different in kind, or only in degree, from "guarantees" of a risk-free macroenvironment in a home market? Surely not! Indeed, in the summer of 1980, which country risk analysts for non–U.S. companies, let alone U.S. commentators within their own market, would have predicted Ronald Reagan to win the presidency and would have predicted the GOP to win the Senate? Further, even if they had, which such analysts would have predicted the initial sweep of both houses to produce the planned deficit of such proportions, the lowered inflation, increased unemployment, lowered industrial production, fluctuating, but high-level interest rates and the so-strong dollar? And, if those predictions could not be made, and if it is accepted that Reaganomics represented a massive, discrete shift in the direction of social and economic policy, why then classify *foreign* country risk as different and special? The risk of nonprediction and the risk of being faced with the fait accompli surely seems to be no different in kind in foreign countries from the one faced in the U.S. macroeconomic structure in this case. Further, to emphasize the point even more, what contingency plans did most U.S. companies have available to accommodate the massive change? What different methods of operation, what new strategies did they employ to avoid the high interest costs? The low demand? Businesspeople are not helpless, but we should not pretend that they have the foreknowledge of such shifts and risks, even in their own markets, or the ability to make massive use of such information even if they did.

Insurance is the classic answer to risk. Some foreign exchange risks can be insured or minimized by hedging. The costs are certain, the risks are reduced. For many companies, however, a better insurance is simply the wide spread of their operations through several countries, with several currencies and, just as important, several different basic economies and factors affecting those economies. Although a worldwide recession is possible, a company with operations in several markets is more likely to show some successes to offset cataclysmic losses. A Mexican devaluation is difficult to recover from quickly if Mexico is the only foreign location; it can be more easily adjusted to if earnings from other major countries continue to flow. Spotting of low-risk, high-reward countries can be, and is, practiced. Some companies will invest in only the most creditworthy and high-potential markets. Others require higher hurdle rates of ROI before investing in less desirable locations. In deciding whether to invest or not, all of these strategies seem wise.

How can the direct foreign investor manage international risk? Greater knowledge, wisely applied, must help; but, as noted, there remains much business risk in the U.S. or home market, from a change in the sovereign government, and no amount of analysis of social, political, or tribal lore will eliminate that. Total avoidance of overseas investment will avoid country risk; it will also limit market potential and growth. Selective avoidance of the riskiest, that is, the most unpredictable, markets can be easily practiced; a spread of investment in several countries will provide a useful insurance, spreading the risk of a calamity in one over the potential successes in others.

The major skills, preinvestment, come in balancing the risk–reward ratio, in choosing markets of greatest size and potential, and investing accordingly. The greatest skills postinvestment, however, are little different from home-market skills, that is, a continual focus on business fundamentals within the overall business strategy. Thus, no matter the corporate objective, it will be greatly aided by financial controls, by focus on inventories and receivables, by treasury decisions on financing, and by planning focus on strengths, weaknesses, opportunities, and problems. The major differences in international operations are the multiplications of significant factors in the external environment and the fact that the unit of exchange is likely to show even more fluctuation in value than the home currency. (And we must acknowledge that inflation has caused significant changes in the value of that home currency.) Operating overseas *is* different from operating in only a home market, but it is not different in *kind* for many industries that truly operate, manufacture, and sell in the foreign market. It is only different in *degree*.

In answering the three initial questions, this perspective offers no panacea. Will analysis allow predictions? Possibly, but it will offer no certainties and little aid in timings. Will the predictions be actionable? Possibly, but mainly before an investment is made; trends are interesting, but they do not often constitute actionable impacts for ongoing business. Are there any actions available to be taken? Maybe, but once the investment has been made and most leverage lost, a company's main strategic thrusts of risk avoidance can only be along tried and true focus on business fundamentals, which should be followed in any case.

Is this to be entirely negative? Certainly not. There is a risk in getting out of bed every morning. There is a business risk in a child's lemonade stand. There are certainly risks in operating an international business, but there are also rewards. A wise businessperson can and does strike a balance in their pursuit.

CHAPTER 5

Organizational and institutional responses to international risk

RAYMOND VERNON

My mandate is to deal with the organizational and institutional responses that foreign direct investors have developed in their efforts to deal with international risk. The boundaries of that mandate are not very sharp.

One problem in drawing the boundaries is to define an institutional response. By implication, some responses to risk exist that are thought to be separable from institutions; I have had some difficulty in picturing what those responses may be. I hope I shall be forgiven therefore if, from time to time, this discussion wanders beyond the organizational and institutional dimensions into areas that some would regard as economics.

A second problem in drawing the boundaries of this chapter has been to decide which of the many different types of international risk could usefully be addressed. In one respect, the decision on boundaries is easy. This chapter is concerned both with the risks that arise from the investor's ignorance and with the risks that arise from random error. In other respects, however, the boundaries are less easily drawn. Direct investment internalizes a set of international transactions that otherwise would be conducted at arm's length with independent buyers or sellers, and one major purpose of this internalization is to avoid some of the risks that exist when dealing with such independent parties. Accordingly, a direct investment commonly represents a response to certain kinds of international risk. An exploration of this phenomenon seems almost indispensable as a preliminary for exploring the responses to the risks associated with the direct investment itself.

This paper profited considerably from the reactions of Brain Levy and L. T. Wells, Jr. to an earlier draft. Stephen Baral and Jack Dulberger assisted in the research.

Direct investment as a response to risk

The desire of managers to internalize certain transactions as a way of avoiding risk is a phenomenon that is encountered in domestic as well as international settings, occurring most commonly when the number of firms in the market is small, when the surrounding environment is uncertain, and when the representations or commitments of the parties concerned are difficult to verify or enforce.[1] Nevertheless, numerous writers have observed that the internalization of certain transactions is likely to be especially important as a risk-reducing measure when the transactions straddle national boundaries (Caves 1973, p. 117, Buckley and Casson 1976, pp. 33–59, Casson 1979, pp. 45–62).

Establishing the foreign subsidiary

The drive for internalization, it is generally agreed, stems from the firm's view that there is some marked imperfection in the market for the product or service concerned, a view that stimulates the firm to create its own internal market and to accept the narrowing of choice that is commonly involved in that decision. Two types of industry in which such internalization is particularly common are the exploitation and processing of oil and minerals and the development and application of advanced technologies. Not surprisingly, therefore, these industries prove to be heavily overrepresented among foreign direct investors (Vernon 1971, pp. 4–17, United Nations 1978, pp. 45–6).

In the case of raw materials, large indivisible costs and high barriers to entry keep the numbers small. The entry barriers are created in part by the difficulties of achieving agreements with host countries on the terms of entry and in part by the size of the capital commitment needed to finance the extensive developmental work and infrastructure that go with the launching of large raw material projects.[2] Meanwhile, the dispersed location of overseas operations and the tenuous

---

[1] See Williamson (1975, pp. 82–131), Bernhardt (1977, pp. 213, 215), Porter (1980, pp. 306–7), and Scherer (1980, pp. 78, 89–91, 302–4). For a survey of recent literature on the incentives for vertical integration, see Kaserman (1978, pp. 483–510); also Jensen, Kehrberg, and Thomas (1962, pp. 378–9, 384).

[2] On the economics of backward integration in the raw materials industries, see for instance, Gort (1962, ch. 6) and Teece (1976, pp. 105, 115–18).

links among the participating parties create uncertainties and hamper fact finding to a degree that is especially acute.[3]

The entry barriers that are typical in the technologically advanced industries are of a different kind, but are commonly no less formidable. They are created by the fact that a considerable expenditure of money and time is commonly required while firms accumulate the necessary knowledge, skills, and reputation that may be necessary for the effective marketing of the product. Like the raw material industries, too, the high-technology firms typically incur developmental costs in the launching of new businesses that are relatively high when compared with the actual costs of production (Freeman 1974, p. 126, Hochmuth 1974, pp. 145–69, Brock 1975, pp. 27–41, 57, Measday 1977, pp. 266–8, Parker 1978, pp. 112–19). After beginning production, individual firms characteristically experience a persistent decline in production costs that appears to be a function of their accumulated production, a fact that represents an added deterrent for newcomers (Hartley 1965, pp. 122–8, Abernathy and Wayne, 1974, pp. 74–141, Conley 1981).

Both the firms in the raw materials industries and those in the high technology industries, then, begin with large sunk costs on which they hope for a return. The importance of reducing uncertainties in industries that have such a cost structure has been sufficiently explored. Firms in such industries place more than the usual stress on avoiding variations in output, inasmuch as small variations in output can generate disproportionate swings in their return on investment. But there are some differences in the two types of industry as well.

In the raw materials industries, the firm's problem of securing a stable return on its sunk commitments is exacerbated by the fact that a relatively high proportion of its operating costs is also fixed. Variations in output generate disproportionate fluctuations in net profits. Accordingly, a persistent objective in the strategy of firms in these industries has been to find ways of stabilizing the demand for their output and to safeguard themselves against interruptions in the supply of needed materials.

---

[3] For descriptions of the international oil industry, especially in relation to the issue of vertical integration, see Adelman (1972, pp. 318–19), Cooper and Gaskel (1976, pp. 72–4, 188), Teece (1976, pp. 83–9, 116–17), Mansvelt Beck and Wiig (1977), and Levy (1982). For the nonferrous metals, Charles River Associates, Inc. (1970, pp. 51–7), Bosson and Varon (1977, pp. 46–7), Duke et al. (1977), Banks (1979, pp. 21, 27, 45), Mikesell (1979a, pp. 108–9), and Goohs (1980).

On the demand side, of course, the price elasticities of aggregate demand for an industrial raw material such as iron ore or crude oil are typically fairly low, especially in the short run. Individual firms, however, face a demand curve that is considerably more elastic than that of the industry as a whole, so that the risk of losing customers in a declining market can be fairly substantial. Insurance, in this case, takes the form of acquiring tied customers who do not have the option to shift their sources of supply.

On the supply side, the integrating imperative is just as obvious. Because of high barriers to entry, the suppliers are usually limited in number. For the processor that does not control its own source of supply, any large increase in price or outright interruption in supply, whatever its cause, can be dangerous. But a particularly disastrous type of price increase or supply interruption is one initiated by a supplier that also controls processing facilities downstream, that is, a supplier that is also a competitor in the processor's market.[4] In that case, the supplier may be found taking over the customers of its unintegrated rival.

Events in the oil industry over the past decade have provided occasional illustrations of such a risk turned into reality. At various times during the 1970s, as multinational sellers were faced with reduced supplies of crude oil, they cut off practially all of the unintegrated processors that they had previously supplied, while continuing to supply their own downstream processing facilities and distributors (Commission of the European Communities 1975, pp. 144–5, OECD 1977a, pp. 23, 25, Levy 1982).

Nevertheless, the fact that such risks exist in the oligopolistic industries that process raw materials does not mean the risks always lead to vertical integration. Such integration has a cost. It requires an investment of capital, which has to be justified in terms of expected yield or an equivalent reduction in risk. Moreover, the capital investment entails risks of its own, which may outweigh the risk-reducing aspects of the investment. Besides, the flexibility of the integrated units is reduced as compared with unintegrated competitors; in times of easy supply, the integrated entity is inhibited from turning to cheaper sources of supply and in times of tight supply is restrained from abandoning its captive markets for markets in which profit margins are higher.

Why then is vertical integration so pervasive in the raw material

---

[4] For a basic statement of this problem, see Caves (1977, pp. 43–5), Porter (1980, pp. 308, 317), and Scherer (1980, pp. 90–1).

industries? The strong tendency toward vertical integration seems to derive from the fact that, in an industry that is only partially integrated, there are always some participants who see themselves especially exposed by that fact; as long as a partial state of integration exists in the industry, a new move toward vertical integration on the part of any firm withdraws a source of supply or a potential customer from the market and thereby increases the perceived risks of those that remain unintegrated. Accordingly, any movement toward integration seems likely to snowball, until all the actors have rendered themselves equally invulnerable by integration.[5] If the markets concerned are global in scope – a situation that clearly exists for oil and aluminum and exists in part for copper and steel – the interactions between the firms will also be global in their reach.

The high-technology industries, as I have already suggested, face a set of risks that differs somewhat from the raw material industries. The challenge to the raw materials industries is to secure a firm link to supplies and markets, a challenge to which it commonly responds with vertical integration. The challenge to the high-technology firm is to secure a reliable return on its unique skills or knowledge. Unlike firms in the raw materials industries, however, those in the high-technology industries rarely exhaust the static and dynamic scale economies that can be exploited at any given production site, so that the costs of setting up another production point can sometimes be fairly high; besides, the relative unimportance of freight costs usually reduces the advantages of creating multiple production sites (Vernon 1977, p. 51). In addition, some high-technology firms such as those in the aircraft industry have been influenced in part by a desire to stay close to the military authorities in their own country, in order to avoid questions of divided loyalty or of security.

Nevertheless, risk-reducing considerations have pushed the firms in high-technology industries to set up overseas subsidiaries for a portion of their foreign business. The most obvious risk leading to direct investment has been that, as the technological edge of the firm is eaten away, foreign countries may begin to bar their products in favor of producers on their own soil.[6] Faced with that risk, firms in

5 For an effort to demonstrate in theoretical terms that equilibrium exists only at the extremes of full integration or full nonintegration, see Green (1974).

6 On "buy-at-home" policies as a nontariff barrier to international trade, see Curtis and Vastine (1971, pp. 202–4), and Cline, Kawarabe, Kronojo, and Williams (1978, pp. 189–94). On the attempts of European governments

high-technology industries have commonly chosen the subsidiary alternative.[7]

But that response, as a rule, has not put an end to the risks to which the firms in high-technology industries have been exposed. The first move of such firms into foreign production sites has usually been limited, consisting of a facility designed to serve the local market. Countries with bargaining power, however, have sometimes obliged foreign firms to develop a more substantive response. In such cases, some firms have responded by establishing a world-scale plant in an important foreign market and shipping some of the output to other countries. That response has been particularly strong in the automobile industry, generating a shift in the location of production facilities, including a shift from the facilities at home; this development is very likely increasing the international flow of components and automobiles (Jenkins 1977, pp. 213–16, Bennett and Sharpe 1979, pp. 177–82, Frank 1980, pp. 102–5).

Once again, therefore, the avoidance of risk has contributed to the growth of foreign direct investment, as enterprises have shuffled their production facilities among countries in an effort to protect their access to the markets that otherwise might be denied to them.

Follow the leader

What the discussion suggests so far is that the foreign direct investment of any firm may represent a response to threats of various kinds. One such risk is that competitors may imperil the foreigner's access to a raw material or a market by making investments of their own. That response, as it turns out, follows some predictable patterns.

Consider a world market, such as the market for nickel or aluminum, dominated by half a dozen leading firms, each capable of observing the main moves of the others. The price elasticity of aggregate

---

to set up and protect national champions in the aerospace and computer industries, see Hochmuth (1974, pp. 145–70) and Jéquier (1974, pp. 195–255). On the restrictions of developing countries, see Robinson (1976, pp. 169–238).

[7] For a discussion of the factors in high-technology industries, such as computers, tending toward vertical integration, see Katz and Philipps (in press). An econometric demonstration that firms in high-technology industries favor subsidiaries over independent licensees to a greater degree than in other industries is presented in Davidson and McFetridge (1981); the analysis is based on data presented in Vernon and Davidson (1979).

demand for the final product, the processed metal, is low; the marginal cost of production in relation to full cost is also low. The challenge for the industry, therefore, is to ensure that no participating producer upsets the existing equilibrium by cutting its prices and enlarging its market share. If that should happen, there is a risk that other producers will also be obliged to cut their prices, thereby reducing the rent for the industry as a whole.

Now assume that in those circumstances, one of the participants, troubled by the risk of being cut off from its existing sources, nevertheless undertakes the development of some new mining properties in a remote corner of the world where no such mining had previously taken place. In circumstances of that sort, history suggests that the other members of the oligopoly are unlikely to be totally ignorant of the geological characteristics of the new areas. In the typical case, they will have some information based on local folklore, observation of outcroppings, or even systematic borings. But the information will be grossly incomplete, thus placing a heavy discount on the value of the most likely estimate. What is the optimum response of the other members of the oligopoly?

Consider the nature of the risk that the others face. The quality of the initiating firm's information is not clear; it may be good or bad. If bad, it may burden the firm with a cost that will have to be absorbed in the rent generated by its other operations. But if good, it may eventually arm the leader with a source of ore whose low cost or strategic geographical location poses a threat to the stability of the oligopoly. If other members of the oligopoly are risk avoiders, they will want to learn about the new location as rapidly as possible. If the acquisition and processing of information take time, the firm that is slow to respond faces the risk of being preempted by the hastier action of a rival firm. Accordingly, the risk avoiders are likely to turn their limited facilities for information-gathering to an examination of the new location, even if that means curtailing their search in other directions.[8] Indeed, some firms may want to commit themselves to the new territories even without all the requisite information. The propensity to move will be enhanced by the expectation that if a sufficient number of members of the oligopoly make a similar move

[8] See, for instance, Cyert and March (1963, ch. 6) and Cyert, Dill, and March (1970, pp. 87–8, 94–5, 107). The effort going into search can be considered a significant investment by the firm, as discussed generally in Arrow (1974, pp. 39–43).

and if all of them eventually prove mistaken, the oligopoly will pass on part of the cost of the error to buyers in the form of higher prices. Hence, the follow-the-leader pattern.

On similar lines, risk-avoiding members of an oligopolistically structured industry will be expected to pursue one another into any substantial foreign market in which one of them has set up a producing subsidiary. In this case, the risk of preemption will be particularly great, inasmuch as the first entrant can be expected to urge the government to impose restrictions on any further imports and to limit the number of foreign producers allowed to set up production facilities in the country. The followers may possess little knowledge about the market's potential; projections about future demand may be inescapably subject to large error, but if the number of possible entrants is limited and if the aggregate demand for the product is thought to be inelastic, the followers can contemplate the possibility of cutting their collective losses by raising the prices.[9]

The urge of members in a tight oligopoly to maintain their relative positions in the industry, even if it entails some risky investments, stems in part from their desire to avoid what they perceive as an even greater risk. There is a common conviction among enterprises in oligopolistic industries that the enterprise is in special danger when its cash flow is diminishing in relation to that of its rivals. Behind that fear lie some strong assumptions about the efficiency of the capital markets. Internal capital is usually thought to be much cheaper than external capital; indeed, external capital is commonly viewed as a scarce, rationed commodity. (See Stigler 1967, pp. 287–92, Eiteman and Stonehill 1979, pp. 346–75. See also the various essays in Heslop 1977.) If oligopolists must match the moves of their rivals in order to maintain equilibrium, those with a reduced cash flow may therefore find themselves out of the competitive running. Worries such as these led a Ford executive to say:

If we don't spend the money, our products will not be competitive. We will not get 25 percent. We will get 20 percent. And if you fall back and take two or three years to recover, soon it will be 20 percent, then 18 percent. Then you can't spend money fast enough to catch up again (*New York Times* December 4, 1975, pp. 1, 9).

[9] The perceptions of prospective lenders in such oligopolistic situations are described in Stiglitz and Weiss (1981, pp. 393–411). These perceptions tend to favor follow-the-leader investors by increasing their ability to borrow.

Although the quotation goes back to 1975, it suggests a certain pre-science regarding the conditions that would prevail in the automobile industry six years later.

The recognition that enterprises tend to move in unison in their foreign direct investments is hardly new, having been advanced as a behavioral proposition at least a quarter of a century ago (e.g., Barlow and Wender 1955, pp. 146, 149). In manufacturing, the evidence is quite extensive and systematic.[10] Now and then, the pattern is so pronounced that it pervades an industry. Outstanding examples have been the wave of investment in semiconductor and microcircuit production in Southeast Asia during the 1960s and the leapfrog patterns of investment among the soap companies and the soft drink companies in Latin America during the same period.

In the raw materials industry, the available data are only impressionistic, but cumulatively they carry some weight. In oil, a surge of investment in the years before the 1930s carried the leading British and American oil companies to the lands surrounding the Gulf of Mexico, from Venezuela to Texas. In the two decades after World War II, another surge of investment greatly expanded oil investments in the countries surrounding the Persian Gulf. Similar waves of investment were to be seen in metallic ores: bauxite investments in the Caribbean area from 1950 to 1965; copper investments in Chile from 1947 to 1958, and in Peru from 1955 to 1960; and iron ore in Venezuela from 1946 to 1960, and in Liberia from 1960 to 1965.

The fact that rival members of an oligopoly tend to move together into a new geographical area, of course, does not conclusively demonstrate that a follow-the-leader pattern exists. A rival possibility, not to be dismissed, is that all of them have been stirred to action by a common stimulus: by the pacification of a hitherto unsafe area, by the appearance of a new consumer market, or by some other such factor. But the empirical evidence is fairly strong for concluding that the follow-the-leader factor is important.

Some of the most obvious illustrations of linked behavior are found in the occasional agreements in the raw material industries under which rivals have explicitly given up the right to act independently. The red-line agreement of 1928 among the world's leading oil companies was one such case. This agreement covered a large portion of the Middle East and remained in force for a decade or two; under its terms, each enterprise undertook not to develop any new fields in the

---

10 The leading work on this point is Knickerbocker (1973). See also Aharoni (1966, pp. 55, 65–6) and Gray (1972, pp. 77, 96–8).

indicated territories except in partnership with the others (see U.S. Federal Trade Commission 1952, pp. 65–7, Jacoby 1974, pp. 29–30, 34–6).

In a very different time and place, other strong illustrations appear of the importance of linkage among members of an oligopoly, albeit not in the form of agreements or consortia. In many markets of the developing world during the 1960s, the leading automobile companies scrambled with one another to set up producing facilities. In at least two cases, that of Argentina and South Africa, the number of firms prepared to enter the scramble and the amount of capacity they were prepared to put in place were so far in excess of prospective market demand as to suggest strongly that some of the investors were reacting to the decisions of the others (Baranson 1969, pp. 46–7, 53, Sundelson 1970, pp. 243, 246–9, and Jenkins 1977, pp. 39–42, 56–8). The seemingly nonrational behavior of the firms could be explained in a number of ways. The explanation I find most plausible, however, is that they were driven by a desire to hold down risk, defining that risk in the terms suggested earlier.

More systematic evidence that the follow-the-leader phenomenon reflects a risk-reducing reaction on the part of the participants in an oligopolistic industry is found in the Knickerbocker study mentioned earlier (1973, pp. 111–44). Knickerbocker found that the degree of the parallel behavior of U.S. firms in any industry was positively correlated with the degree of concentration in that industry – but only up to a point. The strongest patterns of parallel behavior were found in industries in which three or four near-equal firms were the leaders; in industries with an even higher concentration – say, one or two dominant firms, surrounded by a fringe of lesser enterprises – parallel behavior was not as strong. Knickerbocker also found that parallel behavior was a little less pronounced in firms with a relatively high level of technological inputs, where product differentiation was important, than in those with lower technological content. These added bits of information contribute marginally to the credibility of the follow-the-leader hypothesis as a factor in explaining foreign direct investment patterns.

The exchange of threats

Researchers also claim to see risk-reducing objectives in other seemingly imitative investments of the multinational enterprises. It has repeatedly been observed, for instance, that the U.S.-based industries that were generating the highest rates of foreign direct investments in

Europe were much the same as the European industries that more or less simultaneously were investing in the United States (Hymer and Rowthorn 1970, pp. 80–2). One explanation for this behavior is provided by the so-called exchange-of-threat hypothesis. Threatened by the establishment of a foreign-owned subsidiary in their home market, the response of the leading firms in that market is to set up subsidiaries in the invader's home market. This cross-investment conveys a warning to the invading firm that any excessively energetic efforts to compete in the foreign market may be countered by similar efforts in the home market of the invader.[11]

The two-way flows of foreign direct investment in the same set of industries, moreover, may serve to reduce a somewhat different kind of risk, namely, the risk of lagging behind in the global technological race. In many oligopolistic industries, a limited number of multinational enterprises encounter each other in competition in many different national markets. In the computer mainframe industry, IBM, Fujitsu, and Siemens are world competitors; in chemicals, ICI, Dupont, and Rhone-Poulenc cross paths in international markets; and so on. Most multinational enterprises, however, do the bulk of their research and development within their home market (Samuelsson 1974, Ronstadt 1977, pp. xiii–xiv, 2, Lall 1980, pp. 102, 119–20); and, most of these enterprises are greatly influenced by the conditions of the home market as they develop the niche that differentiates their products and processes (Davidson 1976, pp. 207, 216, Franko 1976, pp. 27–44). The U.S. stress on labor-saving, mass-produced products, for instance, was traditionally based on the high cost of labor and the absolute scarcity of artisan skills (see Habakkuk 1962, ch. 3 and 4, Rosenberg 1976, ch. 1 and 3; also Rosenberg 1969, pp. 17–18).

One risk for multinational enterprises in industries with rapid innovational change is that their rivals in other countries, exposed to different conditions in their home markets, may develop a technological lead that will eventually prove threatening elsewhere. American automobile manufacturers, for instance, were eventually threatened by the Japanese mastery of small fuel-saving automobiles, a capability that the Japanese originally developed largely in response to the special needs of their own market. Aware of the risk of falling behind,

---

[11] Koninklijke Nederlandsche Petroleum Maatschappij (1950, p. 18), *Forbes* (1964, pp. 40–1), Graham (1974, pp. 33–4, 75), Michalet and Delapierre (1975, p. 44). But rival explanations are also offered to explain the cross investment phenomenon; see, for instance, Franko (1976, pp. 166–72).

some multinational enterprises have maintained a constant sur-
veillance over their rivals in other countries and have sought licenses
for foreign technology whenever they felt the need (Abegglen 1970,
pp. 117–28, and Ozawa 1974, pp. 52–6, 67–80). But some have preferred to acquire subsidiaries as a technological listening post in the
territory of their rivals (Franko 1971, pp. 8, 14–15, 23, Michalet and
Delapierre 1975; see also Vernon 1980, pp. 150, 153–4, and *Business
Week* 1980, pp. 55, 59, 121). When that has occurred, the multina-
tionalizing process has been the firm's response to a risk generated by
the action of its competitors.

Joint ventures as risk reducers

Once a firm has determined that an international investment may be
desirable as a means of reducing risk, it is still faced at times with the
possibility of going it alone or investing in partnership with others.
The choice among the various alternatives is commonly affected by
questions of risk. But once again, the risks to be avoided are of various
kinds.

Consortia of foreigners

For reasons already discussed, firms in the raw material industries
typically place a high premium on reducing the risks of the unforeseen, such as wars, strikes, and earthquakes. But in operations in
which scale economies are large, such diversification can be costly,
especially on the part of the smaller firms in the oligopoly. The solution is for such firms to multiply their sources by joining others in a
number of consortia. (For aluminum, the subject is fully explored in
Stuckey 1981.) That response has had the effect of producing various
consortia composed of firms engaged in the common exploitation of a
raw material in a country that is foreign to all of them.

Consortia of this sort in raw materials industries, however, also
respond to another risk that has already been noted: the risk that a
rival firm might be in a position to upset the stability of an oligopoly
by securing its materials at an especially advantageous cost. This second motive is, of course, difficult to distinguish from the first.

Some consortia in the raw materials industries, however, are
formed with still a third group of risks in mind, namely, the category
that is usually described as political risk. In practice, political risk can
be of many different types. It can arise because of a host country's
hostility to some specific foreign country and its nationals; or because

of a host country's hostility to foreigners in general, irrespective of nationality; or because of a host country's efforts, without hostility to any foreigners in particular or in general, to improve an existing bargain.[12]

Whatever the variety of political risk may be, a consortium composed of foreigners of different nationalities is ordinarily seen as reducing the risk. If the risk to be reduced is a host country's hostility to one country, the consortium can be seen as diluting the exposure of any firm that is based in that country. If the risk is a deterioration in the position of foreigners in general, without regard to any particular country, the consortium can be seen as a counterforce that may be able to enlist the support of a number of different governments.

Although consortia among foreigners also are to be found in the manufacturing industries, especially those that require large-scale and heavy investment, such consortia are relatively uncommon. Occasionally, consortia of this type are imposed on the manufacturing firms by host governments. Foreign automobile producers in Peru and Mexico, for instance, have been compelled to merge their production activities in order to reduce the number of automobile types in the country and to achieve some obvious economies of scale.[13] But the reduction of risk is also a factor in such consortia.

One reason why consortia among foreign firms are less common in manufacturing than in mining or oil production is that manufacturing firms generally have better ways of diversifying their portfolios of direct investment. Although some foreign-owned manufacturing subsidiaries produce goods for export from the countries in which they are located, most market the bulk of their production within the host country (Vaupel and Curhan, 1973, pp. 376–7, Curhan, Davidson, and Suri 1977, pp. 392–3, 398–9, Tables 7.2.1 and 7.2.6, U.S. Department of Commerce 1977, pp. 318–19, Tables III.H.1 and III.H.2). Firms in manufacturing, therefore, can often diversify their market risks by setting up subsidiaries in a number of different countries, relying on transportation costs or protective devices in each market to buffer them from outside competitors. Firms engaged in

[12] For illustrations, see Moran (1974, pp. 110–36), Thunell (1977, p. 99), Krasner (1978, p. 117), Radetzki and Zorn (1980, p. 186); also Zorn (1980, pp. 225–6).

[13] Pressures of this sort are usually applied informally by administrative means and so are difficult to document. But see Turner (1973, p. 101). For data on the trend to greater concentration of automobile producers in Latin American countries, see Jenkins (1977, pp. 145–50).

extractive activities, however, typically sell their products in world markets, so that high-cost production sites represent a real handicap. With fewer locations from which to choose, the raw materials firms find themselves obliged to turn more often to the consortium possibility in achieving adequate diversification.[14]

Finally, if the factors specified thus far were not enough to explain the lesser use of consortia by manufacturing firms, the nature of their strategies would provide a sufficient explanation. Unlike the raw materials producers, manufacturers commonly build such strategies on product differentiation, building up distinctive trade names and unique services to customers as their route to success. The consortium approach in any market, combining the offerings of rival producers, would be incompatible with a product-differentiating strategy.

Joint ventures with local firms

When manufacturing firms take local partners with an eye to reducing risk, the risk they generally have in mind is political risk. To be sure, multinational enterprises have a number of other reasons for setting up joint ventures with local stockholders. In some cases, they have no choice; host governments lay down and enforce a joint venture requirement (Turner 1973, United Nations 1973, pp. 83–4, Robinson 1976, United Nations Economic and Social Council 1978, pp. 22–3). In other instances, the decision to take a local partner may free the subsidiary of various discriminatory restrictions, such as disqualification from selling to government enterprises or borrowing from local banks. In still other cases, the joint venture may represent the right decision on the part of both partners simply on the basis of the classic choice of a profit-maximizing firm. It may allow both partners to put slack resources to work in a single entity; it may allow each of the partners to earn returns on their investments that were higher than their respective opportunity costs; and it may reduce the risks to the multinational enterprise of securing local distribution channels, while reducing the risks to the local distributor of securing assured supplies (Dubin 1976, pp. 27–43, Radetzki and Zorn 1979, pp. 57–61). The objective of reducing political risk, however, is ordinarily of some importance in such arrangements (see especially Franko 1977, p. 29, Pfeffer and Nowek 1976, p. 332, Caves 1970, pp. 283–302, Hogberg 1977, pp. 6–25, Tomlinson 1970, p. 5).

---

[14] Indicative of the more limited opportunities of the raw materials firms are data in Vernon (1971, pp. 39, 62).

Apart from the direct testimony of businesspeople, the sense that risk reduction must be playing some significant role in the decision to set up joint ventures is supported by a number of studies of the behavioral patterns of the multinational enterprises. Two analyses, when interpreted in tandem, point in that direction. One of these studies offers strong evidence for the view that, as manufacturing firms gain experience in manufacturing in any market, they tend to assign a lower level of risk to that market. The second study concludes that the less experienced the firm, the higher its propensity for entering into joint ventures with local partners.

The first study, linking experience to perceived risk, covered the introduction and subsequent dissemination of 406 new products by fifty-seven large U.S.-based multinational enterprises during the period from 1945–75 (Vernon and Davidson 1979). In the early decades of that period, the firms were slow to establish production units for these products abroad. But the products introduced in the latter decades were produced abroad with much greater alacrity and in many more locations. By breaking down the data by firms and products, the factors that contribute to this trend became more evident. For instance, firms with a high proportion of exports transferred more rapidly and more extensively than those with a low proportion; firms with several different product lines established production sites abroad more rapidly in their principal product lines than in less important lines; firms that had made many prior transfers responded more rapidly than those that had made only a few; and all firms responded more rapidly in countries to which they had made many previous transfers than in countries to which they had made a smaller number.

The study that links experience levels with the propensity to enter into joint ventures consists of an exhaustive analysis of the behavior of the 2,800 foreign manufacturing subsidiaries of 186 U.S.-based multinational enterprises over a fifty-year period. In various ways, the data linked increased foreign experience with a decline in the propensity of the firm to use joint ventures (Stopford and Wells 1972, p. 99).

More suggestive evidence on the connection between risk and joint ventures comes from another direction. It has been commonly observed that for any foreign-owned enterprise the risk of nationalization rises as the firm loses its capacity to offer a scarce resource to the host country, such as technology, capital, or access to foreign markets (Vernon 1971, pp. 46–52, Krasner 1978, pp. 138–42, Jodice 1980, pp. 204–5, Kobrin 1980, pp. 65–88). At the same time, several studies suggest that firms that appear to be in a relatively weak bargaining position in relation to host governments, that is, firms that have little to offer the country, tend to use joint ventures more than firms in a strong bargaining position (Stopford and Wells 1972, pp. 120, 150–6, Fagre and Wells in press).

Most of the studies cited here are less than conclusive, being dogged by difficult problems of multicollinearity and multiple causation. But cumulatively they lend a considerable degree of plausibility to the hypothesis that risk avoidance is a substantial factor in the decision of foreign-owned enterprises to take local partners.

Joint ventures with state-owned enterprises

A special category of joint venture that has grown somewhat in recent years is partnerships between foreign firms and enterprises owned by the state. The oil-processing industries of the oil-exporting countries contain numerous examples of such enterprises (Ghadar 1977, pp. 17–46, Turner and Bedore 1979, pp. 13–36). But they are found in many other industries as well.

The reasons for such arrangements have been fairly well studied.[15] From the viewpoint of foreign partners, many of the reasons for entering into agreements with state-owned enterprises are the same as those that argue for local private partners: freedom from special restrictions, access to local resources, and protection from political risk. Foreign firms generally assume, however, that each of these factors gains a little strength when the partner is a state-owned enterprise. Whether the foreigner actually acquires greater immunity from political risks by entering into partnership with the state, however, seems quite uncertain; when enough experience develops for researchers to explore the question adequately, the likelihood is that a complex answer will emerge.

One difference between partnerships with private local firms and partnerships with the host state lies in the evolution of the local partner's interests over time. In a significant proportion of the joint ventures, the private partnership interest is held by a large number of local stockholders,[16] who commonly have even less power than public stockholders in the United States. In other cases, local stockholdings are more highly concentrated and fewer in number, but many of

[15] The subject is dealt with in Vernon (1979, pp. 7–15) and Aharoni (1981, pp. 184–93).
[16] For detailed data see Vaupel and Curhan (1973, pp. 309–19).

these stockholders, having received their equity interests as a gift, are content to play a passive role and to provide the protective coloration the foreigner has bargained for. Only a fraction of these joint ventures, therefore, represent active partnerships.

Managers of state-owned enterprises, on the other hand, generally find themselves much more actively involved in their partnerships with foreigners. Being exposed to the political process in the home country, state managers are often torn between buffering the foreign partner against political pressures in order to maintain the partnership, or swallowing up the foreign partner's interest in order to demonstrate their national commitment. In the Middle East oil industry, according to one study, those motivations have shifted over time in predictable patterns, ending characteristically in the nationalization of the foreigner's interest (Bradley 1977, pp. 75–83 and Ghadar 1977, pp. 25–7).

To be sure, oil may not prove to be a representative case, especially because of the period covered in existing studies. In other times and other industries, state-owned enterprises may see advantages in clinging to a foreign association, especially if technology or foreign market access is needed. But the recent history of the oil industry does suggest some of the difficult judgments that foreigners have been obliged to make when contemplating the use of joint ventures as insurance against risk.

Other arrangements for avoiding risk

In an effort to reduce some of their various risks, firms have often been pushed to establish foreign subsidiaries, and, in an effort to reduce the risk to their subsidiaries, they have sometimes been compelled to enter into joint ventures. But there have been instances in which no subsidiary, whether joint venture or wholly owned, has seemed able to reduce their risks on balance. Such subsidiaries simply appeared to be substituting one set of risks for another – the risk of expropriation, for instance, for the risk of preemption by a competitor. Faced with such unpalatable alternatives, enterprises have sometimes groped toward some intermediate arrangement hoping to minimize both kinds of risks. These intermediate arrangements have commonly involved long-term contracts of various sorts.

Such contracts have taken a variety of forms. In both raw materials and high-technology industries, some long-term contracts have authorized and obligated foreign firms to exercise managerial functions over extended periods (Bostock and Harvey 1972, Fabrikant 1973,

Smith and Wells 1976, pp. 45–9, Zorn 1980, ch. 12). Some of these arrangements have contemplated cash flows for the foreign firm whose discounted value was not very different from the expected stream generated by an analogous direct investment. In fixing the appropriate discount rate, of course, either stream would have to be recognized as subject to risks of various sorts. But in some of these cases, one would probably have been justified in discounting the anticipated income from fees paid under managerial contracts at lower rates than those applicable to the streams anticipated from foreign direct investments.[17]

Yet long-term contracts simply substitute one set of risks for another. In practice, long-term contracts for the sale of raw materials have often turned out to be nothing much more than a statement of intentions on the part of the parties. Critical elements of the contract, such as prices and quantities, have been subject to repeated renegotiations. In their efforts to reduce uncertainties of this kind, one party or another has sought to introduce various kinds of sanctions. Buyers of raw materials, for instance, have made loans to raw materials producers with provisions for immediate repayment whenever the producers failed to deliver specified quantities, and producers have insisted that buyers must forfeit their rights to interest on such loans whenever the buyers failed to accept specified quantities.

Despite such provisions, large elements of uncertainty have remained. Buyers have been accused of delaying the arrival of their vessels in order to avoid picking up shipments of bulk cargoes; sellers have been accused of stimulating their governments to impose export embargoes in order to avoid delivering their products. Moreover, businesspeople have had reservations about the enforceability of their contracts, especially when enforcement could only be achieved through the use of foreign courts.

For firms in the high-technology industries, long-term contracts have typically taken the form of a licensing agreement with independent producers in foreign countries. Such licenses have normally been written with various restraints. These restraints have sought to ensure that the licensee would not impart the information acquired under the license to an unauthorized third person; that the licensee

---

[17] See, for example, Mikesell (1979b, pp. 52, 56–7). OPEC members' purchases of petroleum management services are generally at a price approaching the return on an equivalent direct foreign investment by the oil companies; see Eiteman and Stonehill (1979, p. 242).

would confine its use of the information to some specified geographical territory; and finally, especially when the licensee was authorized to use the licenser's trademark, that the licensee would produce the product in accordance with some specified standards. Each of these conditions, it is apparent, is aimed at reducing the licenser's risks: the risk of unauthorized appropriation, the risk of competition among license holders, and the risk of impairment of a valued trademark through inadequate quality control.

But long-term licenses, like long-term bulk purchase contracts in the raw materials industries, have had their limitations. Licensers have been aware that licensees can often disregard the contract because the sanctions for violation are notoriously limited. Information that has once been divulged cannot be retrieved; the licensee, therefore, may have little or nothing to fear from losing the licenser's goodwill. On top of that, if the foreign licenser is obliged to pursue its remedies in the home courts of the licensee, court orders directing the licensee to observe the terms of the contract and money damages for breach of contract may prove difficult to obtain.

Apart from the possibility that the courts may not be blind to the foreign nationality of the licenser, there is also the possibility that the underlying legal position of the licenser may be weak. A licenser that holds a strong patent position on an invention in its own home market will sometimes find that the patent protection on the same invention issued by foreign governments is much less secure (Maier 1969, pp. 207–31, Horowitz 1970, p. 539, Penrose 1973, p. 768, Scherer 1976). Moreover, in recent years, various developing countries have adopted laws outlawing the geographical restraints and other restraints that licensers have heretofore found useful to impose on their foreign licensees, further reducing the usefulness of that approach (OECD 1977b, UNCTAD 1979, pp. 24–39, also Naryenya-Takirambudde 1977, pp. 71–3).

Perhaps the most tenuous arrangements for the avoidance of risks in host countries entail payments that in U.S. law and practice would be classified as bribes. The justification for condemning bribes can sometimes be couched in rational terms. In a country whose officials do not solicit bribes, for instance, the foreign offerer of a bribe contributes to the destruction of a public good – the competitive market – an act that could conceivably be costly to all those in the market, including the offerer. But arguments of that sort are not the real stuff of the debate. One side finds bribery prima facie offensive and refuses to use it, whatever the consequences; the other thinks it totally entrenched, presenting an inescapable hurdle for those who wish to operate in certain foreign markets.[18] Any "rational" discussion of the use of bribes as a risk-insuring device is therefore likely to be offensive to one side of the debate and unsatisfying to the other. It is almost inescapable, too, that such a discussion will be seen as an apologia for the practice.

There is perhaps one point worth making nevertheless. The problem of bribery is either a smaller one or a bigger one than is ordinarily described. In the interest of reducing their risk in various developing countries, foreign investors are often obliged to make various payments that are not labeled as bribes. Influential local figures are commonly offered blocks of stock in what is then dubbed a joint venture, at prices well below their reasonable value. Local government officials are appointed to directorships in the enterprise, with appropriate emoluments. Ironically, such measures are often applauded as a sign of the foreign investor's responsiveness to local sensibilities. In this shadowy area of risk avoidance, the line between international chicanery and local adaptation will never be clearly drawn.

The analytical challenge

The avoidance of risk is a quintessential element in the strategy of foreign investors. As a rule, the decision to invest is motivated by a desire to reduce risks of various sorts: the risk of government restrictions on foreign imports, the relative unenforceability of the investor's rights under law or contract, and above all, the risk of preemptive action on the part of a competitor. Risk avoidance also affects the form of the investment; some forms of joint venture help the investor with limited resources to diversify more widely, whereas other forms of joint venture are thought to reduce political risk. On the other hand, even as a direct investment reduces one set of risks, it exposes the investor to another set, including the risk of expropriation. Accordingly, firms often attempt to establish a firm link with foreign markets or foreign sources of materials by long-term arrangements short of investment, but these too produce uncertain results.

The firms involved in the making of these complex judgments

[18] For some of the more serious explorations of this subject see Kobrin (1976, pp. 105–11), U.S. Securities and Exchange Commission (1976), U.S. Senate (1976), Jacoby et al. (1977, pp. 125–45), Kugel and Gruenberg (1977, pp. 113–24), Kennedy and Simon (1978, pp. 1–5, 118–20).

come predominantly from industries that are oligopolistic in structure. Because their risks are those that arise in the never-never land of oligopoly, where individual firms can affect prices and the actions of rival firms are interdependent, the analytical power of our microeconomic concepts proves somewhat limited. Those risks are often more easily analyzed in game-theoretic terms than in the familiar paradigms of systematic and random variance. To add to the difficulties, foreign direct investors are not usually investors in the usual sense; a critical portion of their investments commonly takes an intangible form, entailing assets that have no ready market price. Even the cost of such assets offers little help; such assets as technology or access to markets are provided at near-zero marginal cost.

As a result, the role that risk plays in international direct investment cannot be captured by minor addenda to the principles of finance, such as calculating the appropriate risk adjustment for a target rate of return or computing the appropriate price to be paid for a hedge. Foreign direct investors will resort to a series of stratagems for reducing the uncertainty in their environment that do not fit easily into the mainstream discussions of risk. Faced with that fact, this chapter has discussed, for want of a better term, the "organizational and institutional" responses of such investors to risk. But it is only a matter of time before the economics profession will formalize those responses in ways that incorporate them within the discipline. Indeed, that process is already well under way.

References

Abegglen, J. C. (ed.). *Business Strategies for Japan* (Tokyo: Sophia University, 1970).

Abernathy, W. J., and Kenneth Wayne. *The Bottom of the Learning Curve: The Dilemma of Innovation and Productivity* (Boston: Division of Research, Graduate School of Business Administration, Harvard University, 1974).

Adelman, M. A. *The World Petroleum Industry* (Baltimore, Md.: Johns Hopkins University Press, 1972).

Aharoni, Yair. *The Foreign Investment Decision Process* (Boston: Division of Research, Graduate School of Business Administration, Harvard University, 1966).

"Managerial Discretion," in Raymond Vernon and Yair Aharoni (eds.), *State-Owned Enterprise in the Western Economies* (London: Croom Helm, 1981).

Arrow, K. J. *The Limits of Organization* (New York: Norton, 1974).

Banks, F. E. *Bauxite and Aluminum: An Introduction to the Economics of Nonfuel Minerals* (Lexington, Mass.: Lexington Books, 1979).

Baranson, Jack. *Automotive Industries in Developing Countries* (Baltimore, Md.: Johns Hopkins University Press, 1969).

Barlow, E. R., and I. T. Wender. *Foreign Investment and Taxation* (Englewood Cliffs, N.J.: Prentice-Hall, 1955).

Bennett, David, and K. E. Sharpe. "Transnational Corporations and the Political Economy of Export Promotion: The Case of the Mexican Automobile Industry." *International Organization*, vol. 33, no. 2, Spring 1979, pp. 177–201.

Bernhardt, I. "Vertical Integration and Demand Variability," *Journal of Industrial Economics*, vol. 25, no. 3, March 1977, pp. 213–29.

Bosson, Rex, and Bension Varon. *The Mining Industry and the Developing Countries* (New York: Oxford University Press, 1977).

Bostock, Mark, and Charles Harvey (eds.). *Economic Independence and Zambian Copper: A Case Study of Foreign Investment* (New York: Praeger, 1972).

Bradley, David. "Managing Against Expropriation." *Harvard Business Review*, July–August 1977, pp. 75–83.

Brock, G. W. *The U.S. Computer Industry* (Cambridge, Mass.: Ballinger, 1975).

Buckley, P. J., and M. Casson. *The Future of Multinational Enterprise* (New York: Holmes and Meier Publishers, Inc., 1976).

Business Week. "The Reindustrialization of America," June 30, 1980, pp. 55–146.

Casson, M. *Alternatives to the Multinational Enterprise* (London: Macmillan Press, 1979).

Caves, R. E. "Uncertainty, Market Structure and Performance: Galbraith as Conventional Wisdom," in J. W. Markham and G. F. Papenek (eds.), *Industrial Organization and Economic Development* (Boston: Houghton Mifflin, 1970).

"Industrial Organization," in J. M. Dunning (ed.), *Economic Analysis and the Multinational Enterprise* (New York: Praeger, 1973).

American Industry: Structure, Conduct, Performance (Englewood Cliffs, N.J.: Prentice-Hall, 1977).

Charles River Associates, Inc. "Economic Analysis of the Copper Industry." Prepared for the General Services Administration, March 1970.

Cline, W. R., Noboru Kawarabe, T. O. M. Kronojo, and Thomas Williams. *Trade Negotiations in the Tokyo Round: A Quantitative Assessment* (Washington, D.C.: The Brookings Institution, 1978).

Commission of the European Communities. *Report by the Commission on the Behavior of the Oil Companies in the Community during the Period from October 1973 to March 1974.* EEC Studies on Competition-Approximation of Legislation, no. 26 (Brussels: European Economic Communities, December 1975).

Conley, Patrick. "Experience Curves as a Planning Tool," in R. R. Rothberg (ed.), *Corporate Strategy and Product Innovation* (New York: Free Press, 1981).

Cooper, B., and T. F. Gaskell. *The Adventure of North Sea Oil* (London: Heinemann, 1976).

Curhan, J. P., W. H. Davidson, and Rajan Suri. *Tracing the Multinationals: A. Source Book on U.S.-Based Enterprises* (Cambridge, Mass.: Ballinger, 1977).

Curtis, T. B., and J. R. Vastine, Jr. *The Kennedy Round and the Future of American Trade* (New York: Praeger, 1971).

Cyert, R. M., W. R. Dill, and J. G. March. "The Role of Expectations in Business Decision Making," in L. A. Welsch and R. M. Cyert (eds.), *Management Decision Making* (London: Penguin Books, 1970).

Cyert, R. M., and J. G. March. *A Behavioral Theory of the Firm* (Englewood Cliffs, N.J.: Prentice-Hall, 1963).

Davidson, W. H. "Patterns of Factor-Saving Innovation in the Industrialized World." *European Economic Review*, vol. 8, no. 3, October 1976, pp. 207–17.

Davidson, W. H., and D. G. McFetridge. "International Technology Transactions and The Theory of the Firm." Unpublished, Amos Tuck School, Dartmouth College, 1981.

Dubin, Michael. "Foreign Acquisitions and the Spread of the Multinational Firm." Unpublished DBA thesis, Harvard School of Business Administration, 1976.

Duke, R. M., R. L. Johnson, H. Mueller, P. D. Quaffs, C. T. Roush, Jr., and D. G. Tarr. *Staff Report on the United States Steel Industry and International Rivals.* Bureau of Economics, Federal Trade Commission, Washington, D.C., November 1977.

Eiteman, D. K., and A. I. Stonehill. *Multinational Business Finance* (2nd ed) (Reading, Mass.: Addison-Wesley, 1979).

Fabrikant, Robert. *Oil Discovery and Technical Change in Southeast Asia: Legal Aspects of Production-Sharing Contracts in the Indonesian Petroleum Industry* (Singapore: Institute of Southeast Asian Studies, 1973).

Fagre, Nathan, and L. T. Wells, Jr. "Bargaining Power of Multinationals and Host Governments." *Journal of International Business Studies,* in press.

Forbes. "The Game that Two Could Play." Vol. 94, no. 11, December 1, 1964, pp. 40–1.

Frank, Isaiah. *Foreign Enterprise in Developing Countries* (Baltimore, Md.: Johns Hopkins University Press, 1980).

Franko, L. G. *The European Multinationals, European Business Strategies in the United States* (Geneva: Business International, 1971).

The European Multinationals (Stamford, Conn.: Greylock Publishers, 1976).

Joint Venture Survival in Multinational Corporation (New York: Praeger, 1977).

Freeman, Christopher. *The Economics of Industrial Innovation* (London: Penguin Books, 1974).

Ghadar, Fariborz. *The Evolution of OPEC Strategy* (Lexington, Mass.: Lexington Books, 1977).

Goohs, C. A. "United States Taxation Policies and the Iron Ore Operations of the United States Steel Industry." Unpublished, J. F. Kennedy School, Cambridge, Mass., Spring 1980.

Gort, Michael. *Diversification and Integration in American Industry* (Princeton, N.J.: Princeton University Press, 1962).

Graham, E. M. "Oligopolistic Imitation and European Direct Investment in the United States." Unpublished DBA thesis, Harvard School of Business Administration, 1974.

Gray, H. P. *The Economics of Business Investment Abroad* (New York: Crane, Russak and Co., 1972).

Green, J. R. "Vertical Integration and the Assurance of Markets." Harvard Institute of Economic Research, Discussion Paper 383, October 1974.

Habakkuk, H. J. *American and British Technology in the Nineteenth Century* (Cambridge: Cambridge University Press, 1962).

Hartley, Keith. "The Learning Curve and its Application to the Aircraft Industry." *Journal of Industrial Economics,* vol. 13, no. 2, March 1965, pp. 122–8.

Heslop, Alan (ed.). *The World Capital Shortage* (Indianapolis: Bobbs-Merrill, 1977).

Hochmuth, M. S. "Aerospace," in Raymond Vernon (ed.), *Big Business and the State* (Cambridge, Mass.: Harvard University Press, 1974).

Hogberg, Bengt. *Interfirm Cooperation and Strategic Development* (Ghoteborg: b BAS ek. fhoren, 1977).

Horowitz, Lester. "Patents and World Trade." *Journal of World Trade Law,* vol. 4, no. 4, July–August 1970, pp. 538–47.

Hymer, Stephen, and Robert Rowthorn. "Multinational Corporations and International Oligopoly: The Non-American Challenge," in C. P. Kindleberger (ed.), *The International Corporation: A Symposium* (Cambridge, Mass.: MIT Press, 1970).

Jacoby, N. H. *Multinational Oil* (New York: Macmillan, 1974).

Jacoby, N. H., Peter Nehemkis, and Richard Eells. *Bribery and Extortion in World Business: A Study of Corporate Political Payments Abroad* (New York: Macmillan, 1977).

Jenkins, R. O. *Dependent Industrialization in Latin America: The Automobile Industry in Argentina, Chile, and Mexico* (New York: Praeger, 1977).

Jensen, H. R., E. W. Kehrberg, and D. W. Thomas. "Integration as an Adjustment to Risk and Uncertainty," *Southern Economics Journal*, vol. 28, no. 4 April 1962, pp. 378–84.

Jéquier, Nicolas. "Computer," in Raymond Vernon (ed.), *Big Business and the State* (Cambridge, Mass.: Harvard University Press, 1974).

Jodice, D. A. "Sources of Change in Third World Regimes for Foreign Direct Investment, 1968–1976." *International Organization*, vol. 34, no. 2, Spring 1980, pp. 177–206.

Kaserman, D. L. "Theories of Vertical Integration: Implications for Antitrust Policy." *The Antitrust Bulletin*, vol. 23, no. 3, Fall, 1978, pp. 483–510.

Katz, B. G., and Almarin Phillips. "Government, Technological Opportunities, and the Emergence of the Computer Industry," in Herbert Giersch (ed.), *Emerging Technology* (Kiel: Institute of World Economics, in press).

Kennedy, Tom, and C. E. Simon. *An Examination of Questionable Payments and Practices* (New York: Praeger, 1978).

Knickerbocker, F. T. *Oligopolistic Reaction and Multinational Enterprise* (Boston: Division of Research, Graduate School of Business Administration, Harvard University, 1973).

Kobrin, S. J. "Morality, Political Power and Illegal Payments." *Columbia Journal of World Business*, vol. 11, no. 4, Winter 1976, pp. 105–10.

"Foreign Enterprise and Forced Divestment in LDCs." *International Organization*, vol. 34, no. 1, Winter 1980, pp. 65–88.

Koninklijke Nederlandsche Petroleum Maatschappij, N. V. *The Royal Dutch Petroleum Company 1890–1950* (The Hague, 1950).

Krasner, S. D. *Defending the National Interest* (Princeton, N.J.: Princeton University Press, 1978).

Kugel, Yerachmiel, and G. W. Gruenberg. "Criteria and Guidelines for Decision Making: The Special Case of International Payoffs." *Columbia Journal of World Business*, vol. 12, no. 3, Fall 1977, pp. 113–23.

Lall, Sanjaya. "Monopolistic Advantages and Foreign Involvement by U.S. Manufacturing Industry." *Oxford Economic Papers*, vol. 32, no. 1, March 1980, pp. 102–22.

Levy, Brian. "World Oil Marketing in Transition." *International Organization*, vol. 36, no. 1, Winter 1982, pp. 113–33.

Maier, H. G. "International Patent Conventions and Access to Foreign Technology." *Journal of International Law and Economics*, vol. 4, no. 2, Fall, 1969, pp. 207–31.

Mansvelt Beck, F. W., and K. M. Wiig. *The Economics of Offshore Oil and Gas Supplies* (Lexington, Mass.: Lexington Books, 1977).

Measday, W. S. "The Pharmaceutical Industry," in Walter Adams (ed.), *The Structure of American Industry* (New York: Macmillan, 1977).

Michalet, C. A., and Michel Delapierre. *The Multinationalization of French Firms* (Chicago: Academy of International Business, 1975).

Mikesell, R. F. *The World Copper Industry: Structure and Economic Analysis* (Baltimore, Md.: Johns Hopkins University Press, 1979a).

New Patterns of World Mineral Development (New York: British-North American Committee, 1979b).

Moran, T. H. *Multinational Companies and the Politics of Dependence: Copper in Chile* (Princeton, N.J.: Princeton University Press, 1974).

Naryenya-Takirambudde, Peter. *Technology Transfer and International Law* (New York: Praeger, 1977).

New York Times. "Ford Regroups for the Minicar Battle." December 4, 1975, pp. 1, 9.

Organization for Economic Cooperation and Development (OECD). *Restrictive Business Practices of Multinational Enterprises,* Report to the Committee of Experts on Restrictive Business Practices (Paris, 1977a).

Transfer of Technology by Multinational Corporations (Paris, 1977b).

Ozawa, Terutomo. *Japan's Technological Challenge to the West, 1950–1974: Motivation and Accomplishment* (Cambridge, Mass.: MIT Press, 1974).

Parker, J. E. S. *The Economics of Innovation,* 2nd ed. (New York: Longman, 1978).

Penrose, E. T. "International Patenting and the Less-Developed Countries." *Economic Journal,* vol. 83, no. 331, September 1973, pp. 768–86.

Pfeffer, Jeffrey, and Philip Nowek. "Patterns of Joint Venture Activity: Implications for Antitrust Policy." *The Antitrust Bulletin,* vol. 21, no. 2, Summer 1976, pp. 315–39.

Porter, M. E. *Competitive Strategy: Techniques for Analyzing Industries and Competitors* (New York: Free Press, 1980).

Radetzki, Marion, and Stephen Zorn. *Financing Mining Projects in Developing Countries* (London: Mining Journal Books, 1979).

"Foreign Finance for LDC Mining Projects," in Sandro Sideri and Sheridan Johns (eds.), *Mining for Development in the Third World: Multinational Corporations, State Enterprises and the International Economy* (New York: Pergamon Press, 1980).

Robinson, R. D. *National Control of Foreign Business Entry: A Survey of Fifteen Countries* (New York: Praeger, 1976).

Ronstadt, R. C. *Research and Development Abroad by U.S. Multinationals* (New York: Praeger, 1977).

Rosenberg, Nathan. "The Direction of Technological Change: Inducement Mechanisms and Focussing Devices." *Economic Development and Cultural Change,* vol. 18, no. 1, pt. 1, October 1969, pp. 1–24.

Perspectives on Technology (Cambridge: Cambridge University Press, 1976).

Samuelsson, H. F. "National Scientific and Technological Potential and the Activities of Multinational Corporations: The Case of Sweden." Mimeographed. Report to the OECD Committee for Scientific and Technological Policy, 1974.

Scherer, F. M. "Antitrust and Patent Policy." Mimeographed. Seminar on Technological Innovation, sponsored by U.S. National Science Foundation and the Government of the Federal Republic of Germany, Bonn, April 1976.

Industrial Market Structure and Economic Performance (Skokie, Ill.: Rand McNally, 1980).

Smith, D. M., and L. T. Wells, Jr. *Negotiating Third World Mineral Agreements: Promises as Prologue* (Cambridge, Mass.: Ballinger, 1976).

Stigler, G. J. "Imperfections in the Capital Market." *Journal of Political Economy,* vol. 75, no. 3, June 1967, pp. 287–92.

Stiglitz, J. E., and Andrew Weiss. "Credit Rationing in Markets with Imperfect Information." *American Economic Review,* vol. 71, no. 3, June 1981, pp. 393–409.

Stopford, J. M., and L. T. Wells, Jr. *Managing the Multinational* (New York: Basic Books, 1972).

Stuckey, J. A. "Vertical Integration and Joint Ventures in the International Aluminum Industry." Unpublished doctoral thesis, Harvard University, 1981.

Sundelson, J. W. "U.S. Automotive Investments Abroad," in C. P. Kindleberger (ed.), *The International Corporation* (Cambridge, Mass.: MIT Press, 1970).

Teece, D. J. "Vertical Integration in the U.S. Oil Industry," in E. J. Mitchell (ed.), *Vertical Integration in the Oil Industry* (Washington, D.C.: American Enterprise Institute, 1976).

Thunell, L. H. *Political Risks in International Business: Investment Behavior of Multinational Corporations* (New York: Praeger, 1977).

Tomlinson, J. W. C. *The Joint Venture in International Business* (Cambridge, Mass.: MIT Press, 1970).

Turner, Louis. *Multinational Companies and the Third World* (New York: Hill and Wang, 1973).

Turner, Louis, and J. M. Bedore. *Middle East Industrialization: A Study of Saudi and Iranian Downstream Investments* (Westnead, Farmborough, Hants, UK: Saxon House, 1979).

UNCTAD. *The Role of Trade Marks in Developing Countries* (New York: United Nations, 1979).

United Nations Economic and Social Council, Commission on Transnational Corporations. *Transnational Corporations in World Development: A Reexamination* (New York: United Nations, 1978).

United Nations, Department of Economic and Social Affairs. *Multinational Corporations in World Development* (New York, 1973).

U.S. Department of Commerce, Bureau of Economic Analysis. *U.S. Direct Investment Abroad, 1977* (Washington, D.C.: Government Printing Office, 1981).

U.S. Federal Trade Commission. *The International Petroleum Cartel* (Washington, D.C.: Government Printing Office, 1952).

U.S. Securities and Exchange Commission. *Report on Questionable and Illegal Corporate Payments and Practices* (Washington, D.C.: Government Printing Office, May 12, 1976).

U.S. Senate Committee on Banking, Housing and Urban Affairs. "Prohibiting Bribes to Foreign Officials." *Committee Hearings* (Washington, D.C.: Committee Print, May 18, 1976).

Vaupel, J. W., and J. P. Curhan. *The World's Multinational Enterprises: A Source Book of Tables* (Boston: Division of Research, Graduate School of Business Administration, Harvard University, 1973).

Vernon, Raymond. *Sovereignty at Bay* (New York: Basic Books, 1971).

Storm Over the Multinationals (Cambridge, Mass.: Harvard University Press, 1977).

"The International Aspects of State-Owned Enterprises." *Journal of International Business Studies*, Winter 1979, pp. 7–15.

"Gone are the Cash Cows of Yesteryear." *Harvard Business Review*, November–December 1980, pp. 150–5.

Vernon, Raymond, and W. H. Davidson. "Foreign Production of Technology-Intensive Products by U.S.-Based Multinational Enterprises." Report to the National Science Foundation, no. PB 80 148638, January 1979.

Williamson, O. E. *Markets and Hierarchies: Analysis and Antitrust Implications* (New York: Free Press, 1975).

Zorn, Stephen. "Recent Trends in LDC Mining Agreements," in Sandro Sideri and Sheridan Johns (eds.), *Mining for Development in the Third World: Multinational Corporations, State Enterprises and the International Economy* (Elmsford, N.Y.: Pergamon Press, 1980).

Perspective: Organizational strategies for coping with country risk

JAMES R. STREET

I would like to comment on several key points of Professor Vernon's excellent treatment of the topic of risk, drawing on the experience of my company in responding to risk and drawing on the behavior pattern of others in the oil and petrochemical industries. The decade of the 1970s was not kind to the international competitive stance of the U.S. companies. As a result of the problems we encountered, thinking globally is no longer an option for corporate management. It is now essential, not only for the health of the corporation, but also, in some cases, for survival.

The first example I will examine is an organizational response to a raw material supply interruption: the oil embargo of 1973. This event brought with it a new regime of hydrocarbon economics and new dimensions of risk to the oil and petrochemical industry and to the total economy. What was the needed organizational response? It was twofold: first, to determine ways of managing the risk of supply interruptions of the raw material on which our industry is based, and second, to deal creatively with a complex international situation. Security of hydrocarbon supply became the number one corporate objective.

Our institutional response to this risk was to seek out arrangements with an oil-rich country, Saudi Arabia, which has the largest oil reserves in the world. During the early period after the embargo, my company began negotiations with the kingdom of Saudi Arabia. Our objective was to secure entitlements to purchase crude oil by entering into a joint venture to build a petrochemical complex. We also looked for sources of secure supply in our own hemisphere and became a major purchaser of crude oil from Mexico.

A petrochemical venture in itself represents a major commitment of capital and labor resources. To build such a plant in the Saudi Arabian desert, under conditions that were considerably different from those of any past experience, represented a major challenge in managing a financial risk. Our approach was to develop strategies for each risk variable such that the overall venture would meet corporate profitability standards. Our objective was to be as indifferent as possible, in a financial sense, to whether the plant was built in Saudi Arabia or the U.S. Gulf Coast.

How was this accomplished? First, the project is a joint venture with the host government. This was not only a requirement of the venture, but it was also a risk-reducing strategy. The Saudi kingdom is responsible for the development of all infrastructure, all resources needed for such a complex. Secondly, we decided to use only proven technology well known to us. We wanted no risk here. The higher cost of construction and of operations had to be offset by beneficial arrangements on the cost of raw materials. One by one, and over the course of six years, negotiations proceeded until we and Saudi Arabia were satisfied with the arrangement. The entire venture could be put in the context of defensive risk management.

Now, with construction under way, we have seen a rapidly changing availability of crude oil over the past eighteen months. We are all aware of the considerable change in demand that occurred when the price of crude oil increased nearly fifteenfold in less than a decade. Demand for crude oil in the United States has declined from an average annual increase of about 7 percent to a slightly negative growth rate for the foreseeable future. As Professor Vernon notes, historically the price elasticity of aggregate demand for industrial raw materials such as iron ore or crude oil has been fairly low. In this light, do we still view hydrocarbon security as a priority issue? Yes, we do, but this is where a corporation must take a long-run view.

Recently, it has become somewhat of a liability to have term arrangements for crude oil with spot prices significantly lower. This has put some majors in the oil projects business at a disadvantage compared to some of the independents who mostly purchase spot crude. This is seen as a short-term situation as the market equilibrates.

Professor Vernon is quite right that there is no such thing as a genuine long-term international contract. However, our arrangement with Saudi Arabia is a special situation that we entered into for a secure source of hydrocarbons over the long term. We are pleased with the arrangement because it represents a long-term commitment. It gives us an improved position in dealing with an area of high uncertainty: raw material availability. Our response represents one approach to managing raw material security risk on a global scale. It is an approach that others have followed as the United States accommodates to the realities of a changing raw material base.

The next subject of Professor Vernon's chapter, which struck a very responsive chord, was vertical integration. The merits of vertical integration are frequently debated. But it seems to be an inexorable process in raw-material-dominated industries such as the petrochemical industry. I agree with Professor Vernon that vertical integration is a way to manage risk and that it is not the only alternative. We see, however, in the petrochemical industry, a strong move to "network couples." By this I mean the industry treats the primary material, intermediates, and final products as if they were a single product, taking the profitability across the "network" during a period of oversupply.

An example is producers who are integrated back to the primary raw material. During a period of oversupply, they can price the end product at the marginal cost of all their raw materials and place the producer that must buy their intermediate material at a competitive disadvantage. We see this kind of behavior in the current oversupplied petrochemical market during this period of economic downturn. Vertical integration becomes a defensive strategy to manage the risk of becoming a noncompetitive supplier.

Sellers of an intermediate material to a market with a high degree of vertical integration can find that they have to price their material at a low level to keep their customers in business. If their customers are unable to compete and lose their market share, this can place merchants in the position of being secondary swing suppliers to the market. One strategy for a merchant in this position would be to enter in a strong "business couple," through creative contractual arrangements, with a major player in a downstream market. This is what Professor Vernon calls "entering horizontal arrangements with other firms." We certainly see a trend toward this sort of risk-reducing strategy in the petrochemical industry. We also see the trend spreading as an international strategy where the downstream market can be global. One approach would be to enter into a joint venture with an international partner to supply intermediate products from a domestic plant to the finished product plant located in the partner's country.

The United States' and Western Europe's growth rates for many base industries are slowing down to levels near their GNP. This places an increasing emphasis on international investments in developing countries as a means for sustaining growth and as a defensive strategy. I think that the chemical industry will continue to seek international investments in order to (1) acquire hydrocarbon supplies by investing in oil-rich countries such as Saudi Arabia, Mexico, Canada, and Indonesia; (2) neutralize threats to export markets from emerging petrochemical industries in developing countries by joining them; (3) participate in growth markets; and (4) exploit managerial and technological skills in other markets.

U.S. petrochemical exports have grown at a real rate of 10 percent for the last eight years at the expense of Western Europe and by taking advantage of the growing demand in the "Pacific Rim" area. Many of the projects in developing nations and in Canada are aimed at these Pacific Rim export markets. Obviously, one way for a firm to keep its exports and continue to grow would be to participate in joint ventures in developing countries. Therefore, one strategy for reducing the risk of losing export markets is to join with those who constitute the threat. Professor Vernon addresses this in the section of his chapter that describes "joint ventures as risk reducers."

A highly successful strategy for developing an international position and reducing such risk is to "seed" a foreign market with exported material to build a position. After establishing a sales position, an indigenous plant can be built. Production risk can be managed by selecting a product and technology with which the firm has considerable experience. The foreign-based plant is often a joint venture to allow smooth penetration of the market utilizing the skills and position of the local partner. Gradually, other investments can follow until an entire network is established. The strategy is usually based on raw material or technological position. Many U.S. firms are following this strategy for developing a position in areas of high-growth potential.

Many ventures are with the state government that wishes to establish a petrochemical industry based on its hydrocarbon raw material. Such ventures are usually awarded on a competitive bid basis. We also see transnational ventures in which an intermediate material is made in one country and finished in another. Vertical integration can be done on an international scale.

In commenting on Professor Vernon's observations on high-technology industries, I wish to draw from my experience in the life sciences business as an example of the need for an international strategy. The agricultural chemical business has many factors that have led most companies to emphasize an international strategy.

First, it is a research-intensive industry. Cost must be distributed over a large market to be competitive. Second, the cost of development is high. Regulatory approvals are generally secured outside the United States first. This means that a new pesticide can be launched and experience gained in other markets. This experience can be used to advantage in the United States. Third, often only one world-scale plant is needed. Fourth, the United States is the largest market. Fifth, some of the major growth areas are in developing countries. Thus, it can be seen that long-term viability requires an international strategy.

The same reasoning applies to the drug industry, and the same patterns have been carried out. We also foresee the emerging field of biotechnology evolving in a similar manner.

There is also the fear, as Professor Vernon points out, that competition will get ahead in cumulative experience – in manufacturing cost and technological development from international investments – and will use this advantage in the domestic market. In the base chemical industry, an international player might have the opportunity to move ahead several generations in technological development by constructing significantly more plants than a domestic-only player. I believe this is a compelling reason why industries tend to move together, as Professor Vernon observes.

I believe this will become more and more the pattern as Western European investors continue to move aggressively in the United States and the United States seeks ways to participate in the rapidly growing markets in the developing countries. The supply uncertainty of raw materials and the need to find new growth markets will continue to serve as an impetus to international investments for raw-material-based industries. U.S. industry must learn how to compete even more aggresively in a global market.

I agree with Professor Vernon that the risks investors face in international markets are not unique to these markets. We recently conducted a feasibility study with a group of other companies to evaluate the construction of a petrochemical complex in Alaska. The assessment we had to go through in dealing with local government, local citizenry, environmental regulations, higher construction costs, new markets, and so on, resembled, in most respects, the same sort of process that one would have to go through with a foreign investment. The study assessed financial risk by determining the conditions under which the venture would be feasible. We were able to determine the values that would be required to make this a viable venture with manageable financial risk. However, we concluded that the necessary economic conditions, both energy and product values, did not exist at this time.

Additionally, I must point out that the techniques of risk assessment cannot be reduced to decision analysis using Monte Carlo simulation. Risk of financial loss for foreign investment must be managed just as it is managed in any domestic investment. Each segment of the venture must be analyzed for risk and a determination made if there is a strategy for managing the risk. These risks must be considered in the context of the risk capacity of the firm. Many ventures today are too large and complex and involve too much financial risk for one firm to undertake alone.

Approaching the risk involved in international investment must become a normal part of business management. Our culture and our institutions must learn to be at ease with international uncertainties. And decision makers will have to learn to cope with a new set of increasingly complex issues in managing a global portfolio. Industry looks to the business schools to produce graduates who are comfortable with risk management and who think globally. We need fresh approaches to infuse a new dynamism into our business community. I would certainly encourage frequent interchanges between academia and industry on this subject.

CHAPTER 6

Insuring against country risks: descriptive and prescriptive aspects

HOWARD KUNREUTHER AND
PAUL KLEINDORFER

Introduction

Multinational firms face grave uncertainties today with respect to their investment strategies that involve other countries. In particular, there has been an increasing awareness by international managers of the difficulty of predicting the future political and economic climate likely to exist in a foreign country. One only has to look at the following headlines from *The Economist* during the first few months of 1981 to see graphically the types of uncertainties that exist in different parts of the world:

Iran and Iraq: A New Front in a Slow War? (January 3, 1981)
El Salvador: Final Offensive to the Next? (January 17, 1981)
Ecuador and Peru: The Oil War (February 7, 1981)
Poland: A Shaky Kind of Peace (March 21, 1981)
Arab-Israel Conflict: Steam from the Middle East's Back Burner
(March 28, 1981)

These illustrative examples of the unstable world situation coupled with the continuing interest by multinational firms in investing abroad have motivated two broad questions that this chapter addresses: (1) How do multinational firms and insurers deal with the problems of international risk in making their decisions as to what investments to undertake in foreign countries? (2) What role can

The research reported in this chapter is partially supported by the Bundesministerium für Forschung und Technologie, F.R.G., contract no. 321/7591/RGB 8001. While support for this work is gratefully acknowledged, the views expressed are the authors' own and are not necessarily shared by the sponsor. Our thanks to Harold Barnett, Eric Burke, David Bell, Richard Herring, Joanne Linnerooth, and Jim Vaupel for helpful discussions during the preparation of this chapter. The constructive comments of John Cox on the original version are gratefully acknowledged.

analytic approaches, including insurance mechanisms, play in better managing risk and uncertainty in international transactions?

The first question is of a descriptive nature, and the second one has a prescriptive flavor. A basic theme of this chapter is the importance of undertaking descriptive analysis before making prescriptive recommendations. In the next section we develop a conceptual framework that highlights the importance of integrating these two components of the analysis. The third and fourth sections probe into the actual decision processes utilized by investors and insurers in coping with international risk (question 1). The concluding section addresses ways to improve the process through prescriptive analysis (question 2).

In order to make the analysis more concrete we will illustrate the theoretical concepts with an actual problem facing Indonesia: whether to invest in facilities that will provide the United States with liquefied natural gas. This case illustrates that companies planning to invest in projects that rely on actions by the United States may face similar types of political and economic risks as do American-based firms contemplating projects in less-developed areas of the world.

A conceptual framework

The problems we will be focusing on are associated with insurance decisions of multinational firms undertaken to protect their foreign investments against so-called country risks. In order to discuss this problem in a real-world context, it is necessary to understand the nature of country risk, the relevant institutional arrangements, and the decision processes of the interested parties. These three elements form the descriptive component of the conceptual framework. Prescriptive analysis can then be undertaken with a clearer understanding of the relevant information and constraints facing multinational firms and insurers. Figure 6.1 depicts these four elements of the conceptual framework, each of which will now be described in turn.

Nature of country risk

Raymond Vernon (1971), in his classic study *Sovereignty at Bay*, described the remarkable development of multinational enterprises and their potential conflicts with national governments. Ten years later in a retrospective view of his book, Vernon (1981) pointed out that the central question facing multinational firms is, "How do the sovereign states propose to deal with the fact that so many of their enterprises

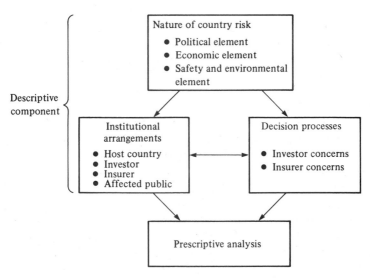

Figure 6.1. Elements of conceptual framework

are conduits through which other sovereigns exert their influence?" This question implies that any multinational firm must seriously consider the possible reactions that countries will have to their investments. Insurers must similarly focus on the probability of specific losses and the likely consequences to the investor firms. Other chapters by Dunn, Eaton and Gersovitz, Shubik, and Vernon discuss the nature of these country risks facing firms and insurers, and we will only briefly allude to them here. Several categories of country risk need to be considered.

Political element: Risks under this heading are connected with actions taken by a country in response to political and social developments. Some of the possible developments that are likely to have adverse consequences for specific investments are as follows:

> Inconvertibility of currency
> Repudiation, default, or rescheduling of loans
> Expropriation of facilities
> War, revolution, or insurrection
> Sabotage of facilities

The social climate within the country must also be taken into account by firms who require formal approval for their proposed investment at the local, municipal, and state government level. One only has to witness the changing history of nuclear power to recognize that what appeared to be an investment that would be tacitly approved by the public in the 1950s and 1960s has been viewed very differently in recent years (Hohenemser et al. 1977).

Economic risk: Here one has to distinguish between external and internal risks. By *external risks* we are referring to the adverse effects caused by events outside the control of the host country. For example, one must consider the likelihood and consequences of changing prices and uncertain future demand for goods that are produced by a proposed project. The degree of uncertainty on the returns from an investment will influence the final decision on whether or not it should be undertaken.

Internal risks refer to direct actions taken by the host country that have an impact on the project. For example, the government of a country can subsidize an internal producer of a competing product in order to threaten the profitability of a foreign investment. Changes in labor laws and working conditions can raise production costs so the investment is less competitive on world markets.

Safety and environmental risk: Here we are referring to direct losses to the investment itself and the indirect consequences to others. Natural disasters, such as floods, earthquakes, or fire, can cause severe damage to a facility or plant. There can also be man-made disasters such as explosions, which can damage the facility and may also kill or severely injure employees or individuals residing nearby. A set of other harmful effects such as pollution, noise, and environmental degradation may also be created by a particular project. Both the investing firm and potential insurers will want to know the extent of their liability from any of these negative impacts.

Institutional arrangements

Figure 6.1 identifies the four interested parties who are involved in the decision process with respect to the problem of managing international risk.

Host country: We assume there is an expressed interest in having funds invested in a particular country. In many cases the host country will not be able to give credible assurances that such an investment, if approved, will be immune to the effects of political risks.

Investor: Multinational firms often can invest in a number of different projects, each of which will be viewed differently by them. Funds can be allocated for modernization or expansion of an existing enterprise in a host country, for a new facility, or for exploration of natural resources (e.g., gas, oil, minerals). The project can be jointly owned by the investor and a firm in the host country or it can be controlled entirely by the investing firm. With respect to the organizational structure, corporate investment planners have the responsibility for collecting data and judging the relative attractiveness of specific projects. They are frequently assisted by outside experts who have specialized knowledge of the host countries (Rummel and Heenan 1978).

Insurer: Today governmental and private insurers provide various forms of political risk insurance. Within the private sector Lloyd's has written protection against war damage to sea shipments since the early 1800s, but only within the last ten years have they begun to write insurance against other political risks. In 1978, the private market was broadened when the American International Group began offering different types of political risk coverage (Ralston 1981). In addition, other large companies, such as the Insurance Company of North America (INA), have recently also offered coverage against selected political risks.[1]

Another form of insurance coverage is through the Federal Credit Insurance Association (FCIA), which represents approximately fifty private insurance companies and has the backing of the Export– Import Bank. This insurance is available only for goods and services exported from the United States. At the governmental level the Overseas Private Investment Corporation (OPIC) was formed in 1969 to encourage U.S. companies to invest in less-developed countries by offering insurance against political hazards such as expropriation and war. Before providing coverage, OPIC must be assured through bilateral agreements between the United States and the host country that its rights are recognized (West 1980).

In most other Western countries similar governmental agencies provide insurance against expropriation, inconvertibility, war, revolution, and insurrection.[2] The central banks of other developing coun-

---

[1] INA wrote its first policy in 1792 on a merchant sea captain's life and then went on to insure international cargo (Cathey 1981).

[2] For example, in 1971, France set up two systems to protect the foreign investments of their companies, one managed by its foreign trade bank BFCE (Banque Francaise pour le Commerce Exteriur) and the other by

tries frequently provide loan guarantees that enable investors to obtain funds from the Eurocurrency market in currencies not native to their country.

Affected public: The local populace may have little say regarding the investment decision itself even though they are the ones most directly affected by the negative environmental consequences such as noise and pollution. Once the project is in place this group may be the primary cause of government actions to expropriate a facility, if the perceived economic returns to them are overwhelmed by social and environmental costs. Predicting the attitudes and decision processes of the affected public is a difficult task given the diversity in cultural and social values within a country and between countries. These aspects are discussed in more detail by Shubik and Dunn (this volume).

Decision processes

To explain and predict the responses by multinational firms and insurance companies to international hazards requires a closer look at their decision processes. By *decision processes* we mean the way these parties structure their perceived alternatives, the data they have collected, the evaluation of the alternatives, and their final choice.

Before the investor and insurer can evaluate the relative attractiveness of a particular alternative there needs to be a clear understanding of the elements comprising risk. We will utilize the language of decision analysis to formulate the problem, although we recognize that in practice firms may not undertake such a formal approach.

Consider a particular project that has been proposed by a host country to a multinational firm. In Figure 6.2 we depict a specific investment, Project A, where there are n possible events, each of which has a certain likelihood of occurring and an associated outcome. The investor assigns probability Φ_i to the occurrence of each event i; C_i represents the consequence to the project if this event occurs. Some events in the host country (e.g., political or economic stability) will yield positive profits whereas others (e.g., social conflict) may produce losses. The insurer may have a different representation of the tree but the formal structure will be the same as shown in Figure 6.2.

In practice, constructing a decision tree is difficult for problems

COFACE (Compagnie Francaise d'Assurance a l'Exportation) (Chavlier and Hirsch 1981).

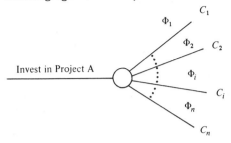

Figure 6.2. Events and consequences of firm's investment decision

such as international risk since there is an extremely sparse data base on which to specify events or estimate probabilities and consequences of different outcomes with any statistical precision. It is also difficult for the relevant parties to formulate a causal model on which to base a contingent structure of probabilities and consequences.

Investor concerns: The decision process of the key individuals or groups in the multinational firm specifying investment priorities will be influenced by the institutional structure of the organization. Two elements play an important role in influencing the collection and processing of data for choosing between proposed projects: the allocation of responsibility for the consequences of decisions and the use of simplified decision rules by organizations.

Allocation of responsibility: In their classic study of the behavioral theory of the firm, Cyert and March (1963) theorized that each part of the organization has a set of independent goals and constraints that guide its actions. We hypothesize that this feature of the organizational structure plays a key role in the foreign investment decision by many firms. Corporate investment planners are held responsible for the outcomes of their decisions with respect to particular projects. For this reason they try to share responsibility for uncertain outcomes with others and to avoid negative outcomes. There is thus a reliance on experts for advice, as well as a tendency to favor projects in foreign countries where investment planners feel they understand the situation very well.

Simplified decision rules: Organizations prefer to develop simple decision rules that enable them to avoid collecting information on future events (Cyert and March 1963). For this reason investors are likely to utilize threshold models of choice whereby projects are approved only if the corporate risk manager perceives the chances of a given event to be below an acceptable risk level. Acceptable risk levels themselves might vary according to the country, the nature of the risk, and the economic stakes involved.

If the problem is structured in this way, firms can avoid undertaking a detailed analysis of the consequences of different events. If Φ_i^* is the acceptable risk level for a project of (type) i, then the decision rule under a threshold model is simply: Accept i if its assessed risk level $\Phi_i \leq \Phi_i^*$; otherwise reject the project. One can justify this heuristic in terms of the attention that needs to be devoted to each investment decision. By specifying a cutoff point for examining specific projects, the investment planner is using a simple heuristic for comparing and pooling decision outcomes across projects of the same type and for reducing the time spent on collecting data and examining alternatives (Borkan and Kunreuther 1979).

Insurer concerns: Insurance firms face additional problems of uncertainty that revolve around information asymmetries. Specifically, the insurer has limited information regarding the risk characteristics of firms' investment decisions now as well as in the future. This asymmetric information between the insurer and the insured creates problems of adverse selection and moral hazard. These problems are likely to be greater in the international hazard area due to the lack of published information on which to base estimates of probabilities and future expected losses from a foreign investment.

Adverse selection: This is caused by the inability of insurance firms to fully discriminate among different types of risks in specifying premiums. The insurance industry may thus attract a portfolio of investors whose risk exposure is worse than average. In order to cover costs, premiums would have to be raised above the average costs of all investors facing the risk in question, possibly excluding some of the better risks because of high premiums. Eventually, rates may be so high that only the poorest risks, if any, are willing to insure, and the market fails. This spiral effect has been discussed widely in the economics and insurance literature (see Arrow 1971). For adverse selection to occur, investors must have better information on the nature of their risks than private insurance firms.

Moral hazard: This refers to the limited ability of the insurer to predict changes in the investor's behavior after they are insured. Multinational firms may then be less concerned with a project's success than if they had to bear the entire risk themselves. If insurers do not anticipate these behavioral shifts, then premiums will be inadequate to cover their expected losses.

Government regulations: Insurers are very concerned with the role of governmental regulations on their operations and on market structure. For example, U.S.-based insurance firms have become increasingly concerned over barriers to entry in marketing insurance in other countries.[3] Such regulations can strongly affect efficiency of risk pooling by insurance firms. They also adversely affect the competitive process by restricting market entry.

Prescriptive analysis

An understanding of the institutional arrangements and decision processes of investors and insurers toward country risk provides insights into ways of improving the management of risk and uncertainty in international transactions. Our interest in this chapter will be on two areas of prescriptive analysis. In the final section, we will consider how political risk assessment can be improved within the multinational firm itself. We also will consider cooperative institutional arrangements between the private insurance industry and the government in providing wider insurance coverage against international risks.

How investors deal with international risk

In this section we utilize our conceptual framework to provide more detail on the decision processes that multinational firms are likely to utilize in coping with the problems of international risk. We motivate our discussion with a real-world example: the problem faced by Indonesia as to whether it should invest financial resources in constructing facilities for shipping liquefied natural gas (LNG) abroad. In particular, we focus on the question, "Should Indonesia enter into a formal contract with United States firms to supply a specific quantity of LNG over the next twenty years?" Simplified models of the choice process based on this particular problem are constructed, even though we are aware that the actual decision-making process is far more complicated

---

[3] Personal conversation with John Cox, President of Insurance Company of North America.

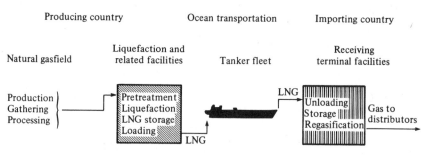

Figure 6.3. Major segments of a liquefied natural gas project

than our treatment implies. The exercise is thus designed to stimulate ideas as to ways one can describe investor behavior in a more realistic manner.

Problem formulation

Liquefied natural gas is a potential source of energy requiring a fairly complicated technological process for transportation and storage that has the potential, albeit with low probability, of creating severe losses. For purposes of transportation and storage, natural gas is liquefied to reduce its volume hundreds of times. It is then shipped in specially constructed tankers and received at a terminal where it undergoes regasification and is then distributed to different parts of the country, mostly by pipelines with the remainder carried by trucks or railcars. Due to the volatile nature of these liquids, there are potential catastrophic losses associated with explosions of a tanker or with a fire at a receiving terminal. Figure 6.3 depicts major segments of an LNG project.

Indonesia became a logical source of gas supply to other countries after Mobil Oil Indonesia announced in late 1971 that it had discovered large reserves of natural gas in northern Sumatra (i.e., the Arun field). The United States then expressed interest in buying Indonesian LNG. In 1972, the principal decision facing Pertamina, the Indonesian state-owned oil company, was whether it wanted to construct a liquefaction and loading facility for shipping LNG abroad.

Although it was not investing money in facilities in other countries, Pertamina faced the possibility that the United States would not construct a site for receiving LNG. In this sense, the United States plays the role of the host country with the associated set of political and social risks facing Pertamina regarding the approval process of the receiving and regasification terminals in California.[4] Since the proposed contract was for twenty years there were also economic risks associated with the project. Given the large investment costs required for constructing the Indonesian facilities, all of which are borne by Pertamina, there was some concern over the stability of future markets for LNG due to the uncertainty of future world energy prices.

Institutional arrangements

Each real-world problem involving foreign investments has a special set of institutional arrangements that reflect the regulatory and political structure of the involved countries. In our specific example the investor, Pertamina, could only enter into any contract on shipping LNG abroad after it was approved by the Indonesian government. With respect to the host country, the United States, two gas utilities in California (Pacific Lighting Corporation and Pacific Gas and Electric) formed a partnership to import LNG from Indonesia through a subsidiary, PacIndonesia. Any contract signed between PacIndonesia and Pertamina was subject to approval by the Federal Power Commission.

Other parties also had a stake in the final decision. For large-scale investments, such as LNG facilities, a substantial portion of the required funds is provided by long-term loans. The lenders, who include banks and insurance companies, utilize other people's money and thus are obliged to repay in full. Hence, before undertaking the financing of such projects, they will try to obtain some form of insurance against possible losses from the aforementioned risks. In the case of Indonesia, lenders to Pertamina, which included the Eurocurrency market, were guaranteed repayment of any financial loss by the Indonesia Central Bank (Office of Technology Assessment 1980). Hence, the risk from the proposed investment was assumed by the government directly rather than by the state-owned company.

Decision processes

Use of decision trees: Let us first turn to the question of how the investor is likely to evaluate whether to commit funds to a particular project. In the case of Pertamina, the decision was undoubtedly influenced by its estimate of the probability that California would approve the siting of an LNG terminal. Pertamina was entirely at risk with respect to the

4 California was proposed as the state where LNG would be received from Indonesia.

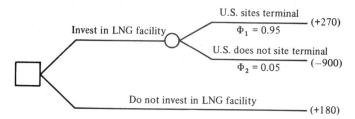

Figure 6.4. Decision tree for evaluating Pertamina's options

investment costs of its liquefaction and loading facilities.[5] To keep the analysis simple, suppose that in 1972, Pertamina feels the United States is its only potential customer of the LNG[6] and the company estimates the probability of California's not siting a facility to be Φ_1 = .05. Should this scenario develop we assume that the cost of converting the Indonesian facility to other uses would involve a net loss of $900 million. If California did construct a receiving terminal, then Pertamina anticipates that its total discounted profit on the investment would be $270 million. The Indonesian firm knows that if it does not invest in liquefaction facilities it could invest its resources in government securities that are known to yield $180 million with certainty.

The relevant branches and outcomes for the decisions to invest in LNG facilities and to not invest in LNG facilities are depicted in Figure 6.4. If one were using the criterion of maximizing expected or average return on investment, then the LNG facilities would be deemed attractive.[7] In reality the actual situation is much more complicated than Figure 6.4 implies. There are questions with respect to the final terms of the contract, the future prices of different forms of energy, the costs in constructing the liquefaction and loading facility, and various social and political factors that may affect the proba-

[5] A *force majeure* clause in that contract absolved the United States from any obligation to pay for gas should California not site a facility.

[6] In reality, Japan also expressed interest in possibly purchasing LNG, although negotiations on a contract did not begin until 1973.

[7] The expected return for investing in the LNG facilities is simply the sum of probabilities times consequences, i.e., Pertamina would prefer to invest rather than not (211.5 vs. 180). If, however, Pertamina's management were strongly risk averse so there was a high disutility assigned to the large loss then the reverse preference might hold. See Raiffa (1968) for a discussion of how utilities and disutilities can be introduced into this analysis.

bilities, consequences, and causal links between events. Each of these uncertainties could be represented in a more complicated decision tree, and Pertamina would then be faced with the difficult task of providing estimates of these additional parameters.

As we pointed out in the previous section, the lack of a good statistical data base makes it unlikely that Pertamina actually followed this formal analysis process. We do not know exactly how the company went about making its decision, but we can suggest factors that may have influenced its data collection and processing activities. Our conjectures are derived from related research on how firms behave with respect to country risk (see Vernon, this volume) coupled with empirical data on individual and organizational behavior toward low-probability events.

Systematic biases: Due to the lack of a good statistical data base, past experience with the host country is likely to be an important element in determining whether to invest in a particular project. Most firms feel they do not have a good understanding of the relationship between events and managerial contingencies from historical data to estimate the probabilities and consequences of future events on particular investments. Kobrin (1981) points out that impacts of political risks on firms are rarely documented, with the exception of expropriation. As a result, firms frequently focus on recent events to the exclusion of others in making their judgments. Undue importance may be placed on dramatic events, such as a student riot or a palace coup, which suggest that the country is unstable when, in fact, it is not (Rummel and Heenan 1978). Economists who have studied corporate risk management feel that too much time is devoted by multinationals to worrying about these headline-grabbing events and not enough attention is given to studying erratic shifts in foreign laws and regulations that steadily erode corporate profits (*Business Week* 1981).

Kelly (1981) provides empirical evidence on the role of past experience in the foreign investment decision-making process through a study of 105 multinational firms, all in the Fortune 500. She points out that if a firm has suffered recent losses from political risks, it tends to use a finer screen and undertakes a more detailed and sophisticated analysis of this factor before making future decisions.

This type of biased behavior on the part of firms has been well documented in field survey and controlled laboratory experiments. Tversky and Kahneman (1974) have labeled this pehnomenon "availability," whereby one judges the probability of future events by the ease with which one can remember past ones. An example of the availability bias from the field of financial investment is provided by Guttentag and Herring (1981). They indicate that several European banks (e.g., the Fugger Bank, the Bardi, and the Peruzzi) became insolvent during the Middle Ages because of default on large loans by sovereign borrowers. These rulers had a history of paying back small loans. By focusing only on the number of times loans were repaid it appeared as if the sovereign had a favorable record when, in fact, he was a very risky customer.

Nisbett and Ross (1980) provide anecdotal and case history evidence that suggests that individuals give more weight to information that is vivid, concrete, and easily recalled. The authors point out that the availability heuristic is a prime determinant of the effect of vividness on causal inference, since graphic information is more likely to be remembered than bland data.

Empirical studies on consumer decision making with respect to low-probability events reveal similar behavior. For example, few individuals voluntarily protect themselves against the financial consequences of natural hazards until after a disaster occurs. Kunreuther et al. (1978) have documented the importance of past experience as a critical variable in the insurance purchase decision against flood and earthquakes by statistically analyzing data from face-to-face interviews with 3,000 homeowners, half of them insured and the other half uninsured. A comment from a homeowner in a flood-prone area illustrates the importance of past experience in determining his attitude toward future coverage:

I've talked to the different ones that have been bombed out. This was their feelings: the $60 in premiums they could use for something else. But now they don't care if the figure was $600. They're going to take insurance because they have been through it twice and learned a lesson from it (Kunreuther et al. p.112).

Similar behavior was observed in earthquake areas of California. Following the Santa Barbara quake of 1978, insurance agents noted a sharp increase in demand for coverage (MacDougall 1981).

The media can play a key role in highlighting certain events, which then increases their salience as perceived by the public. As a result there is often a tendency to estimate the probability of a particular event to be much higher than it actually is. Combs and Slovic (1979) undertook a study of the frequency with which two newspapers reported various causes of death. They found that violent deaths due to homicides, accidents, and natural disasters were overreported, whereas disease-related deaths were underreported. These biases in coverage corresponded closely to biases found in a previous study (Lichtenstein et al. 1978) in which people were asked to judge the frequency of these same causes of death. Their findings suggest that there may be similar biases with respect to political risk if firms focus on headlines as a basis for judging the magnitude of the risks facing a particular investment.

Role of regret: The absence of both a detailed statistical data base and a causal model of political and economic risk places an enormous responsibility on the shoulders of corporate investment planners, who are likely to be highly sensitive to the potential losses when committing funds to a project. We hypothesize that one of the important factors influencing the decision on whether or not to invest in a particular project is how much the responsible individual will regret each choice on the basis of possible outcomes. Savage (1954) has defined the concept of regret as the difference between the level of assets that the decision maker obtains when a given event occurs and the best that one could have done had one known that this particular event would actually happen. Bell (1982) has used this concept in a similar manner.

Figure 6.5 illustrates regret for the simplified problem treated earlier. The choice between investing and not investing is characterized by two attributes, the first one being the actual consequence C_i, and the second one indicating the amount of money that would have been earned had the other action been taken.

Before recommending that Pertamina invest in LNG facilities the planner would compare the outcomes under both branches of "Invest in LNG facility," with the return from a certain investment should it not "Invest in LNG Facilities" (i.e., +180). If the event represented by Φ_1 occurs, then there is no regret. If the event associated with Φ_2 is realized, then the planner would be subject to a regret of 1,080 (i.e., 900 + 180). This represents the difference between the actual consequence and the best outcome that could have been obtained had the planner known in advance that Φ_2 would occur, and hence would have opted not to invest in LNG facilities. A similar analysis would be undertaken in evaluating the regret in the decision "Not Invest in LNG Facilities."

If regret is an important factor in the decision-making process, then investment planners will base their decisions partly on potential returns and partly on foregone returns. If the foregone returns are

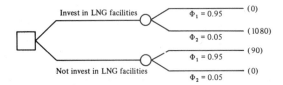

Figure 6.5. Regret as part of Pertamina's decision tree

sufficiently large and regret is weighed heavily in their process, then the managers may prefer not to take the responsibility for having made a "bad" decision even if the probability of this outcome is relatively small.

Regret can be avoided by partly shifting the responsibility for taking actions to others. Hopple and Kuhlman (1981) point out that firms are increasingly relying on country and area specialists in making their decisions. Investment planners can also utilize personal contacts in the host country where an investment is planned. These sources of information provide firms with a more detailed rationale for justifying investment actions.

The principal disadvantage of this strategy, when there is no insurance, is that it frequently leads to a lack of diversification across countries because of large transaction costs associated with finding experts and personal contacts from many different nations. Guttentag and Herring (1981) have noted a tendency of some banks to concentrate most of their foreign investments in a few countries. This opens them up to the possibility of large losses should these governments refuse to honor foreign debts. The bank's strategy of not diversifying its portfolio widely may appear to be economically sound given the advantages of specialization. On the other hand, the lack of perfect capital markets increases its probability of going bankrupt should foreign investments be threatened by events such as expropriation or inconvertibility of currency.

Threshold models: An additional way to reduce the possibility of regret is not to undertake any actions unless the probability of failure is below a given threshold level. To illustrate, suppose Pertamina used a threshold model for screening out projects. It would then specify an acceptable risk level Φ^*, which would be used as a criterion for approving or disapproving a project. If the risk associated with failure Φ_2 was less than Φ^* then the project would be approved, subject to the additional condition that the expected rate of return for success was above an acceptable level. If $\Phi_2 > \Phi^*$, then the project would be rejected no matter how high the rate of return would be. Looking at the data in Figure 6.4, the LNG liquefaction and loading facility would be approved if $\Phi^* > .05$ and \$270 million were considered an acceptable return on the proposed investment.

In a study of thirty-eight companies considering foreign investments, Aharoni (1966) provides empirical evidence on the importance of threshold models for initially screening out projects that have high risk. Kelly (1981) finds similar behavior on the part of the 105 firms she investigated. Investment planners made decisions on the basis of acceptable rates of return and acceptable risk levels. Each situation was looked at on its own merits without any attempt to undertake any type of portfolio or covariance analysis across projects, as would be implied by an optimization model. This type of decision rule reduced the costs of collecting and processing large amounts of data and avoided uncertainty. It thus conforms to the hypotheses advanced by Cyert and March (1963) in their behavioral theory of the firm.

Consumers and government agencies, as well as business organizations, use threshold models to avoid having to focus on the consequences of extremely low probability events. In making insurance decisions, an individual frequently concludes that if the probability of a flood or earthquake is below some given level Φ^* then "It won't happen to me." Hence, it is not worth worrying about the potential consequences. In such a case insurance protection is not even considered (Slovic et al. 1977; Kunreuther et al. 1978). Government regulatory agencies such as the Nuclear Regulatory Commission use threshold rules to evaluate the decision to license plants. If they deem the probability of a severe accident to be below Φ^* then they do not worry about the consequences and may overlook design features of a plant that could produce a very serious accident (Jackson and Kunreuther 1981).

Taken together, the empirical evidence supports the hypothesis that multinational firms behave in a manner consistent with concepts from the behavioral theory of the firm. The lack of a rich statistical data base and causal model of risk creates special burdens on the investment planner. Actions are justified and regret is avoided through the use of experts and personal contacts. Threshold models and acceptable levels of performance are also used as a guide to selecting projects. Finally, little effort is made to deal with the portfolio of risks. Rather, each project is evaluated on its own merits without comparisons between other potential investments.

Pertamina's decision problem

Let us now return to the specific uncertainty facing Pertamina: determining the probability that the United States will actually site an LNG receiving terminal in California. There are great difficulties in providing an estimate of this probability because of the complex nature of the decision-making process in the United States with respect to the siting of large-scale technologies such as nuclear power plants or LNG terminals.

The siting process: For one thing, the decision affects many different individuals and groups in society rather than being confined to the normal relationship of a private market transaction such as when a consumer purchases food or an appliance from a store. In the siting decision, each of these groups has its own objectives, attributes, data base, and constraints (Kunreuther, Linnerooth, et al. in press).

In the case of the LNG terminal in California several different parties were concerned with the siting decision. The first was the applicant for the terminal, Western LNG Terminal Associates.[8] Also involved were government agencies at the federal, state, and local level. The Federal Energy Regulatory Commission (FERC) determines whether a proposed LNG project is in the public interest and should be allowed. The California Coastal Commission has the responsibility of protecting the California coastline, the California Public Utilities Commission (CPUC) is the principal state body involved in power plant issues, and the state legislature sets up the rules of the siting process. Finally, there are public interest groups such as the Sierra Club and local citizens' groups. Each of these different parties interacted with each other at different stages of the decision process with respect to the siting of a terminal. Their concerns centered around three different classes of attributes: economic aspects, environmental aspects, and risk aspects.

A second feature of the siting problem is the absence of a statistical data base on which to base reliable estimates of the different economic, environmental, and safety risks associated with a proposed project. Experts are likely to differ on their estimates of the consequences of an LNG terminal, and each of the different parties will use

---

[8] This was a special company set up to represent the LNG siting interests of the three gas distribution utilities: Southern California Gas Company, Pacific Gas and Electric, and El Paso Natural Gas Company.

those quantitative figures that best suit their purposes (Lathrop and Linnerooth 1982).

As a result of conflicts between the parties involved in the LNG siting debate, today (eight years after initial applications were filed for three terminals in California), no final decision has been made as to whether one will actually be built. The Los Angeles facility was ruled out because of seismic risk and Oxnard was rejected because the risk to the population of a catastrophic accident was perceived to be too high. Only Point Conception remains a possibility. In 1978, this site was approved, conditional on its being a seismically safe harbor. The final report on the safety of the facility has not yet been issued by the FERC and CPUC.[9]

Pertamina's investment strategy: Despite these uncertainties with respect to the resolution of political and social forces affecting the siting decision in California, Pertamina decided to invest in a liquefaction and loading facility. In taking this action Pertamina protected its investment in two ways. First, it negotiated and signed a contract with Japan in 1973 to ship LNG from its new facility. By diversifying its portfolio, Pertamina was not locked into one potential customer. It actually began shipping LNG to Japan in August 1977 from its new plant (Wood, 1979). Second, given its concern with increasing demand for LNG by Japan, Pertamina has renegotiated its contract on a month-to-month basis with PacIndonesia (the U.S. firm) since October 1977. Pertamina has the right to cancel at any time without any attached penalty. With the recent expansion of the Japanese market for LNG there is now no guarantee that the United States will receive liquefied gas from Indonesia even if a terminal in California is eventually approved.

The other uncertainty that Pertamina faced with respect to the profitability of its LNG facility is the future of world energy prices. The company resolved this problem through contract negotiations. Soon after the initial contract between PacIndonesia and Pertamina was signed in 1973, the world price of oil rose sharply. Since this contract was not tied to an increase in energy prices, the Indonesian government refused to approve it. A final version was eventually

9 A detailed description of the California siting decision appears in Kunreuther and Lathrop (1982) and Linnerooth (1980). A descriptive model of choice indicating the nature of the political and social risks and how they play a role in siting decisions can be found in Kunreuther, Linnerooth et al. (in press).

approved in 1978. It includes an escalation clause reflecting changes in the Indonesian crude oil export prices.[10] In the case of Japan, because the initial contract was tied to the price of world oil and automatically reflected the increase, it did not have to be renegotiated (Western LNG Terminal Associates 1978).[11]

How insurers deal with international risk

In this section we will investigate the role played by private and government insurers against political risk. Our object is to provide some perspective on current institutional arrangements and decision processes before discussing proposals for change.

Problem formulation

If a multinational firm could entice private insurance firms to protect its foreign investments against political and economic risk, then the responsibility for a loss would be effectively shifted to another party. As pointed out, private insurance firms have been reluctant to offer coverage because of the absence of accurate data on which to base actuarially fair rates. In fact, political risk is at the opposite end of the spectrum from the risk of dying, for which there are highly sophisticated mortality tables upon which life insurance premiums are based. An additional problem facing private firms is that large amounts of money are at stake. Insurance contracts for political risks can involve coverage and premiums in the millions of dollars.[12] Should the company be expropriated by the host country, then the resulting loss to the insurance firm could represent a sizeable proportion of its assets unless it can engage in reinsurance contracts.

Institutional arrangements

The only private firms who are now marketing insurance coverage are large companies, such as the Insurance Company of North America, or consortia such as the American International Group or the

---

[10] Further information on this is contained in Office of Technology Assessment (1980).

[11] Vernon (this volume) provides insights into the usefulness of long-term contracts when there are economic risks.

[12] Personal conversation with Hugh Sinclair, President of Insurance Company of North America Multinational Insurance Corporation (INAMIC). See also *Business Week* (1981).

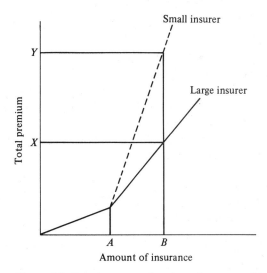

Figure 6.6. Premiums as a function of amount of insurance for small and large insurers

Chubb Group of Insurance Companies (Cathey 1981). We hypothesize that this type of concentration is due to the different degrees of risk aversion between large and small firms. Figure 6.6 illustrates this point with a simple diagram relating the premium charged to the amount of coverage offered. For small amounts of coverage (until $A) both large and small firms are assumed to be risk neutral as indicated by the straight line. For amounts in excess of $A the small firms become more risk averse relative to the larger companies or consortia. If $B of protection were demanded by a multinational firm, then the large company would want to charge a premium of $X, whereas the small firm would require a larger premium of $Y in order to be willing to undertake this insurance. After market adjustment, only the large firms would provide insurance for risks of type B to multinational investors and these large insurers will make monopoly profits, because there are only a limited number of suppliers of coverage. If both insurance firms and multinational corporations overestimate the probability of a potential loss, the prices for a given amount of coverage will be even higher, thus increasing monopoly profits.

What impact will this type of equilibrium have on changes on the supply side? We anticipate that as more insurance firms become knowledgeable about political risk, they will enter the market and compete away monopoly profits through lower premiums. This is consistent with a recent article in *Business Week* (1981) predicting that current high levels of profits in the political risk area would soon be eroded by the entry of new private insurance companies into the market.

Multinational firms also rely heavily on OPIC for insurance coverage against political risks in developing countries. Since this governmental program was established in 1969, it has come under close scrutiny by congressional committees. One of the most controversial issues associated with OPIC is whether it is likely to involve the United States in the foreign affairs of other countries than would otherwise be the case.

In the Senate Foreign Relations Committee hearings of 1974, the U.S. Ambassador to Jamaica testified that additional guarantees by OPIC related to $500 million of investments in Jamaican alumina/bauxite facilities would have been interpreted by the Jamaican government as an indication of lack of confidence by the U.S. government in the Jamaican economy and political leadership. Hence, he refused to concur in OPIC's proposal (Griffin 1976). Based on this testimony and other evidence presented at the hearings, the Senate committee concluded that some involvement in host country politics was inherent in the nature of the OPIC program. On the other hand, the House subcommittee disagreed with these criticisms. It claimed that, "OPIC provides an institutional framework which can help insure that US private corporate activities in the LDCs do not unnecessarily precipitate conflicts directly involving the US government" (Griffin 1976, p. 639).

In the fall of 1981, Congress extended the life of OPIC for four more years. The only major change in OPIC's new charter was to slightly broaden the scope of countries where OPIC is allowed to write political risk insurance. Previously, its mandate restricted OPIC, except in unusual circumstances or when dealing with mineral and energy projects, to countries with a per capita income of less than $1,000 (in 1975 dollars). Their new character has increased this to $2,950 (in 1979 dollars).[13]

Decision process

Both private firms and OPIC face potential problems of adverse selection and moral hazard in issuing insurance to multinational firms.

---

[13] Private conversation with Robert L. Jordan of OPIC.

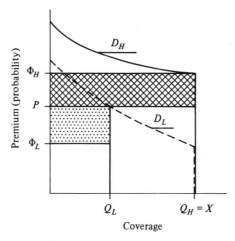

Figure 6.7. The adverse selection problem

Adverse selection: To illustrate adverse selection consider the simplified case where there are an equal number of each of two types of project, low and high risk, but the insurer cannot distinguish between them. Low-risk projects have a probability Φ_L of a loss of X dollars whereas high-risk projects face a probability $\Phi_H > \Phi_L$ of a loss of X dollars.[14] Insurers assume that the probability of a loss is the average of the two probabilities $\Phi = (\Phi_L + \Phi_H)/2$. They base their premium P per dollar coverage on this estimate.

Figure 6.7 depicts the phenomenon of adverse selection due to this imperfect information by the insurer. Investment planners are assumed to be risk averse, to estimate the probability of a loss correctly, and to choose an amount of insurance that maximizes some objective function (e.g., expected utility). The demand curves for high- and low-risk projects are then given by D_H and D_L, respectively, with full coverage purchased if $P \leq \Phi_i$, $i = L, H$.[15] Q_L units of coverage will be purchased for low-risk projects and Q_H units for high-risk investments. The expected loss to the insurer on high-risk projects (shown

---

[14] We are assuming that there are only two states of nature: loss of X dollars or no loss.

[15] Risk-averse customers will always demand full protection if the premium per dollar coverage is below the probability of a loss and they do not have a budget constraint.

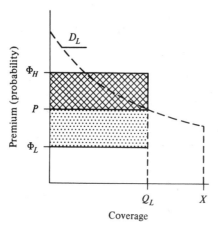

Figure 6.8. The moral hazard problem

by the hatched area in Figure 6.7) exceeds the expected gain from low-risk ones (the dotted region).

One way for insurers to counteract the adverse selection problem, when they do not have good information on the respective risks, is to market price–quantity policies. Under this system, the insurer offers a set of policies for which the premium per dollar of coverage rises as the amount of coverage rises. Investors with riskier projects will tend to opt for higher coverage and consequently will pay higher premiums per dollar of coverage; investors with less risky projects will tend to select lower coverage and lower premiums per dollar of coverage. The analytic properties of this system have been investigated by Rothschild and Stiglitz (1976). For such a set of policies to function effectively some monitoring system must be instituted by insurance firms to ensure that no entity attempts to protect itself against a large loss by purchasing multiple low premium–low coverage policies from several different insurers.[16]

Moral hazard: The moral hazard problem is illustrated in Figure 6.8 for a set of low-risk projects. The multinational firm and the insurer both assume at the time the investment is made that there is a proba-

---

[16] Kleindorfer and Kunreuther (in press) have investigated the robustness of these types of price-quantity policies for the case where potential insured individuals misperceive the probabilities of a loss.

bility Φ_L that it will fail. Based on the demand curve D_L, the investment planners purchase Q_L units of insurance at P dollars per unit. Once coverage is bought, investors are less vigilant than anticipated (and than they would have been in the absence of coverage) so that the actual probability of a project failure increases to Φ_H. As a result insurers face an expected loss for each project, shown by the cross-hatched area in Figure 6.8, instead of an expected gain, indicated by the dotted area.

The possibility of moral hazard as a result of a firm's purchasing insurance from OPIC was suggested by the Senate Foreign Relations Committee following its 1974 hearings. It felt that insurance purchased from a U.S. government-sponsored program such as OPIC

> may lull the companies into a false sense of security and induce them not to make the necessary adjustments to changing local conditions when a healthy relationship between host country and companies would require it.
>
> Moreover, it is the belief of the Committee that government insurance may at times increase the likelihood of expropriation. Expropriation is viewed by some radical governments as a means of striking a blow at the United States Government (Griffin 1976, p. 638).

Prescriptive analysis

The preceding descriptive analysis and case study make clear that there are several impediments to a feasible or workable sharing of political risks between multinational firms involved in direct foreign investments and insurers. Concerning firms, the complexities involved in assessing such risks give rise to organizational reactions characterized by single project–single country myopia, by organizational diffusion of responsibility and regret, and by uncertainty avoidance. Such organizational behavior can result in various inefficiencies, including improperly diversified investments, problems of organizational monitoring and control, and inappropriate protective reaction to unfolding events.

These reactions at the firm level only compound the normal problems that insurers face in providing coverage against large risks. It is not surprising, therefore, that the role of insuring political risks has been assumed for the most part by government agencies such as OPIC.[17] One may argue, of course, that some governmental involve-

---

[17] *Business Week* (1981) estimated that multinationals worldwide paid some $600–700 million in political risk premiums in 1980, with about $500 million going to government agencies.

ment in insuring these risks is desirable given their strategic ramifications. Nonetheless, private industry has demonstrated significant efficiency advantages over governmental operations in other areas, so reliance on private market mechanisms has prima facie desirable characteristics.[18]

Our discussion of prescriptive analysis is divided into two parts. We first focus on ways that corporations might improve their assessment procedures, so that they have a better understanding of the hazards for which they seek insurance. We then conclude by proposing an alternative insurance program with which private industry can play a more prominent role in providing coverage against international hazards.

Improving risk assessments by investors

The preceding descriptive analysis suggests several areas in which political risk assessment might be improved. We briefly review here recent research of interest under two headings: process improvements and organizational design.

Process improvements: It should be recognized that the problem of political risk assessment is a special case of the general problem of risk assessment. In recent times, the increasing technical and social complexity of industrial society has given rise to a concerted research effort to develop publicly and scientifically defensible methods for assessing social and technological hazards. It would take us too far afield to review this literature here, but some of its major conclusions deserve stress in the present context.[19]

First, one may broadly describe the process of risk assessment as involving two interrelated tasks:

1. Determining the structure of the contingent events and decisions relating to the risk in question. Figure 6.4 is a very simple example of such a structure. This representation in so-called decision-tree fashion depicts the possible events and consequences resulting from different scenarios.
2. Estimating the probabilities and consequences of each scenario.

[18] See Blankart (1980) for a survey of comparative results on public versus private provision of goods and services. These empirical results strongly support the view that private industry has cost advantages relative to governmental provision of goods.

[19] Recent research on the role of risk assessment in an institutional context can be found in Conrad (1980).

Concerning the second task, recent research has provided a variety of subjective and analytical methods of assessment. However, the more fundamental problem in the political risk assessment area is the first task, determining the "right" decision tree (i.e., a decision tree whose causal links to the risks in question are not just specious). The Indonesian case study indicates how difficult this task is, as it calls for an intricate knowledge of the events or scenarios in another country that may condition or cause significant political change. Although it would be foolish to expect a perfect understanding in advance of such scenarios, recent research on corporate planning and risk assessment has shown that the use of new corporate planning methodologies can be of help here.[20] By a formal analysis of alternative assumptions and their consequences, these methods enlarge the set of scenarios considered and lend added plausibility and understanding to the chains of events that may produce negative outcomes. In the end, of course, nothing substitutes for the wisdom and intuition of the participants in such planning processes. Nonetheless, this research suggests that although political risk assessment is intrinsically subjective, one can substantially improve even wise intuition by instituting explicit and formal procedures.

One of the most promising assessment procedures for evaluating the political risks is SPAIR, an acronym for subjective probabilities assigned to investment risks. This approach, developed at Shell Oil Company (see Meisner 1976 and Gebelein et al. 1978), requires experts to evaluate different global scenarios (some of which they may generate themselves). Each expert provides qualitative judgment on the likelihood that certain events such as civil disorder, war, expropriation, price controls, taxation changes, and export or production restrictions will occur.

These assessments are then converted into probability estimates on the basis of how strongly a particular proposition is supported or refuted by the expert. The elicitation technique is similar to the Delphi procedure because it uses opinions solicited through a questionnaire. Unlike the Delphi method the SPAIR procedure does not force a panel consensus.

The approach also incorporates a Bayesian updating procedure if new information becomes available. For example, suppose that Per-

---

[20] See Ackoff (1974) and Kleindorfer (1982) for a review of recent research on planning methods and risk assessment. Zeleny (1979) and Hogarth and Madridakis (1981) discuss recent field and experimental results on group processes and forecasting.

tamina brought a group of experts to estimate the probability that California would site an LNG terminal. One individual might have estimated the probability that a terminal would *not* be sited as Φ_1 = .05. After learning that two of the three proposed sites were rejected, this individual might revise the estimate downward using data on previous real-world scenarios as a basis for updating the probability.[21]

Organizational design issues: Many of the problems of country and project myopia observed in multinational corporations are due to the necessity of organizing corporate activities around specific (large) projects and geographical regions. Oftentimes such specialization represents the appropriate tradeoff between responsibility and control in disaggregating corporate worldwide activities into manageable chunks. Moreover, political risks form only one piece of the more complicated puzzle of business and foreign exchange risks for a given geographical region or group of investment projects.

These considerations can be evaluated operationally by considering the costs and benefits of alternative organizational designs, for example, organizing by region, by project, or by functional area. Each of these organizational forms has certain corporation-specific benefits for the planning and control of activities. The final choice of organizational structure is then dictated by those dimensions of corporate performance most critical for responsibility and control.

Kelly's (1981) analysis of the organizational structure of international operations reveals considerable diversity in the ways in which firms organize, including structuring corporate activities by geographical divisions (19 percent), by global product divisions (34 percent), having international operations organized under an international division (22 percent), or by matrix organizations (23 percent). This variety reflects the absence of general truths regarding efficient organizational design. For example, organizing by product groups may make sense from an operational viewpoint, whereas assessing and monitoring political and foreign exchange risks would be much simpler under a regional organization. Combining these two criteria can be accomplished, through additional managerial resources, by forming a matrix organization with primary operational control vested in the product group while simultaneously giving a regional coordinator the authority to collect and monitor information on all corporate activities in a given region.

[21] A more detailed discussion on how Bayesian techniques can be used to revise political risk estimates appears in Hopple and Kuhlman (1981).

Compromise solutions such as matrix organizations have begun to prove their worth in coping with a variety of information and control tradeoffs in organizational design.[22] Indeed, one may view organization design generally as the evaluation of how different organizational forms fare with respect to competing long- and short-run planning and control dimensions. Here, just as with decision process problems, the key to improvement is an explicit analysis of alternatives and their consequences.

In reviewing the preceding discussion on prescriptive measures for the firm, the fundamental problem of dealing with the risks of international hazards appears to be the cost and/or unavailability of accurate information concerning probabilities and consequences of different events and the organizational responses that such uncertainty evokes. In part, these problems are a generic feature of the complexity of doing business in the international arena. However, these informational issues do suggest benefits from sharing data across insurers. In the next section, we consider such an "information partnership" in more detail, as we investigate appropriate informational and insurance roles for government and private insurers in the political risk area.

Alternative insurance programs

The foregoing discussion points out that there are currently only a few large private insurers willing to enter the political risk area in the U.S. market. Outside the United States, the situation is even more skewed, with political risk insurance almost entirely in the hands of governmental agencies. Considering only the U.S. market, we have hypothesized that smaller insurers are unwilling to enter this market because of the large uncertainties involved and because their small asset base would not allow them to provide coverage against the catastrophic loss potential of many political risks. To encourage more private firms to enter the political risk market, thus promoting competition and innovation, the following steps could be pursued: (1) facilitate the pooling and sharing of information between the federal government and private industry, and (2) expand the current OPIC-backed political risk reinsurance program.

The first of these measures is designed to increase the quality and ease of obtaining information concerning country risks. The second measure is designed to decrease maximum exposure of firms in given

---

22 See Galbraith (1973) for a detailed discussion of matrix organizations and their relationship to other organizational design issues.

areas through excess-loss reinsurance. Taken together, these measures could increase the quality of risk assessment procedures by insurers and promote competition.

Pooling and sharing of information: Concerning the pooling of information, governmental agencies now serve as the major source of information for political risk assessment for private insurers. However, such information is located in many different agencies. Our proposal, simply, is to further facilitate the exchange of information on risks and claims by setting up a coordinating agency, possibly through OPIC.[23]

In setting up or expanding any agency to deal with information pooling, it would be very important to have private industry's involvement in determining what data, both in form and content, would be useful. Currently, some private insurers are using a project region–maximum coverage grid to classify risks (and claims history). One would hope that a classification scheme of this sort would be devised in cooperation with private insurers and the government. The pooling arrangements should be sufficiently attractive to motivate private insurers to provide their company data on claims settlements for inclusion in the statistical data base. All private member insurance firms in such an information-sharing consortium would then have access to this data base and related backup material and could learn from the experience of others in making future underwriting decisions.

In addition to this historical data base, one would also expect certain future-oriented studies (e.g., information on relevant country risk factors and expert prognoses) to be put in the archives of the coordinating agency. Much of this material is now available only in an ad hoc fashion through the respective country desks in the Departments of State and Commerce. In the end, of course, political risk assessment is a highly uncertain enterprise, even after all possible sources have been examined. The point we are making here is that U.S. suppliers of political risk insurance, both private and government, should realize the immense importance of sharing relevant information on risk assessment.

Government reinsurance: Another reason that private industry has been reluctant to insure large foreign investments against political risk is

---

[23] West (1980) argues that OPIC already has considerable informational advantages and is better informed than its typical multinational investor client.

the possibility of their incurring severe losses that may threaten their solvency. Private reinsurance companies have also been reluctant to share this risk. Government reinsurance may therefore be desirable. By agreeing to share the risk in this way, the government also has an implied responsibility to protect U.S. investments. This involvement will most likely be taken into account by governments who are considering acts that might imperil foreign investments.

Currently, OPIC, through the Overseas Investment Reinsurance Group (OIRG), does reinsure private insurers writing policies for developing countries and for mineral and energy exploration projects. What we are suggesting is an expansion of these reinsurance activities to provide excess loss insurance, with long time horizons, in the political risk area generally. By continuing OPIC's past premium policies (which have provided a self-sustaining margin of profit and reserves), such an expanded reinsurance program would provide incentives for additional private insurers to enter the political risk insurance market.

A prototype example of the type of reinsurance program we have in mind is provided by the Federal Riot Reinsurance Program, currently administered by the Federal Insurance Administration under the Federal Emergency Management Agency (FEMA). This program provides excess-loss reinsurance to private insurers against urban disorders of various sorts. The government's only role here is to provide protection against very large losses. The program has had no major financial or administrative problems since its inception in the late 1960s. Indeed, the Riot Reinsurance Program may be phased out during the current administration on the grounds that private reinsurance markets have now grown to the point where this program is superfluous. This changing institutional structure suggests the importance of federally backed riot (and crime) reinsurance in stimulating the growth of private (re-)insurance. In the same spirit, the proposed expansion of current OPIC activities to broader reinsurance coverage for political risk may be viewed as encouraging the further development of private insurance firms' involvement in this area. Moreover, one may expect that the strategic and informational advantages of OPIC would ensure a continuing important role for this agency in the reinsurance market for political risk coverage offered by private U.S. firms.

References

Ackoff, R. (1974). *Redesigning the Future: A Systems Approach to Societal Problems.* New York: Wiley.

Aharoni, Y. (1966). *The Foreign Investment Decision Process.* Cambridge, Mass.: Graduate School of Business Administration, Harvard University.

Arrow, K. (1971). *Essays in the Theory of Risk Bearing.* Chicago: Markham.

Bell, D. (1982). "Regret in Decision Making Under Uncertainty." *Operations Research,* 30 (September-October): 961–81.

Blankart, C. B. (1980). "Bureaucratic Problems in Public Choice: Why do Public Goods Still Remain Public?" in K. W. Roskamp (ed.), *Public Finance and Public Choice.* Paris: Cujas.

Borkan, B., and H. Kunreuther (1979). "Contingency Planning Against Low Probability Events." *Best's Review,* 80: 106–12.

Business Week (1981). "Insuring Against Risk Abroad." (September 14): 59–62.

Cathey, P. (1981). "Hedge Overseas Bets with Risk Insurance." *Iron Age,* (August 12): 33–5.

Chavlier, A., and G. Hirsch (1981). "The Assessment of the Political Risk in the Investment Decision." *Journal of Operational Research,* 32: 599–610.

Combs, B., and P. Slovic (1979). "Newspaper Coverage of Causes of Death." *Journalism Quarterly,* 56: 837–43.

Conrad, J. (1980). *Society, Technology and Risk Assessment.* New York: Academic Press.

Cyert, R., and J. March (1963). *A Behavioral Theory of the Firm.* Englewood Cliffs, N.J.: Prentice-Hall.

Galbraith, J. (1973). *Designing Complex Organizations.* Reading, Mass.: Addison-Wesley.

Gebelein, C. D., C. Pearson, and M. Silbersh (1978). "Assessing Political Risk of Oil Investment Ventures." *Journal of Petroleum Technology,* (May): 725–30.

Griffin, J. (1976). "Transfer of OPIC's Investment Insurance Programs to Private Insurers: Prospects and Proposals." *Law and Policy in International Business,* 8: 631–56.

Guttentag, J., and R. Herring (1981). "A Framework for the Analysis of Financial Disorder," in Blume, Crockett, and Taubman (eds.), *Economic Activity and Finance.* Cambridge, Mass.: Ballinger.

Hogarth, R. M., and S. Madridakis (1981). "Forecasting and Planning: An Evaluation." *Management Science,* vol.27, no.2 (February): 115–38.

Hohenemser, C., R. Kasperson, and R. Kates (1977). "The Distrust of Nuclear Power." *Science,* 196: 25–34.

Hopple, G., and J. Kuhlman (1981). *Expert-Generated Data: Applications In International Affairs.* Boulder, Colo.: Westview.

Jackson, J., and H. Kunreuther (1981). "Low Probability Events and Determining Acceptable Risk: The Case of Nuclear Regulation." Professional Paper, PP-81-87, May, Laxenburg, Austria: IIASA.

Kelly, M. (1981). "Foreign Investment Evaluation Practices of US Multinational Corporations." Ann Arbor, Mich.: UMI Research Press.

Kleindorfer, P. (1982). "Group Decision Making Methods for Evaluating Social and Technological Risk," in H. Kunreuther and E. Ley (eds.), *The Risk Analysis Controversy: An Institutional Perspective.* Berlin: Springer-Verlag.

Kleindorfer, P., and H. Kunreuther (in press). "Misinformation and Equilibrium in Insurance Markets," in J. Finsinger (ed.), *Economic Analysis of Regulated Markets. Pt. 3: Insurance Markets.* London: Macmillan.

Kobrin, S. (1981). "Political Assessment by International Firms: Models or Methodologies." *Journal of Policy Modeling,* 3: 251–70.

Kunreuther, H., R. Ginsberg, L. Miller, P. Sagi, P. Slovic, B. Borkan, and N. Katz (1978). *Disaster Insurance Protection.* New York: Wiley.

Kunreuther, H., and J. Lathrop (1982). "Siting Hazardous Facilities: Lessons from LNG." *Risk Analysis*, 1: 289–302.

Kunreuther, H., J. Linnerooth, J. Lathrop, H. Atz, S. MacGill, C. Mandl, M. Schwartz, and M. Thompson (in press). *Risk Analysis and Decision Processes: The Siting of LEG in Four Countries*. New York: Springer-Verlag.

Lathrop, J., and J. Linnerooth (1982). "The Role of Risk Assessment in a Political Decision Process," in P. Humphreys and A. Vari (eds.), *Analysing and Aiding Decision Processes*. Amsterdam: North Holland. IIASA.

Lichtenstein, S., P. Slovic, B. Fischhoff, M. Layman, and B. Combs. (1978). "Judged Frequency of Lethal Events." *Journal of Experimental Psychology: Human Learning and Memory*, 4: 551–78.

Linnerooth, J. (1980). "A Short History of the California LNG Terminal." Working Paper WP-80-155. Laxenburg, Austria: IIASA.

MacDougall, A. (1981). "Earthquake Insurance: Is it Worth It?" *Los Angeles Times*, March 8.

Meisner, J. (1976). "Processing and Evaluating Expert Opinion." Paper presented at the Second European Congress on Operations Research, Stockholm.

Nisbett, R., and L. Ross (1980). *Human Inference: Strategies and Shortcomings of Social Judgment*. Englewood Cliffs, N.J.: Prentice-Hall.

Office of Technology Assessment (1980). "Alternative Energy Futures, Pt. 1, The Future of Liquefied Natural Gas Imports." Washington, D.C.: Government Printing Office.

Raiffa, H. (1968). *Decision Analysis*. Reading, Mass.: Addison-Wesley.

Ralston, A. (1981). "The Struggle to Protect Worldwide Investment." *Risk Management*, 28: 70–8.

Rothschild, M., and J. Stiglitz (1976). "Equilibrium in Competitive Insurance Markets: An Essay in the Economics of Imperfect Information." *Quarterly Journal of Economics*, 90: 629–49.

Rummel, R., and D. Heenan (1978). "How Multinationals Analyze Political Risk." *Harvard Business Review*, 56: 67–76.

Savage, L. (1954). *The Foundations of Statistics*. New York: Wiley.

Slovic, P., B. Fischhoff, S. Lichtenstein, B. Corrigan, and B. Combs (1977). "Preferences for Insuring Against Probable Small Losses: Insurance Implications." *Journal of Risk and Insurance*, 44: 237–58.

Tversky, A., and D. Kahneman (1974). "Judgment Under Uncertainty: Heuristics and Biases." *Science*, 185: 1124–34.

Vernon, R. (1971). *Sovereignty at Bay*. New York: Basic Books.

(1981). "Sovereignty at Bay Ten Years After." *International Organization*, 35: 517–29.

West, G. (1980). "Underwriting and Management Policies of the Overseas Private Investment Corporation." Paper presented before International Risk Management Symposium on Managing Country Risk. New York City, January.

Western LNG Terminal Associates (1978). "Indonesian LNG Project Case History." Mimeographed.

Wood, W. (1979). "Chronology and History of PacIndonesia Project," in R. Petsinger and R. Vance (eds.), *LNG Terminals and Safety Symposium*. Flushing, N.Y.: Scholium.

Zeleny, M. (1979). "Intuition: Its Failures and its Merits," in B. Persson (ed.), *Surviving Failures*. Atlantic Highlands, N.J.: Humanities Press, pp. 172–83.

Perspective: Country risk insurance, an insurer's view

JAMES M. WYBAR

Kunreuther and Kleindorfer's chapter (this volume) contains some extremely valuable information, analysis, and insight into the present state of the country risk generated by the investment by our multinational corporations in foreign countries. In the process some assumptions are made that are subject to challenge, and some overemphasis is placed on the desirability of the development of empirical actuarial data and its application to premium determination for the insuring of this risk. It should be recognized that throughout the insurance business, with the possible exception of life insurance and broad-spectrum forms of property and casualty insurance such as private passenger automobile and homeowners, the data and actuarial projections for rate making are less than complete. Actuarial practice is as much an art as a science.

One of the elements that enters into that rate-making process is the period of time over which the data have been collected and the increasing reliability that derives as the period of time increases. A case could be made for comparing country risk exposure with catastrophe exposure in that each has the element of high probability of occurrence of loss over the entire portfolio of risks, but a low probability within each individual risk in a given period of time. The probability of loss for each risk increases as the length of time increases in both cases. The probability of the event's happening in any given time span also increases as a larger segment of the total portfolio of risks of that class is included in the expectancy field.

We know with certainty, for example, that each spring in the United States there will be tornadoes, and that each fall in the Western Hemisphere there will be hurricanes. The exact location and severity or number of either of these events within a given time period of one year, three years, or five years are extremely unpredictable. If we lengthen the time, retaining the same geography, to 100 years, then the predictability of the location and the frequency within that time period increase significantly. This same concept can be applied to country risk since we know with certainty that there will be expropriation of foreign investment by a host country; there will be deflation of currency with the attendant loss of capital value; there will be insurrection and revolutions and other uprisings, and the other events comprising country risk.

The historical data on a broad geographical base over time of each of these events are available and can be utilized in the development of the premium necessary to successfully underwrite country risk on individual exposures.

The process, however, can only be expected to be reasonably successful if there are enough risk-taking participants in the insurance market to accumulate the data and to generate a competitive climate for the available business. If the number of risk takers remains as it is now, that is, extremely small, then the market will not be fully served. This limited capacity will continue to result in unavailability of insurance for all but the apparently least risky applicants.

Kunreuther and Kleindorfer suggest an adverse selection against the insurer as a result of the inability to properly select risks and the superior knowledge of the insured utilized against the insurer. It is true that insurers are at a disadvantage in developing information relative to the specific risk, but they have the advantage of the broader scope of experience resulting from involvement in many of the kinds of risks to be assumed. That experience has equipped them to identify the critical kind of information needed and to develop it accordingly in their assessment of the risk and its pricing.

The authors also suggest a moral hazard problem that is based upon the insurers' limited ability to detect changes in the insured's behavior. By the transfer of risk to an insurer, it is suggested that adverse circumstances created by outside factors will instigate changes in the insured's behavior that will result ultimately in an increase in the risk not originally contemplated. This situation indeed can occur. It can be just as problematic in other risks such as a simple fire policy on a commercial enterprise. Instability of the neighborhood and eventual decline of its economic viability followed by increased crime and urban blight can lead to economic failure of an enterprise. The result will be increased hazard through neglect or lack of maintenance, or even destruction through purposeful arson. This scenario is not a great deal different from some of the description of country risk in Chapter 6.

One of the available techniques to reduce this hazard that could be used in the multinational country risk assumption is the use of a participating share or a coinsuring portion of all losses borne by the insured. The effect of this, of course, would be to make the insured participate in any loss, and the only time it would benefit the insured to reduce interest in maintaining the investment would be when their share of the loss would be less than their cost of maintaining the original investment.

We have attempted here to draw some similarities between country risk insurance and other kinds of insurance. It is certainly recognized that these are only similarities and not equivalencies; there are still unique features of country risk insurance. One of these is that U.S. multinational corporations have a very limited choice among insurers. Another very significant feature, and partly a consequence of the limited size of the market, is that multinational corporations are not able to satisfy their demands for long-term insurance, at least at any kind of guaranteed premium.

If we use Kunreuther and Kleindorfer's example of the liquefied natural gas processing plant and reverse the political situation so that it involves a U.S. investment in Indonesia, we can demonstrate this need. If we assume that the reserves of natural gas are estimated to be a fifty-year supply at the anticipated output, then obviously the value of the plant, which was $900 million, reduces at one-fiftieth of that each year. A desired commitment from the buyer's view would be for the insurance to be guaranteed for the entire life of that plant with the amount of insurance reducing on the depreciated basis. Given the present state of the art, it would obviously be impossible to guarantee a fixed rate or premium for that length of time, and in the normal contractual terms, the insurer is always left with the ability to not renew the contract. This phenomenon itself leaves the insured with an additional, totally unmeasurable risk. This same guarantee, of course, is not available in the more mundane domestic policies. The availability of a broad choice of alternative suppliers of insurance in that case, however, eliminates the concern.

The problems discussed in Chapter 6 relative to the attention paid by risk managers in assessing risk to the "headline-grabbing events" and the tendency to downplay the more frequent and subtle shifts in foreign laws and regulations are not unlike the problems faced by standard insurance companies in other lines. As stated earlier, country risk has many similarities to catastrophe-exposure risk. The focus is traditionally on short-term catastrophes such as a violent windstorm in the form of a hurricane or tornado, or a flood or earthquake. The reality is that many catastrophic conditions do not attain the same level of visibility. These include such phenomena as droughts or sustained cold spells as occurred in the United States in 1979 and 1982 and in Europe in 1982. These cold spells have significant impact on the loss record of insurance companies and will eventually be identified as catastrophe losses. The volcanic eruption of Mount St. Helens in the spring of 1980 received considerable attention in the insurance industry, but the losses produced by the extreme cold of the first quarter of 1982 were far greater and received much less notice.

In the field of country risk, the same phenomenon occurs when revolutions, insurrections, or overthrows of government receive significant attention. An encroachment on anticipated profit or even the imposition of a loss brought about by administrative actions such as environmental protection laws or capital controls does not receive the same level of concern in the pricing process.

Kunreuther and Kleindorfer's treatment of the decision process indicates that the risk manager might well use a threshold model in analyzing the acceptable risk level for any individual project. The authors relate this to the consumer's purchase of or decision to purchase flood or earthquake insurance, with the event's low probability of occurrence and high probability of severity of loss. It should be noted here that risk managers sometimes have alternatives to insurance. For instance, government loans have been utilized for international expansion when such expansion was desirable from a political standpoint. These loans could easily have a forgiveness feature if in fact the capital created by them were expropriated by the foreign country. In the case of individual consumers, history dictates to them that the loss suffered by their failure to purchase insurance may be relieved by other governmental action such as low-interest loans or outright relief grants. It would seem that the potential for these forms of relief must be part of the decision-making process.

In their summary of the decision-making process, Kunreuther and Kleindorfer note that the investment planner will evaluate each project on its own merits, ignoring the "portfolio investments." This is undoubtedly true and the assumption of the risk other than the business risk becomes a province and function of the insurance mechanism. Having once evaluated the business risk of the individual project and found it acceptable, investment managers must proceed to make the investment decision. Having done so many times, they are now exposed to a significant loss if one or more of those investments is lost to country risk. The function of the insurance mechanism is to eliminate or at least reduce the effect should such loss occur. This is not unlike the investment manager's decision to open a store in a certain shopping area because a market study indicates that the return on investment from that store will be as great or greater than investments used in other ways. The consideration of the loss of that store due to fire or other catastrophe is transferred as part of the insurance mechanism.

There is some question as to whether the hypothesis presented in the discussion of institutional arrangements in Chapter 6 is complete. It is true that the larger the risk, the smaller the likelihood that a small company will accept that risk. The probable reason for this, however, is the lack of ability or capital to develop the skills necessary to properly underwrite such risk assumption. Given the number of large risks available and the expertise needed to properly underwrite and service such risks, it becomes uneconomical for all participants in the insurance mechanisms to compete in insuring each of those risks. In planning marketing efforts companies will target those risks where they perceive the greatest expected return on investment. Effectively, this means that the largest number of insurance companies, which are small to medium in size, will not offer insurance for most large risks – the large risk is not an economical venture. The small company could not charge a higher premium than a large company and so it would reject the underwriting of such a risk.

Carried to the next extension, which deals with the multinational risk and the international insurance market, the smaller company, without some pooling arrangement, is unable to develop the necessary expertise to successfully compete in that marketplace. This is an important concept to bear in mind in the later discussion of ways to increase the supply of country risk insurance.

Kunreuther and Kleindorfer also suggest that monopoly profits will be available to the participants in this limited marketplace. But because of the subjective nature of the rating structure, the opposite result is also possible. An inadequate premium level could produce significant losses without the ability to spread those losses. As we argued, if insurance is overpriced, there will be little demand and poor financial results.

The authors' assertion that high profits probably induce additional entrants into the multinational and political risk field is probably valid. Increased entry may also be a consequence of overcapacity and depressed rate levels internationally for almost all forms of property–casualty insurance. In an effort to increase the underwriting profit or reduce the underwriting loss, together with a desire to increase cash flow for investment purposes, new sources of underwriting profit are being constantly sought. If there is indeed an excess profit in the political or country risk insurance field, new entrants will decrease prices and eventually reduce monopoly profits. Early in 1982, the AIG (American International Group), which has been underwriting country risk for some years, organized a separate company for this activity. During the same time, the AFIA (American Foreign Insurance Association), a competitor of AIG, began underwriting country risk.

The "Prescriptive Analysis" section of Chapter 6 begins by suggesting that the problem of assessing the large risk based upon inadequate data and unpredictable actuarial results, a problem parallel to that confronting the investment manager, is the principal deterrent to increases in the supply of country risk insurance. A more likely explanation is that many insurance companies are not aware of country risk insurance opportunities or they have regarded the risks-adjusted return as less attractive than that available in other activities. It is also true that the federal government has not lent its support to an intensive marketing effort. This may be the result of the insurance industry's past defense of state regulation and its opposition to being included in antitrust laws, which have generated an extremely wary relationship with the federal government. Its relationship with the federal government has been one of "keep the nose out of the tent."

It may also be relevant to note that the insurance industry is much less concentrated in the United States than in most other countries. The recent merger of two Norwegian companies produced a market share in that country of 31 percent for the new entity. In the United States, it is highly unusual for any company in any single state to acquire more than 3 or 4 percent of the total market share. As indicated earlier, the limited expertise in country risk insurance would be available only to the largest companies, and it is obvious that the largest companies number very few.

The pooling mechanism that brings together many smaller companies to provide the necessary capital to bear large risks has been used many times in the past. Examples of these are abundant in the fire insurance field where the dollars of risk become significant at times. Other programs have been utilized in the same way in the involuntary risk market. There are pools of companies that have been created legislatively or voluntarily to assume not only large risks, but also those risks that are considered to be less than desirable. Such pools operate in Workers' Compensation and in the fire insurance and automobile liability fields.

Given the proper incentive by government and the opportunity for profit that apparently exists, there is no reason to believe that pools or pooling arrangements could not be generated to underwrite insurance against the country risk. The AIG is an example of one of these, but it involves larger companies for the most part. Similar pools could be created to underwrite the same kinds of coverage, but including in their membership much smaller entities.

The present worldwide capacity for insurance and reinsurance is more than adequate to provide the total capacity needed for the assumption of these risks. Pools have been put together, for instance, to insure offshore oil rigs for which the amount of insurance is well in excess of $100 million for a single rig. A catastrophe developing out of a North Sea storm could elevate that loss by a significant multiple of the number of rigs that might be involved in that single storm-related catastrophe. There is no reason to believe that the country risk exposures of multinational corporations could not receive adequate protection from this large capacity currently available worldwide.

The reinsurance mechanism now in place could easily be utilized to spread that risk throughout the worldwide capacity and protect any individual participant in the pool or other arrangement from insolvency. The involvement of such international markets in the insurance and reinsurance process would also help to add some stability to the risk itself since the likelihood of any one country's insurers' or reinsurers' being involved in a loss precipitated by that country's government actions would to some extent deter such actions.

It is my considered judgment that there is no need for federal reinsurance of this risk and that given the proper friendly government environment, OPIC itself could be eliminated and the marketplace satisfied by the actions of the voluntary private enterprise system. There is, however, one inducement that the federal government could supply but that is not likely to be forthcoming. It is the same inducement that would probably have made flood insurance available in the voluntary market and avoided the highly controversial Federal Flood Program from being put in place. This deals with the matter of taxation on short-term profits and reserves and the income from reserves. The country risk, like the flood risk or other catastrophe risk, is extremely uncertain with respect to frequency and severity. The experience over any short period of time is certain to be erratic and might be, for some extended period of time, extremely profitable. However, the ultimate loss will eventually happen and must be paid for. In order to accommodate this, it would be beneficial to all if the tax laws recognized this need to reserve. Income generated could be used to reduce premiums chargeable, and the risk assumption would be much more desirable from the standpoint of the insurance carrier. This kind of favorable government attitude would be conducive to the growth and stability of this market.

The history of the government's involvement in insurance reinsurance has been less than successful, and any suggestion that this problem could be solved by a similar program is extremely doubtful. Kunreuther and Kleindorfer cite the Federal Riot Reinsurance Program. What they fail to reveal is that the reserves built up under the Riot Reinsurance Program were, in fact, utilized to pay the excessive losses over premiums developed under the Federal Crime Insurance

Program. This fact was revealed when Gloria Jimenez, the past Federal Insurance administrator, retired from her office.

Country risk as presented in Chapter 6 is an insurable one even though it may not completely satisfy the classic definition of an insurable risk. It is just as much so as many other kinds of catastrophe risk, and the needed coverage must be provided. The available rating process is in many ways similar to that used in other classifications of insurance and would be based upon long-term considerations with some subjectivity added to the actuarial calculation. This in no way makes it either impossible or unsound to proceed along those lines.

The assessment-of-risk technique used by investment managers in such situations is not entirely different from that used by the same managers for placing and utilizing capital on a domestic basis. The difference lies in the inability to measure effectively the unknown hazard created by the country risk. In domestic situations, the unknown hazards such as fire and windstorm are insurable on a standard policy basis. There is no reason to believe that the same technique cannot be used to insure the unknown hazard of the country risk parallel to the way in which other risks are insured – risks that are generated by the investment of that capital. In assessing individual projects, investment managers can follow the procedure they now use in the domestic market and again assume that the insurance mechanism will provide for the unknown hazard.

The insurer in the meantime can also be cognizant of the fact that the hazard can change because of some deteriorating political situation and the attendant lack of attention to the risk by the insured because it is insured. This contingency can be controlled by utilizing a participating insurance or coinsurance mechanism. This device is frequently used in other lines of insurance to serve essentially the same purpose, that is, to control moral hazard. The fact that the present insurance product is provided by a limited number of practitioners is a reflection of the highly competitive situation with respect to property and casualty insurance in the United States. The competition for the utilization of capital within most of these companies because they are relatively small has meant that opportunities for providing country risk insurance have been ignored. The need to generate expertise in the field to enable entry into it has been a deterrent to most companies, and consequently the marketplace has been left to a few large companies together with a few pools. The successful use of pools indicates that they are an acceptable mode for providing insurance. Except for the competition for capital, there is no reason why the expansion to additional pooling arrangements could not be made, given a favorable government environment. The favorable government environment is one that would promote the utilization of domestic insurers for the assumption of this country risk of our multinational corporations. At the same time there is some reluctance on the part of the insurance industry to deal with the federal government, since for the most part it wishes to retain state regulation and its freedom from the antitrust laws. It is felt by many in the industry that any request for cooperation from Washington will generate inquiries into the status quo and perhaps destroy it.

In addition to a favorable environment in the sense of marketing, an impetus could be given to the supply of country risk insurance by favorable tax legislation that would permit the retention of reserves over long periods of time, since losses in this kind of business are erratic with respect to short periods of time.

The capacity to underwrite country risk insurance is available within the domestic company markets utilizing reinsurance on a worldwide basis to spread the risk and level the operating results. The international market, in return, has an extremely adequate capacity and would be readily available. Currently, more insurance and reinsurance are available in the worldwide marketplace than can be utilized. Given an adequate opportunity for profit and a favorable government environment, the need for country insurance for multinational corporations will be quickly and easily satisfied.

Index